Use and Abuse
of
America's Natural Resources

Use and Abuse
of
America's Natural Resources

Advisory Editor

STUART BRUCHEY
Allan Nevins Professor of American
Economic History, Columbia University

Associate Editor

ELEANOR BRUCHEY

REPORT

IN REGARD TO THE

RANGE AND RANCH CATTLE BUSINESS

OF THE

UNITED STATES

BY

JOSEPH NIMMO, Jr.

ARNO PRESS

A NEW YORK TIMES COMPANY

New York • 1972

Reprint Edition 1972 by Arno Press Inc.

Use and Abuse of America's Natural Resources
ISBN for complete set: 0-405-04500-X
See last pages of this volume for titles.

Manufactured in the United States of America

Publisher's Note: Only the map which could
be produced in black and white has been
retained for this edition.

––––––––

Library of Congress Cataloging in Publication Data

Nimmo, Joseph, 1837-1909.
    Report in regard to the range and ranch cattle
business of the United States.

    (Use and abuse of America's natural resources)
    Reprint of the 1885 ed., which was issued as
Treasury Department document no. 690, Bureau of
Statistics.
    1. Cattle trade--United States. 2. United
States. Bureau of Statistics (Treasury Dept.)
II. Title. III. Series. IV. Series: United States.
Treasury Dept. Document no. 690.
HD9433.U4N54 1972   338.1'7'6200973   72-2860
ISBN 0-405-04524-7

REPORT

IN REGARD TO THE

RANGE AND RANCH CATTLE BUSINESS

OF THE

UNITED STATES.

BY

JOSEPH NIMMO, JR.,
CHIEF OF THE BUREAU OF STATISTICS,
TREASURY DEPARTMENT.

MAY 16, 1885.

WASHINGTON
GOVERNMENT PRINTING OFFICE
1885.

TREASURY DEPARTMENT,
Document No. 690,
Bureau of Statistics.

TREASURY DEPARTMENT,
Washington, D. C., May 16, 1885.

The following report on the range and ranch cattle business of the United States has been submitted to the Secretary of the Treasury in compliance with the following resolution of the House of Representatives, dated February 17, 1885:

"*Resolved,* That the Secretary of the Treasury be requested to transmit to this House such information as he may be able to communicate at an early day in regard to the range and ranch cattle traffic of the Western, Southwestern, and Northwestern States and Territories, with special reference to the bearings of that traffic upon the internal and foreign commerce of the United States."

iii

CONTENTS.

REPORT.

Page.

MAPS.

11991 R C——II

THE RANGE AND RANCH CATTLE BUSINESS OF THE UNITED STATES.

INTRODUCTORY REMARKS.

The portion of the United States now extensively devoted to grazing, and commonly known as the range and ranch cattle area, is delineated as accurately as it has been possible, upon Map No. 1, at the end of this report. This territory embraces about 1,365,000 square miles, and constitutes, approximately, 44 per cent. of the total area of the United States exclusive of Alaska. It is as large as all that portion of the United States situated east of the Mississippi River, together with the States of Minnesota, Iowa, Missouri, Arkansas, and Louisiana. Its area is also equal to that of Great Britain and Ireland, France, Germany, Denmark, Holland, Belgium, Austria, Hungary, Italy, Spain and Portugal, and one-fifth of Russia in Europe, combined.

By referring to Map No. 2, showing the distribution of the annual rainfall, and to Map No. 3, showing the distribution of the spring and summer rainfall of the United States, it will be seen that the range and ranch cattle area, as delineated on Map No. 1, very nearly corresponds with the great dry area of the interior. By referring to Map No. 4, which is a hypsometric sketch of the United States, it will also be seen that the portion of the country situated between the Mississippi River and the Pacific coast, and elevated more than 1,500 feet above the level of the sea, corresponds pretty nearly with the dry area and with the range and ranch cattle area.

By virtue of its characteristics of soil, rainfall, elevation, and natural food supply, this comparatively dry area is especially adapted to pastoral pursuits, and it appears to be probable that a large part of it will never be available for any other purpose. The mean annual rainfall of this area is, however, much greater than was at an early day supposed. At that time it was erroneously called the Great American Desert. It is now known to embrace a considerable amount of land available for agricultural purposes as the result of a sufficiency of rainfall or through irrigation. The early explorers appear to have been misled as to the capabilities of this area.

The expression "range and ranch cattle" in this report applies to cattle which, from the time they are dropped until they are shipped to market, seek their own food, water, and shelter, as did the buffalo, the deer, and the elk before them, and which are subject only to the restraints of herding.

The distinction between the "range" and the "ranch" cattle business herein observed, is that the former designation applies to the raising and fattening of cattle upon public lands, or upon unfenced lands generally, where the herds of different proprietors freely range and intermingle; whereas the "ranch" cattle business is carried on within inclosures, belonging to cattlemen on which only their own cattle graze.

The very fact that the range-cattle business is most profitably carried on in a large way, and that its successful prosecution involves organization and co-operative work, appears to have suggested at an early day the conduct of the business under corporate ownership and management. Accordingly this has been one of the marked features of the enterprise almost from the beginning.

Incorporated companies, chartered under the laws of this country as well as under the laws of foreign countries, are now extensively engaged in the cattle business from Southern Texas to the northern border line of the United States.

It is proposed, first, to describe the origin and development of the range and ranch cattle business in this country. The subject naturally divides itself geographically and historically into two grand divisions, viz: First, the range and ranch cattle business of the State of Texas; and, second, the range and ranch cattle business of the vast area situated north and northwest of Texas, an area which has been opened to pastoral pursuits during the last twenty years. Throughout the principal part of the area last mentioned, the cowboy has superseded the Indian, and the Texas steer has supplanted the buffalo.

THE RANGE AND RANCH CATTLE AREA OF TEXAS

Texas has an area of 274,356 square miles, or 175,587,840 acres, exceeding in area the thirteen original States of the Union.

The raising of cattle in Texas had its origin long before the admission of that State into the Union. The original or native cattle of Texas are of Spanish and Mexican origin. Their most distinctive physical characteristics are long horns, large and vigorous lungs, small intestinal organization, and small bones. These characteristics appear to be the result of the conditions which for three hundred years have constituted their environment.

Texas cattle exhibit some of the marked self-reliant traits of the wild animal, being strong in the instinct of seeking food and water, and of self-protection against the inclemency of the weather. In the language of the herdsmen they are good "rustlers," which means that they know how and where to find food and water and have the alertness and spirit to seek them upon the vast plains and in valleys and mountain fastnesses where they roam, and even beneath the snows which in the winter, at times, in the more northerly regions, cover their feeding grounds.

Thirty years ago almost the entire area of Texas was one vast unfenced feeding ground for cattle, horses, and sheep. Almost all the cattle of the State were, according to the popular phrase, "on the range"; i. e., grazed upon the public lands. The cattle belonging to different persons were then as now known by brands upon their sides, large enough to be distinguished by a horseman at some distance. This method of designating different ownerships still prevails throughout the entire range and ranch cattle area of the United States. A general supervision of cattle within certain extensive districts is had, by horsemen commonly known as "cowboys." Twice a year the cattle of the different owners and associated owners are "rounded up"; i. e., gathered together in close herds, when the calves are branded, and cattle for slaughter selected out, the rest being allowed to wander off again upon the range. During the last twenty years a great change has taken place in the cattle business of Texas. About half of the area of the State, including the eastern portion, not embraced in the range and ranch cattle area, as shown on Map 1, has been taken up, and is now being cultivated as farms. In this part of the State, cattle are raised as domestic animals, being generally provided with food and shelter in the winter. The range and ranch portion is also to a considerable extent settled up by farmers, especially the eastern and southern portions of the State.

Upon her admission into the Union Texas retained the ownership of her public lands. These lands have been surveyed and divided into townships, sections, and quarter sections in a manner quite similar to that in which the public lands of the United States have been laid out. Texas has, however, pursued a less conservative policy in regard to the disposition of her public lands than has the United States, and the result is, that the ownership of vast areas has been freely acquired for ranch purposes by individuals and corporations. In a few instances single individuals have acquired the ownership of upwards of 250,000 acres. The result of this is that with the exception of the extreme western and extreme northern portions of the State, where herds range on the public domain, the cattle business of Texas has become largely a ranch business. In other words. cattle are, to a considerable extent, confined to the lands of the different owners or associated owners.

The State of Texas is in a marked degree a cattle-breeding State. Its climate is well .suited to that industry, especially in view of the fact that the calves of range cows are, under the prevailing custom as to breeding, dropped at all seasons of the year. Not only do the cows of Texas have more calves during their lifetime than cows upon the ranges of the Northwestern Territories of the United States, but of the total number of cows a larger proportion have calves each year. Also, of the

11991 R C——2

calves dropped, a larger proportion survive in Texas than upon the more northerly ranges and ranches. Differences of opinion exist, however, as hereinbefore mentioned, as to the relative advantages of Texas as a breeding State for cattle. Attention is invited to the various statements upon this point which are expressed by experts. (See Appendices, Nos. 1, 2, 3, 4, and 5.) It is asserted that the State of Texas has to-day as many breeding cows as all the other States and Territories west of the Mississippi River together.

Twenty-five years ago Texas cattle were slaughtered in immense numbers for their hides and tallow. Then the average value of three-year-old steers on the ranch or range was only from $3.50 to $4.50 a head. But a great change has taken place in the cattle interests of that State within a comparatively brief period. Railroads have been constructed, whereby the markets of Kansas City, Saint Louis, and Chicago have been opened to the Texas cattle trade. Those cities have become not only great cattle markets, but also great slaughtering and packing centers, from which live cattle, fresh beef, salted meats, and canned beef are shipped to various parts of the United States, and are also exported to foreign countries. The construction of the Missouri, Kansas and Texas Railroad, the Saint Louis, Iron Mountain and Southern Railroad, and the railroads extending west into the State of Kansas—more especially the Kansas branch of the Union Pacific Railroad and the Atchison, Topeka and Santa Fé Railroad—have been greatly promotive of the cattle interests of Texas.

During the last twenty years another movement from Texas has sprung up and has attained great commercial importance, viz, the driving of young cattle north, to stock the newly opened ranges of the vast Northwestern Territories, including also the Indian Territory, New Mexico, and Colorado. It is estimated that the total number thus driven north, composed mainly of yearling and two-year-old steers, has, since the beginning of the movement, amounted to about 3,000,000.

The opening of these new and enormous commercial possibilities to the cattle-owners of Texas has developed a vast amount of wealth, and has, of course, greatly stimulated the cattle industry of that State. Cattle which about the year 1868 were worth only $4.50 a head advanced in value to $15 and $18 per head. The lands of Texas also greatly appreciated in value, and the general prosperity of the State attracted to it hundreds of thousands of immigrants from other States and from foreign countries. The opportunities for gain and the wild fascination of the herdsman's life have also drawn to Texas many young men of education and of fortune in the Northern States, and even scions of noble families in Europe. This has also been the case throughout the entire range and ranch cattle area of the United States.

Not only is Texas a great breeding ground for cattle, but vast herds are also matured and shipped direct to market from that State. The northern and northwestern portions of the State are well adapted to the maturing of cattle. It is estimated that during the year 1884 about 300,000 cattle were driven from Texas to northern ranges, to be there matured for marketing, and that about 625,000 beef cattle were shipped from Texas direct to the markets of Kansas City, Saint Louis, Chicago, and New Orleans.

THE WESTERN AND NORTHWESTERN RANGE AND RANCH CATTLE AREA OF THE UNITED STATES.

The western and northwestern range and ranch cattle area of the United States embraces the principal part of the Indian Territory, the western portions of Kansas, Nebraska, and Dakota, the Territories of Montana, Idaho, Wyoming, Utah, Arizona, and New Mexico, the States of Colorado and Nevada, and portions of California, Oregon, and Washington Territory.

This vast area, embracing 1,159,907 square miles, or 742,340,480 acres, has within the last fifteen years been largely devoted to the cattle business. The portion of this region in which the raising of cattle is chiefly carried on is, however, distinctively known as "The Plains." These extend from Texas to Montana, a distance of about 1,000 miles, with an average width of about 200 miles, and embracing an area of nearly 130,000,000 acres.

The discovery of the capabilities of this area for grazing purposes is said to have been accidental. The history of this important discovery is thus stated by Mr. Theodore J. McMinn, of Saint Louis:

"Early in December, 1864, a Government trader, with a wagon train of supplies drawn by oxen, was on his way west to Camp Douglas, in the Territory of Utah; but on being overtaken on the Laramie plains by an unusually severe snow-storm, he was compelled at once to go into winter quarters. He turned his cattle adrift, expecting, as a matter of course, they would soon perish from exposure and starvation. But they remained about the camp, and, as the snow was blown off the highlands, the dried grass afforded them an abundance of forage. When the spring opened they were found to be in even better condition than when turned out to die four months previously."

This discovery led to the purchase of stock cattle in Texas to be matured and fattened on the northern ranges, and the trade has steadily grown to its present enormous proportions, accelerated greatly during the past fifteen years by the building of the various railroads in the north and west.

Soon after this discovery of the possibilities of the great dry area of the north for pasturage, the range and ranch cattle trade of Texas debouched upon a territory three times as large as its original habitat. The growth of the business has been one of the marvels of this marvelous age and country The well-known fact that for ages the buffalo had thriven during the winter in Montana, Dakota, Idaho, and Wyoming on natural grasses also inspired confidence that cattle-grazing on the more northerly ranges would be successful.

It is said that about fifty different kinds of nutritious grasses have been found on the northern ranges. The "bunch grass" (*Boutelona oligostachya*), is, however, the most nutritious and sustaining and the most abundant of all. The gramma and buffalo grasses also abound. All of these grasses derive moisture mainly from the melting snows of winter and from the rainfall of the spring months. During the summer months they are cured by the dryness of the air, thus retaining their nutritious qualities through the succeeding autumn, winter, and spring months. When these supplies are temporarily cut off by snow-falls the cattle resort to the white sage-brush and the black sage-brush, which, though not very nutritious, supply the cravings of hunger until the melting of the snows. It has been found in Wyoming and elsewhere that the alfalfa or Lucerne, a plant originally imported from Chili, can be cultivated to great advantage whenever irrigation is possible. It is a most excellent, abundant, and highly nutritious article of food for cattle as well as for hogs. It yields usually from three to four crops a year.

Already the range and ranch business of the Western and Northwestern States and Territories has assumed gigantic proportions. The total number of cattle in this area, east of the Rocky Mountains and north of New Mexico and Texas, is estimated at 7,500,000, and their value at $187,500,000.

The secretary of the Wyoming Stock-Growers' Association has recently reported that since its organization in 1873 it has increased from ten members, representing an ownership of 20,000 cattle, valued at $350,000, to a membership of 435 in 1885, representing an ownership of 2,000,000 head of cattle, valued at $100,000,000.

The range cattle business of the Western and Northwestern States and Territories is carried on chiefly upon the public lands. With the exception of the small percentage of lands the title to which has been secured under the provisions of the homestead and pre-emption laws of the United States, the desert-land acts, or the timber-culture acts, the cattle upon the northern ranges feed upon the public lands of the United States, their owners being simply tenants by sufferance upon such lands.

The great range and ranch cattle business is environed by conditions involving the public interests, which must be described in order the more clearly to meet the requirements of the resolution of the House of Representatives.

Before considering the important questions which arise as to the relations of the business to the general interests of the country throughout the public domain, and the important relation sustained by it to our commercial and transportation interests, it appears advisable to consider the meteorological characteristics of the range and ranch cattle area.

THE CONDITIONS WHICH APPEAR TO DETERMINE THE LIMITED AMOUNT OF PRECIPITATION OF MOISTURE THROUGHOUT THE SO-CALLED DRY AREA OF THE INTERIOR OF THE UNITED STATES, AND THE PRACTICABILITY OF INCREASING SUCH PRECIPITATION.

The consideration of the conditions which determine the limited rainfall throughout the so-called dry area of the United States has an important practical bearing upon the range and ranch cattle business, in view of the efforts which are being made by the Government to increase the amount of precipitation within that area through the culture of forest trees, and also in view of the possible increase of precipitation as the result of artificial irrigation.

The winds which blow eastwardly over the Pacific Slope become heavily laden with moisture from the Pacific Ocean, and mainly perhaps from the great *kuro sivo*, or Japanese current, which sweeps along the eastern shores of Japan and washes the southern shores of the Aleutian Archipelago, the southern and western coasts of Alaska, and the western coast of British America and of the United States.

The several mountain ranges of the western portion of the continent, viz, the Coast Range, the Middle or Sierra Nevada Range, and the more easterly range known as the Rocky Mountain Range, by reason of the low temperature which prevails at and near their summits, condense the moisture of these winds.

This condensation of moisture by mountain ranges causes a large local precipitation. Consequently the winds as they proceed eastwardly beyond the Rocky Mountain Range are depleted of their original supply of moisture. This and the fact that the great range and ranch cattle area is so far removed from the Gulf of Mexico and the Atlantic Ocean, the two other principal primary sources of precipitation, in connection with known meteorological laws regarding the movements of aerial currents, seem fully to account for the small amount of precipitation throughout that area.

The meteorological conditions which determine the amount of rainfall throughout the range and ranch cattle area may, perhaps, be more clearly set forth by considering the probable primary and secondary sources of precipitation of the different sections of the country.

(a) THE PROBABLE SOURCES OF PRECIPITATION OF THE VARIOUS PARTS OF THE UNITED STATES.

In this connection it is a matter of interest to consider the probable sources of precipitation of the various parts of the United States. The force of the following remarks upon this subject may, perhaps, be the better appreciated by referring to the maps at the end of this report, viz, map No. 2, showing the distribution of annual rainfall; map No. 3, showing the distribution of spring and summer rainfall, and map No. 4, a hypsometric sketch of the United States.

The Gulf of Mexico is evidently the chief primary source of moisture of the Gulf States and of the interior, western, and northwestern States, about as far west as the 100th meridian, while the Atlantic seaboard States, and, to a considerable extent, the interior States of the Mississippi Valley and the Lake basin, receive their supply of moisture chiefly from the Atlantic Ocean.

The entire territory west of the Rocky Mountains, embracing the Pacific slope and the great interior basin of Nevada and Utah, undoubtedly receives its supply of moisture almost entirely from the Pacific Ocean.

Moisture borne by the winds from the Pacific Coast also supplies the precipitation throughout that vast mountain region formed by the Rocky Mountain ranges and their spurs—a region fitly termed by Silas Bent the "water dome" of North America. From this immense reservoir of precipitation flow the McKenzie, the Saskatchawan, and the Assiniboin toward the north, the Missouri, the Yellowstone, the Arkansas, the Red, the Rio Grande, and the Colorado toward the east and south, and the Columbia and the Colorado toward the west.

It remains to consider the sources of the rainfall of that immense region which embraces the larger part of the great range and ranch cattle area, and which is situated mainly west of the 99th meridian, north of the 31st parallel, and east of the Rocky Mountains. The elevation of this area above the level of the sea ranges from 2,000 to 10,000 feet, and its average annual rainfall is not over 15 inches. The smallness of this precipitation is clearly illustrated by the fact that the average annual rainfall at Chicago is 37.57 inches; at Leavenworth, Kans., 38.97 inches, at Saint Louis, 37.88 inches; at Nashville, 53.63 inches; at Cincinnati, 44.09 inches; at New Orleans, 64.69 inches; at Buffalo, 37.05 inches; at Washington, 43.30 inches; at New York, 42.68 inches, and at Boston, Mass., 48.21 inches.

A large amount of data in regard to the average rainfall at different points in the United States will be found in a statement furnished to this office by General William B. Hazen, Chief Signal Officer of the United Army. (See Appendix No. 11.)

By referring to Appendix No. 10 the same being a table furnished to this office by Capt. Samuel M. Mills, Acting Chief Signal Officer, it will be seen that west of the Rocky Mountains the principal precipitation occurs during the period of six months from the autumnal to the vernal equinox, and that on the east side of the Rocky Mountains the principal precipitation occurs during the six months from the vernal to the autumnal equinox. The rainfall, however, throughout the interior elevated region east of the Rocky Mountains, takes place chiefly during the months of April, May, June, July, and August.

In attempting here to state the probable sources of the rainfall of the great elevated area of the interior, attention is invited to the following opinions of three gentlemen eminent as meteorologists.

1. In a letter addressed to the chief of this Bureau, under date of February 23, 1885, Prof. Elias Loomis, of Yale College, says:

There is no doubt that the westerly winds which blow over the Rocky Mountains are very dry winds when they reach the eastern slope of those mountains, and they appear to have lost a very considerable part of their moisture by the precipitation which took place on the western slope of the Sierra Nevadas. I have examined this subject in a paper published in the American Journal of Science for July, 1881, and I herewith send you a copy of this paper. As the result of this dryness, the mean annual rainfall between the Sierra Nevadas and the meridian of 100° is, with slight exceptions, less than 15 inches. This is shown by the latest rain-charts published by the Smithsonian Institution.

Throughout all the southern part of the United States east of the Rocky Mountains, with the exception of the Atlantic coast, a considerable part of the rainfall is evidently due to vapor, which comes from the Gulf of Mexico. This influence is very decided up to the parallel of 36°, and is probably felt in a diminished degree still further north.

Near the Atlantic Coast the amount of rainfall is evidently increased by vapor which comes from the Atlantic Ocean. For the remaining portion of the United States east of the Rocky Mountains the vapor which furnishes the rainfall may come, to some extent, from these two sources, but it is chiefly derived from the chain of the Great Lakes, from the rivers, small lakes and collections of water, and from the moist earth.

2. In a letter addressed to the chief of this Bureau, under date of April 9, 1885, Mr. Silas Bent, of Saint Louis, says:

The ocean temperature of the North Pacific remains pretty much the same throughout the year and is, as I have before said, about 70° or 75° F. The temperature of the land, however, along the coasts of Oregon, Washington Territory, and the lower regions of Idaho, is much higher than that of the ocean in the summer time, and much lower in the winter season.

The vapor laden west winds, which come to those coasts from across the Pacific, partake of the temperature of the ocean, and being cooler than the land in summer, are expanded by the contact rather than contracted, and of course yield no precipitation, but in the winter, being warmer than the land, they are contracted by the contact, and give forth the mists and rain which envelop that whole region throughout that season, and which mists and rain are congealed into snow, only when those winds reach the mountains, where the temperature is below the freezing point.

3. In a letter addressed to the chief of this Bureau, under date of March 6, 1885, Capt. Samuel M. Mills, Acting Chief Signal Officer, United States Army, says:

Your questions relate to general theories which are not easily discussed in a few words.

It seems probable that evaporation from the Kuro Siwo is no more important than that from the remainder of the Pacific Ocean.

The southwest wind that north of California passes over the Rocky Mountains and deposits rain on our Pacific Coast, undoubtedly draws most of its moisture from the Pacific Ocean; it loses more of its moisture on the immediate coast than in the neighborhood of the crest of the Rocky Mountains, but is by no means depleted; on the average its dew-point falls about fifteen degrees Fahrenheit before reaching the crest. This corresponds to a loss of about 40 per cent. of its moisture. Having passed the crest it does not furnish any more rain until its 60 per cent. residuum has been increased either by local evaporation or by mixing with moist air from some distant source, such as the Atlantic, Gulf of Mexico, Great Lakes, &c.

The facts hereinbefore presented, showing that the principal precipitation of moisture throughout the great elevated dry area of the interior east of the Rocky Mountains occurs during the summer months, and that the principal precipitation west of the Rocky Mountains occurs during the winter months, and the views expressed by Prof. Elias Loomis, and by Mr. Silas Bent, and by Capt. Samuel M. Mills, of the United States Signal Service, seem to lead to the following hypothesis, viz: that, as stated by Mr. Bent, the winds blowing eastwardly from the Pacific Ocean during the summer months are cooler than the land, and that they are expanded rather than contracted by passing over the land. After passing the Rocky Mountain summit they retain a considerable proportion of their moisture, but not enough generally to produce precipitation, the dew-point being as stated by Capt. Mills, considerably below the temperature of the air. But by mixing with air laden with moisture from the Gulf of Mexico, the Atlantic Ocean, and with vapors which arise by evaporation from the Great Lakes, from rivers and small collections of water, and from the moist earth of the area east of the Mississippi River, as stated by Professor Loomis, such evaporation being abundant during the summer months, the dew-point is reached and precipitation takes place.

The fact that the area here referred to is especially subject to violent atmospheric disturbances, clearly due to the contact of strata of air differing in temperature, amount of moisture and electrical condition, appears to prove the intermingling of air from the Gulf of Mexico, and from the area east of the Mississippi and Missouri Rivers with the winds blowing eastwardly from the Pacific Ocean. This subject is clearly elucidated by Mr. Silas Bent in his interesting article entitled "The Birth of the Tornado," and also in Appendix No. 58.

The great range and ranch cattle area evidently receives its limited supply of moisture from various sources and under exceedingly variable and complex conditions. The subject is one of great public and scientific interest, and it is worthy of a very full and careful investigation by the Government.

THE PRACTICABILITY OF INCREASING THE AMOUNT OF RAINFALL THROUGHOUT THE GREAT INTERIOR DRY AREA.

The question of increasing the amount of rainfall throughout the extensive dry area of the interior of the country is one of the most important economic problems of the age.

The theory is held by some that the culture of trees will tend to increase the precipitation of moisture, and, accordingly, under the provisions of the so-called timber-culture laws, any individual may procure 160 acres of land upon complying with certain conditions as to the culture of trees upon a part of such lands. This theory has its earnest advocates, but it is sharply controverted by others. Perhaps the ablest and most conspicuous of its advocates is Dr. Franklin B. Hough, of Lowville, N. Y., an agent of the Department of Agriculture on Forestry and an eminent writer upon that subject. Dr. Hough has in a letter addressed to the chief of this Bureau briefly stated the reasons upon which his views are based. (See Appendix No. 14.)

There are those who believe that the construction of railroads and telegraph lines throughout the dry area has tended to increase the amount of rainfall in that region.

It is also held by others that the system of irrigation, whereby the water of the streams which come down from the Rocky Mountains and their various spurs is turned upon the dry land, instead of allowing it to run off into the great rivers which flow easterly and empty into the Mississippi River, will tend to increase the rainfall in the dry area, from the copious evaporation which takes place from such irrigated lands. This appears to be a plausible theory, for it is based upon the known course of natural forces, but the extent to which the expedient is available is yet to be ascertained. It is, however, certain that by this means a very large area can be reclaimed to profitable agriculture. As a general rule it is found that the crops of irrigated lands are more abundant and more reliable than those of lands watered by natural rainfall.

Another expedient for obtaining water throughout this vast area is that of sinking artesian wells. By this means a considerable amount of water could be secured for the use of cattle. The effect of this would, however, be to open up extensive areas to grazing now comparatively unavailable, for the reason that they are too remote from water.

It is evident that any practical expedient for increasing the amount of precipitation throughout the dry area will also be the means of supplying, through re-evaporation and recondensation the return to the earth of moisture originally drawn from the great primary source of continental precipitation—the ocean.

It appears to be a well-established fact that in the States of Kansas and Nebraska the limits of the area sufficiently watered by natural rainfall for agricultural purposes has during the last twenty years moved westward from 150 to 200 miles. This seems to present the promise of an extensive reclamation to the arts of agriculture of lands now available only as pasturage. It is believed that this westward extension of the area of agricultural lands is due mainly to the increased amount of evaporation from lands brought under culture in the Western and Northwestern States. The foregoing facts seem to indicate the wisdom of a tentative and expectant policy regarding the disposition of the lands of the dry area now embraced in the public domain, especially in Kansas and Nebraska, and the Territories of Dakota, Montana, and Wyoming. Such lands should not be regarded as necessarily and for all time, merely pastoral lands.

The matters just treated of seem also to suggest the national importance of a careful and extended study of the meteorology and climatology of the great dry area, and a close observation of the effect of all efforts which are being made to secure an increased precipitation of moisture, and thus to reclaim to agriculture a large part, at least, of that vast area.

CHARACTERISTICS OF THE RANGE AND RANCH CATTLE AREA WITH RESPECT TO TEMPERATURE.

The characteristics of the range and ranch cattle area, with respect to temperature during the different seasons of the year, are very clearly exhibited in the census temperature charts, and also in the annual reports of the Chief Signal Officer of the War Department. On Map No. 1, at the end of this report, are delineated the January isothermal lines. These indicate approximately the relative severity of the winter season in various parts of the range and ranch cattle area. It will be observed that these isotherms pay little heed to parallels of latitude. For example, the January isotherm of 30° sweeps in an apparently fantastic course through 14° of latitude, equal to 967 statute miles, between Washington Territory and New Mexico. Such wide departures of the isothermal lines from the parallels of latitude are due mainly to the hypsometric characteristics of the continent, and especially to its orological features. These causes of thermal conditions are very clearly illustrated on Map No. 4, at the end of this report, which map is a hypsometric sketch of the United States.

It will be observed that the point of lowest January temperature along the northern boundary-line of the United States is about where that line is crossed by the Red River of the North, the boundary between the State of Minnesota and the Territory of Dakota. It will also be observed that the mean January temperature rises from a little below zero at that point to 20° above zero in the northern part of the Territory of Idaho, and to 30° above zero where the boundary-line between Washington Territory and British Columbia touches Puget Sound.

The northwest winds which during the winter months blow over Montana and Wyoming, and which also sometimes reach Western Dakota and Nebraska and Northern Colorado, are comparatively warm winds, and evidently come from the Pacific Ocean. They are commonly known as Chinook winds. During certain seasons these winds have been so warm and so long continued as to melt the snows and to break up the ice in the Upper Missouri River and its principal tributaries. As the swelling waters, filled with broken masses of ice, flow onward, they at length reach a point in Dakota or Nebraska where the effect of the Chinook winds has not been felt, and where the Missouri River is solidly frozen. This, in certain instances, has caused widespread and damaging overflows.

It has been found that cattle do not suffer much from the severity of the temperature of the northern ranges so long as they are able to obtain an abundance of nutritious food. This is always the case when the winter snows are light, or when they are blown off the high lands.

The storms most disastrous to cattle are usually those which occur in the latter part of the winter or early spring, and when, after a rainfall, the grasses and shrubbery become covered with ice, and for several days the cattle are almost entirely cut off from their food supply. Losses from the severity of the weather occur in every State and Territory from Texas to Montana. Sometimes it happens, as has been the case during the past winter, that the losses from the severity of the weather have been even greater in Texas than in Montana. Range cattle usually have heavy coats of hair which, when saturated with rain and frozen, cause their sufferings to be much greater than when exposed to extremely cold but dry weather. The regions where losses on account of the weather are least are generally those where the cattle are best able to obtain sufficient food, and where they can readily find natural sheltering places from the violence of the winds.

THE RELATIONS OF THE RANGE AND RANCH CATTLE BUSINESS TO THE INTERESTS OF THE INDIANS.

The massacre of General Custer and his detachment on the 25th of June, 1876, at Little Big Horn, Dakota, near the present location of Fort Custer, led to the adoption of a more stringent policy on the part of the United States Government with respect to requiring the Indians to remain upon their reservations. During the five years following that tragic event our valiant little army, widely scattered over a vast area, had many bloody encounters with the Indians. At last the spirit of resistance was broken, and Montana, Idaho, and Dakota became comparatively safe for the introduction of the range-cattle business, which had already become known in Colorado and Wyoming as a highly attractive enterprise, and a speedy avenue to wealth. In the course of a few years, hundreds of thousands of cattle, almost all of them driven from the State of Texas as yearlings and two-year-olds, were quietly grazing throughout the former haunts of the buffalo, and the cowboy, armed and equipped, a bold rider, and valiant in fight, became the dominating power throughout vast areas where but a few years before the Indian had bidden defiance to the advancement of the arts of civilization. The question of Indian wars was thus forever settled in the region mentioned. Montana, Idaho, and Dakota now afford as much security for life and property as do the States on the Atlantic seaboard.

In the year 1864 a regiment of Colorado militia, under Colonel Chivington, attacked a camp of hostile Indians at Spring Creek, near Kit Carson, and administered to them a punishment which exerted an important influence in breaking the spirit of resistance in the more southerly portion of the range and ranch cattle area. In this section, as at the north, the land has been subdued to the purposes of the miner, the agriculturist, and the herdsman.

The only difficulties now experienced from the Indians result from their leaving their reservations in certain of the Territories. When thus permitted to wander off they frequently steal cattle from the herdsmen. Such incursions are usually made singly or in small bodies.

The National Convention of Cattlemen, held at Saint Louis, Mo., November 17 to 22, 1884, passed the following preamble and resolutions upon this subject:

Whereas the Indians in various sections have virtually been forced by the inadequacy of Government supplies to forage outside of their reservations; and

Whereas, in New Mexico, Arizona, Colorado, Wyoming, Nevada, Montana, and Eastern Oregon and Dakota permits are given each year to irresponsible bands of Indians to roam at will over the lands beyond the limits of their reservations, whereby great damage by fire and depredations is entailed upon the live-stock industry and hostile collision with rangemen made imminent: Now, therefore,

Resolved (1), That it is the sense of this convention that all the covenants of the Government with the Indians should be most scrupulously and honestly carried out.

Resolved (2), That the Indians named in the preamble, having been granted the exclusive use of vast areas of public domain, should be rigidly restricted to the limits of such reservations.

In view of the fact that the Government has adopted, and has long maintained, the policy of preventing hostilities with the Indians by locating them on reservations, upon which white men are not allowed to trespass, and of feeding and clothing the Indians so located, it appears but just to settlers and to those who are pursuing legitimate and useful occupations upon the public lands, whereby the people of the country are better supplied with cheap beef, that the desire of the cattlemen for the better protection of their interests should be respected.

THE OCCUPANCY OF LANDS BY HERDSMEN IN THE INDIAN TERRITORY AND ON INDIAN RESERVATIONS.

Important questions have arisen in regard to the grazing of cattle upon the lands of the Indian Territory and upon Indian reservations.

As shown on map No. 1, at the end of this report, more than three-fourths of the Indian Territory is now embraced in the great range and ranch cattle area of the United States. To a great extent the cattle business in that Territory is carried on by members of the various tribes, the same being either full-blooded Indians, or so-called "half-breeds," and by white men who, by marriage with Indian women, have become identified with the several tribes. But for many years a large part of the Indian Territory was unoccupied by the Indians for grazing or any other purpose. This led at first to the unauthorized, but permitted, occupancy of such lands by herdsmen, chiefly from Kansas and Missouri; but subsequently permits or licenses were granted by the Indians to herdsmen to graze their cattle upon such lands on payment of a stipulated rental to the several tribes to whom the lands belonged, or to whose use they had been dedicated and set apart by the National Government under treaty stipulations.

The Senate of the United States, on the 3d of December, 1884, adopted a resolution inquiring what leases of lands have been made in the Indian Territory, or Indian reservations, for grazing or other purposes, the number of acres embraced by each of such leases, the terms thereof, and the persons, corporations, or associations named therein as lessees, also as to the circumstances under which such leases have been made. The Secretary of the Interior submitted a reply to this resolution under date of January 3, 1885.

He first states that in years past owners of cattle used quite extensively the unoccupied lands of the Indians by sufferance and without any compensation in the nature of rental, except presents to certain influential chiefs apparently for the purpose of winning their favor. It was found, however, that such unregulated occupancy led to waste, by the cutting and carrying off of large quantities of black-walnut and other valuable timber. Finally it was deemed best to allow the Indians to grant to responsible parties the exclusive right to graze cattle within specific limits. By this means waste was prevented, and lands not used by the Indians became a source of revenue to them.

Referring especially to the lands of the Cherokee Nation, the Secretary explains the nature of the tenure of such lands for grazing purposes as follows:

The privilege to graze cattle is but a license and not a lease. It conveys no interest in the lands occupied. It is true that the Indians did attempt to make leases with a fixed period during which the parties would, if the power existed, have all the rights of lessees, but doubting the power to make, as well as the policy of such leasing, I declined to approve the same as a lease, but did treat them as amounting to a license, to be revoked by the Indians at will.

The view taken by the Secretary is that the privilege granted by the Indians to herdsmen simply amounts to the sale of a crop, and in support of the right of the Cherokee Nation to do this he says:

Under the decisions of the courts as to the title by which they hold their lands, and the guarantee pledged them by the United States in the 16th article of the treaty of 1866, can any one question or doubt their right to make such a disposition of the grass growing on their lands as they have made, whether it is called a lease, license, or permit? The land is theirs and they have an undoubted right to use it in any way that a white man would use it with the same character of title, and an attempt to deprive the nation of the right would be in direct conflict with the treaty as well as the plain words of the patent.

During the year 1884 the following amounts were paid to the different tribes of the Indian Territory by individuals and corporations for the privilege of grazing cattle:

Cheyennes and Arapahoes	$77,351 60
Poncas	1,700 00
Otoes	2,100 00
Pawnees	4,500 00
Sac and Fox	4,000 00
Osages	13,160 00
Quapaws	3,000 00
Kiowas	2,080 00
Total	107,891 60

In addition to this the Cherokees have received $100,000 for grazing on the lands known as the Cherokee strip or outlet.

In his report the Secretary of the Interior, while expressing his approval of the policy of leasing, asserts that in his opinion the amounts paid do not constitute an adequate compensation. The payment to the Cheyennes and Arapahoes amounted to only 2 cents an acre, or an average of $12.33 per capita of these tribes. The Secretary asserts his belief that these lands might be leased at from 4 to 6 cents per acre.

It is a fact generally well known that the occupancy of lands in the Indian Territory by white men for grazing cattle, even under such licenses or permits as constitute them simply tenants by sufferance upon assigned lands, and the occupancy also of certain unassigned lands for the same purpose, the title of which lands is in the Government of the United States, has been regarded as a sort of precedent under which persons proposing to become actual settlers have sought to acquire homes upon such unassigned lands, which are commonly known as the "Oklahoma country." These pretensions have invariably been resisted by the National Government. The subject is now being investigated by the Senate Committee on Indian Affairs. As stated elsewhere, it is against the general policy of the Government touching the disposition of the public lands to lease them to cattlemen; therefore it has not been deemed proper to establish any precedent of that sort by leasing lands in the Indian Territory held in trust by the United States for the use of Indians and freedmen.

The granting of permits to graze cattle has also been practiced on the reservations north of the Indian Territory. To what extent this is done cannot here be definitely stated. In a recent letter to this office Mr. E. V. Smalley, of Saint Paul, says:

There seems to be no general rule about leases. On one reservation I visited last summer I found the exclusive privilege of pasturing cattle was leased to a single individual; on another there were several leases, while on still another, that of the Flatheads, the agent did not even allow himself the privilege of having cattle on the range.

After considering the legal points involved in the various questions which had arisen with respect to the right of the Indians to permit white men to occupy a part of their lands for the grazing of cattle, and the right of the United States Government, under the provision of law, of treaty, and of conveyance, to permit white men thus to occupy the lands of the Indians or to obtain the necessary licenses, the Secretary of the Interior, in the document before referred to, clearly and forcibly discusses, first, the questions of property and proprietary rights involved in such leases, or licenses for grazing cattle on Indian reservations, and second, the question of policy as to whether the interests of the Indians and of the people of the United States demand that the Indians should be allowed to continue to own large and valuable tracts of land which are not needed by them, and which might be used for the settlement and development of the country.

Upon the first of these points the Secretary says:

The laws excluding white men from Indian reservations were enacted for the benefit of the Indians. In all cases where the Department has felt that the presence of white men on the reservation was injurious to the Indians they have been removed. In all cases where the Indians have asked their removal the Department has acceded to the wishes of the Indians and caused their removal, without reference to the question whether their presence was injurious or not. On the other hand, if the Indians favored their remaining, they have rarely been disturbed, and never, unless as before stated, their presence was clearly injurious to the Indians. This applies to the uncivilized tribes. But it is manifestly unfair to the Indians to exclude white men from their midst whose presence they desire and declare to be beneficial to them, and it should not be done unless their presence is clearly injurious to the Indians. It cannot be demonstrated that the permission given by the Indians to the owners of cattle to graze them on the Indian lands is injurious to the Indians. Isolation of the Indians from the white man was once thought necessary to protect him from the vices of civilization, but such isolation, even if desirable, has now become impossible. But such isolation is not desirable, and the Indian will become civilized much more readily when he comes in daily contact with white men, and certainly so if such contact is of his own choice and seeking. If the lands so occupied by cattlemen are not required for the grazing of the herds of Indians or for agricultural purposes, the Indians are not only benefited by contact with the whites, but by the compensation received for such grazing privileges.

Upon the second point above noticed the Secretary expresses the following opinion:

I do not propose that the Government shall confiscate these lands, or open them to settlement without proper compensation to the Indians, and while the title is held either by the Indians, or the Government for them, they should be prohibited from intrusion by unauthorized persons, and allowed to receive all the advantages that can be had from the ownership or occupation of such lands. But the interest of the Indians and of the people of the United States demands that they should not be allowed to own large and valuable tracts to the exclusion of the settlers, when such lands are not needed by the Indians. It is a misfortune to any country to have its lands held in large tracts by few owners, and it is the more so if held by owners who neither make use of it themselves nor allow others to do so.

The relation of Indian population to area of reservations is stated as follows with respect to the Indian Territory and the Indian reservations of Dakota and Montana, viz: Crow Creek, Devil's Lake, Fort Berthold, Lake Traverse, Old Winnebago, Ponca, Sioux, Turtle Mountain and Yankton in Dakota, and the Blackfeet, Crow, and Jocko in Montana, each of which is shown upon map No. 1, at the end of this report.

Reservations.	Area.	Population.	Population per square mile.
	Sq. miles.	Number	Number.
Indian Territory	64, 223	82, 334	1. 28
Reservations in Dakota	41, 949	31, 051	. 74
Reservations in Montana	43, 434	14, 775	. 34

How small relatively is this Indian population in proportion to the area of land occupied is indicated by the following comparison, showing the population per square mile of the Indian Territory and reservations in Dakota and Montana and in certain of the States:

Reservations and States.	Population.	Reservations and States.	Population.
	Sq. mile.		*Sq. mile.*
Indian Territory	1. 28	Louisiana	20. 7
Indian reservations in Dakota	. 74	Texas	6. 1
Indian reservations in Montana	. 34	Mississippi	24. 4
Minnesota	9. 80	Ohio	78. 5
Iowa	29. 3	Pennsylvania	95. 2
Missouri	31. 5	New York	106. 7
Arkansas	15. 1	Massachusetts	221. 8

The Indian population of the United States is estimated by the Commissioner of Indian Affairs to be as follows:

The five civilized tribes of the Indian Territory:

Cherokees	23, 000
Creeks	14, 000
Choctaws	18, 000
Chickasaws	6, 000
Seminoles	3, 000
	64, 000
All others	200, 000
Total	264, 000

Upon the subject of the reduction of the size of some of the principal reservations, Mr. E. V. Smalley says in a letter addressed to this office:

"Considerable new territory will be thrown open to the stock industry by the reductions of the large Indian reservations in Dakota and Montana.

"The great Sioux Reservation in Western Dakota could be reduced to one-third of its present dimensions without any injury to the interests of the Indians. Measures are already in progress for cutting down about one-half the area of the Crow Reservation in Montana, which is now about as large as the State of Connecticut. The portion to be released from Indian control is nearly all excellent bunch-grass range. The largest of all the existing reservations is that of the Black Feet, Piegans, River Crows, and other tribes lying between the Upper Missouri and the British boundary, which covers an area about equal to that of the State of Ohio.

" It is proposed by the Indian Commission to establish three small reservations within this Territory and to restore the remainder of the old reservation to the public domain. Nearly all the area which will thus be thrown open to white settlement consists of good grazing land. The Milk River Valley, which now lies wholly within the reservation, is especially valuable for range purposes, combined with farming by irrigation on the bottom lands near the river and its tributaries. In Washington Territory much good grass land has lately been added to the open range country by the reduction of the Moses Reservation.

"To confine the Indians in smaller areas than were assigned to them when they lived by hunting, is to put them in the way of becoming civilized. The game which once furnished them with food and clothing is now gone, and the nomadic life encouraged by the possession of enormous reservations is not favorable to the formation of habits of industry.

"With the opening of new ranges by the reduction of Indian reservations and the better stocking of the existing ranges, the cattle industry has a large field for further development."

Since the vast area over which the Indians once roamed for the mere purpose of hunting and following a nomadic life has been devoted to the use of white men engaged in industrial pursuits, and the buffalo has been driven off, a nomadic mode of life within that region is no longer possible; therefore reservations far beyond the needs of the Indians are to them a curse rather than a blessing. The sentiment that civilization has the right of way to the future on this continent, in its application to the reduction of the size of the great Indian reservations, appears to be dictated not only by sound views of public policy regarding the use of such lands by white men, but also by the moral obligation of according to the Indians just and humane treatment and placing them under such conditions as shall inculcate in them habits of industry and render them self-sustaining.

CAPACITY OF THE RANGES FOR GRAZING PURPOSES.

The capacity of the range and ranch lands of the United States for grazing cattle, differs widely in the several States, Territories, and sections as the result of differences in the quantity and quality of nutritious grasses produced, the water supply, and the extent to which natural shelter is available for cattle during storms. In Texas from five to thirty acres of land per head are required, and on the northern ranges almost the same differences are observable in different localities.

The ultimate limit of the capacity of the entire range and ranch cattle area of the United States for grazing, and the magnitude of its possible annual product can of course only be ascertained from the results of experience. It is evident, from the best available information, that the number of cattle on ranches and ranges in Texas might be greatly increased. Mr. George B. Loving, of Fort Worth, Tex., in reply to inquiries addressed to him by this office, expresses the opinion that by providing reservoirs, sinking artesian wells, and destroying the prairie dogs, which, in certain parts of the State, consume a larger quantity of the nutritious grasses than is consumed by cattle, the number of range and ranch cattle pastured in that State might perhaps be doubled.

It is impossible at the present time even approximately to estimate the proportion of the available range lands in the northern part of the

11991 R C——3

great dry area which are as yet unoccupied, or the extent to which the supply of grasses within the nominally occupied portions exceeds the supply necessary for the sustenance and fattening of cattle now grazing thereupon.

There appears to be a tendency on the part of those who have already occupied the ground to promulgate the idea that the ranges are fully stocked, and that there is, therefore, no room for additional herds. But intelligent observers who have prospected the different parts of the great cattle area north of Texas assert that two, three, or even four times the number of cattle now upon the ranges can be fed upon them.

Experience proves that cattle cannot advantageously graze more than 6 or 8 miles from water. The result is that vast areas now well grassed are of little value on account of their remoteness from water. The rendering of such lands available for the cattle business of course turns largely upon the practicability of procuring thereupon adequate supplies of water by means of artesian wells or by reservoirs for collecting rain-water.

PROFITABLENESS OF THE RANGE CATTLE BUSINESS.

The range cattle business of the western and northwestern portions of the great cattle area of course differs widely in the various localities and sections as to its profitableness. This is due to differences of conditions as to water supply, the quantity and quality of grasses, shelter, the number of calves produced, extent of winter losses, and the management of herds. As a rule the business has yielded large profits. This is clearly indicated by the large amounts of capital which have been invested in it during the last fifteen years. Many large fortunes have been made at the business within a comparatively brief period. Hundreds of men who embarked in the business a few years ago, with exceedingly limited means, are now ranked as " cattle kings." In certain instances women also have successfully engaged in the enterprise, and two or three of their number have already won the soubriquet of " cattle queen."

But like all enterprises yielding extraordinary results in the beginning, competition has in many sections already reduced the average profits approximately to the limits usually attained in commercial enterprises.

Mr. E. V. Smalley states that the usual profits on long-established ranges in Wyoming and Montana vary from 20 to 30 per cent. per annum on the capital invested. The following is from his statement, in Appendix No. 1:

" The average cost of raising a steer on the ranges, not including interest on the capital invested, is usually estimated by the large stockowners at from 75 cents to $1.25 a year. Thus a steer four years old ready for market has cost the owner $4 or $5 to raise. When driven to the railroad he is worth from $25 to $45. A recent estimate, approved by a number of Wyoming ranchmen, places the profit at the end of the third year on a herd consisting of 2,000 cows with 1,000 yearlings, and 35 short-horn bulls, representing in all, with ranch improvements and horses, an investment of about $70,000, at $40,000."

The completion of the Northern Pacific Railroad, and the construction of other railroads in the Territories during the past two or three years, caused the price of range cattle to advance. Thus large profits were realized from the sale of herds.

Generally it is found that the average cost per head of the management of large herds is much less than that of small herds. The tendency in the range cattle business of late years has therefore been toward a reduction in the number of herds, and generally toward the consolidation of the business in the hands of individuals, corporations, and associations. It is stated that a single cattle company in Wyoming advertises the ownership of ninety different brands, each one of which formerly represented a herd constituting a separate property.

In opposition to the tendency toward consolidation, there is also the tendency toward separate ownerships on the part of homestead, pre-emption, and "desert-land" settlers, through the privileges afforded them under the public land laws of the United States.

THE BREEDING OF CATTLE ON THE NORTHERN RANGES.

As already stated, the northern ranges were originally stocked with young cattle, chiefly steers, driven from Texas. For several years it was supposed that Texas must continue to be almost exclusively the breeding ground, and that the northern ranges would for all time be the maturing and fattening ground for Texas cattle. But an impor. tant change has taken place in this regard. The raising of cattle on the northern ranges has met with an encouraging degree of success. At the present time many of the large cattle-owners and herdsmen of Montana, Dakota, Wyoming, Nebraska, and it is believed also of Colorado, are of the opinion that it is more profitable for them to raise their young cattle than to import them from Texas.

It is a well-established fact that cows in Texas produce more calves than cows on the northern ranges. The general opinion appears to be to the effect that about 90 per cent. of the cows of Texas drop calves every year. Wide differences of opinion are, however, expressed as to the increase on the northern ranges. The estimates vary from 50 to 70 per cent. of the number of cows. Hon. Martin E. Post, late Delegate in Congress, from Wyoming, estimates the average increase at from 50 to 60 per cent. of the total number of cows, and the increase from two-year-old heifers at 40 per cent. He adds, however, that every two-cattle raised in Wyoming are worth three raised in Texas.

While Texas cattle are largely purchased for stocking ranges at the north, the policy upon the well-established ranges appears to be quite generally favorable to maintaining and increasing the stocks upon such ranges by keeping a sufficient number of cows and bulls for breeding purposes. This change of policy has led to a disposition on the part of the northern-range cattlemen to oppose the driving of young cattle from Texas to the north, which spirit of opposition has manifested itself in hostility to the proposition for the establishment of a national cattle-trail. In so far as such opposition is based upon considerations of a commercial nature, namely, the shutting off of the competition of Texas cattle-breeders from the northern ranges, it could not, of course, meet any co-operation whatever from the National Government, as that would be to favor the restriction of free competition in a legitimate trade. Nor does it appear to be becoming in the northern owners of herds to seek such protection so long as they enjoy the privilege by sufferance of allowing their cattle to graze upon the public domain.

The practical effect of breeding cattle on the northern ranges and of the efforts made to raise the grade of such cattle by the importation of high-grade bulls is seen in the improved quality of the beef cattle shipped to market from the northern ranges.

THE IMPROVEMENT OF THE BREED OF RANGE AND RANCH CATTLE.

During the last ten or twelve years the thought of the leading range and ranch cattle herdsmen, as well as of settlers, within the great cattle belt has been turned toward the subject of improving the quality of their stock. This has been accomplished, first, by the shipment of young " native " cattle of the States east of the Missouri River to the western and northwestern ranges, there to be matured and fattened for market. Efforts in the direction of improving the breed of range cattle have also been made by crossing the " native " and the Texas cows with bulls of the higher breeds of beef cattle, and chiefly with those of the Short-horn, Hereford, Polled Angus, and Galloway breeds. To what extent it is practicable to improve the grade of cattle on the range that are compelled to seek their own food and water, and such shelter against storms as they can find in valleys and mountain gorges and in the " coulees " of the broken ranges from the time they are dropped until they are driven to the railroad depot for shipment to market, and permanently to maintain such improvement under the conditions mentioned, is yet to be ascertained.

The following remarks upon this point by ex-Governor Crittenden, of Missouri, before the National Convention of Cattlemen held in Saint Louis in November, 1884, are of interest :

" The highest and most successful type of cattle is the product of the highest artificial condition, and you can only maintain this high standard by the continuance of the conditions. Our increasing population requires the observance of these conditions, and it is useless in the opinions of many to refine blood without at the same time supplying and maintaining those artificial aids and surroundings so necessary to the growth, the comfort, and early maturity of the beast. You practical men must be the judges how far those aids must extend.

" I can only say if those aids are extended enough they will pay; if insufficient for the refined blood, loss will ensue. Palace bred animals will wither in a wilderness or in an unprotected condition. Good mangers and good managers produce good cattle, provided good surroundings are had. You must in the growth of cattle do one of two things : breed a race of cattle fitted to the existing conditions or fit the conditions to our high-bred cattle. Which will pay is the question."

It seems to be evident that high-bred cattle, which owe their development by heredity to the care and protection which they have for many generations received at the hands of man, would be likely to retrograde if deprived of such conditions of care and protection upon the bleak ranges of the Northwestern Territories. This suggests the thought that the higher-bred animals are more likely to thrive under the management of actual settlers than under the management of the large herdsmen, for the reason that the settlers are usually prepared to shelter their cattle against the rigors of winter and to supply them with food at times when the natural supply is cut off by snow and ice. The large herdsmen, on the other hand, must, under existing conditions, leave their cattle to struggle for existence against all the adverse conditions of cold, and winds, and weather.

It is, however, the prevailing opinion that the efforts which are being made toward the improvement of the breed of range cattle will result in producing cattle greatly superior in quality, not only to the Texan, but also to the native stock, and marked by physical characteristics adapting them to life upon the range. Important advances have already been made in this direction.

Attention is invited to the interesting and valuable statements upon this subject by Hon. Martin E. Post, late Delegate in Congress from the Territory of Wyoming. Mr. Post refers particularly to the efforts in this direction on the northern ranges. (See Appendix No. 49.)

In Texas also great attention is paid to the subject of the improvement of the breed of range and ranch cattle, and with a gratifying degree of success. Attention is invited to a statement upon this subject by Mr. D. W. Hinkle, of San Antonio. (See Appendix No. 23.)

THE TEXAS CATTLE-TRAIL AND THE MALADY KNOWN AS TEXAS FEVER.

The driving of cattle from Texas to the northern ranges, to be there matured and fattened, is a business which has grown up chiefly during the last fifteen years. Such cattle consist mainly of young steers one and two years old, with a small proportion of heifers. Not only is it found to be a source of profit thus to utilize the extensive northern ranges, but it has been ascertained that the Texas cattle, when driven north, increase in weight more rapidly than if raised and prepared for market on the Texas ranges. It is said that Texas steers driven north at the age of two years will weigh on the average, when four years old, about 200 pounds more than if kept in Texas until they have reached the same age. The quality of their beef is also greatly improved as the result of the migration. This is attributed to the fact that the natural grasses of the higher latitudes are more nutritious than those of Texas and therefore more fattening, and also to the stimulus of the high and dry areas of the northern ranges.

The cattle driven north from Texas embrace, first, beef cattle three and four years old and upwards, in condition for the markets, and, second, young cattle for stocking the northern ranges. The beef cattle ready for marketing are generally shipped at points in Western Kansas, over the Atchison, Topeka and Santa Fé Railroad and the Kansas Pacific Railroad to Kansas City, Saint Louis, and Chicago. The great herds of young cattle driven north to the ranges of Nebraska, Dakota, Montana, Idaho, and Wyoming have latterly been sold chiefly at Dodge City, in Kansas, and at Ogallala, in Nebraska.

Owing to the difficulty of driving cattle through sections of the country to any considerable extent settled and fenced in farms, the markets in Kansas for the sale of Texas cattle have always been located near the western line of settlements, but the influx of population has gradually crowded these frontier markets farther and farther west. In the years 1870, 1871, and 1872 the chief Texas cattle markets of Kansas were at Newton, in Harvey County, on the line of the Atchison, Topeka and Santa Fé Railroad, and at Abilene, in Dickinson County, on the line of the Kansas Pacific Railroad. Later those markets were located at Great Bend, on the Atchison, Topeka and Santa Fé Railroad, and at Ellsworth, on the Kansas Pacific Railroad, and still later they were moved to Dodge City, on the former railroad, and to Hayes City, on the latter. For several years past, however, Dodge City, in Kansas, and Ogallala, in Nebraska, on the line of the Union Pacific Railroad, have been the chief markets for the sale of Texas cattle for the northern ranges. From those points the young cattle have been driven to the ranges of Nebraska, Dakota, Colorado, Wyoming, Montana, and Idaho. The movement has varied in magnitude from year to year, but during the year 1884 it is said to have amounted to about 400,000 head.

THE TEXAS FEVER.

In common with almost all human enterprises, the most promising and beneficial not excepted, the movement of young cattle from the great breeding grounds of Texas to the vast northern ranges is beset by an adverse condition. In this instance it is the destructive bovine disease commonly known as "Texas" fever, but also designated as "splenic" fever, and as "Spanish" fever.

It is proposed to consider this disease in its commercial aspect. Its cause and its pathology are as yet involved in mystery. Wide differences of opinion prevail in regard to both. It has been attributed to bacterial and bacillic organisms, but the existence of such supposed germs throws no light upon the subject, for it is an unsolved problem as to whether they are a cause or an effect of disease. A few general facts of commercial significance, touching the manifestation of Texas fever, appear, however, to be pretty well established. Its cause, whatever it may be, is undoubtedly persistent, and yet it is not invariable as to the circumstances attending its appearance. It is endemic rather than epidemic. The low lands, bordering upon the Gulf of Mexico, are undoubtedly the locality of its origin. This infected area is believed to embrace somewhat more than one half of the State of Texas. On map No. 1. at the end of the report, is shown the line which marks approximately, at least, the northern limit of this area.

So long as cattle born and raised in this Gulf section remain there, Texas fever is unknown among them. But when they are driven or transported to the northern part of Texas, or to the States and Territories of the northwest, they communicate the disease to the cattle of these more northern latitudes. Such infection of northern cattle appears to be invariably the result of their walking over, or feeding upon, the trails along which Texas cattle have passed. The Southern Texas cattle on their way north, in most cases, suffer a constitutional disturbance apparently attributable to change of food and climate, but it is said that usually they are not affected by what is distinctively known as "Texas" fever. This appears to involve the apparent paradox of their imparting a disease which they themselves do not have. Nevertheless there is a consensus of opinion among careful observers indicating that this is really the case, and the opinion appears to command popular belief.

The theory now generally held is, that the cause of the disease exists in a latent state in the cattle of Southern Texas, under conditions of climate and food which produce no impairment of the health of the animal, but that during migration towards the north, such latent cause of disease passes off in fecal matter, and is inhaled or taken into the stomachs of the northern animals when they feed upon the ground over which the Texas cattle have passed. In other words, the disease is believed to be an incident of a changed condition in Texas cattle by acclimatization. It is also a pretty well established fact that it is not, at least to any great extent, contagious. It is held by many that no animal which has taken the disease from the trail can communicate it to his fellows who have not been upon the trail.

The general testimony appears to be to the effect that Texas cattle

driven north have never communicated the disease to other cattle north
of the South Platte River, nor to cattle in the State of Colorado. It
has been assumed, therefore, that the disease is limited as to the sphere
of its manifestation, both by latitude and elevation. It is also the accepted theory that the cause of the disease is eliminated from the systems of the Southern Texas cattle while " on the trail " from their place
of nativity to the ranges of the north. It is also a well established fact
that herds driven slowly are very much less likely to communicate the disease to the cattle in the northern part of Texas and to other northern cattle than when driven rapidly. Experience also proves that the disease is
much more likely to manifest itself during the months of June, July,
August, and September, than during the other months of the year.
That cattle driven from the State of Texas gradually lose the power of
imparting disease as they proceed north, and that the limits of the
area of infection have been approximately determined, appear to be
facts pretty well established.

Mr. N. J. Wilson, of Denver, who is extensively engaged in the range-
cattle business, states that he has been engaged in that business along
the line of the Kansas Pacific Railroad since the year 1869, but has never
had among his herds a case of Texas fever caused by cattle driven from
Texas, although he has handled large numbers of Texas cattle and
allowed them to mingle freely with native cattle. Mr. Wilson also
asserts it as his belief that cattle driven from Texas have never communicated the disease after crossing the Arkansas River at Dodge City,
in the southwestern part of the State of Kansas.

The committee of the Wyoming Stock Growers' Association, charged
with the duty of investigating the subject of Texas fever, reported at
the recent annual meeting of the association, April, 1885, " that Texas
cattle brought from the southern part of Texas are dangerous to our
cattle for about sixty days from the time they leave their native ranges
and that the same cattle can be brought among our stock after sixty
days have elapsed with entire safety."

As somewhat more than sixty days are required in driving cattle from
the southern part of Texas to Wyoming it is evident that there is no
danger to be apprehended in Wyoming from Texas cattle when so
handled. This fact is clearly stated by Hon. J. W. Carey, Delegate in
Congress from Wyoming, and president of the Wyoming Stock Growers' Association, who says:

In so far as my experience and that of others in the cattle business of Wyoming goes
it is found to be perfectly safe to admit to our ranges Texas cattle which are driven on
the trail. By the time they reach Wyoming and Nebraka, when moved in that way,
they appear to lose entirely the liability to impart the socalled Texas fever.

THE PROPOSITION TO ESTABLISH A NATIONAL CATTLE TRAIL.

The extension of settlements in the State of Kansas has, as already stated, gradually forced the main line of the Texas cattle-trail westward to what has for several years past been known as the Fort Griffin and Dodge City trail, Dodge City, Kans., on the Atchison, Topeka and Santa Fé Railroad, and Ogallala, Nebr., on the Union Pacific Railroad, being the two chief markets for the sale of young Texas cattle intended for the northern and northwestern ranges.

But as the trail was forced westward by the settlement of the country, it was apprehended that eventually there might be a lack of the necessary water supplies for the cattle at proper intervals. Accordingly, it was deemed advisable by those who are interested in keeping a practicable trail open to secure the establishment of a national cattle trail, by inducing Congress to set aside a strip of public lands through the national domain in Kansas, Nebraska, and Dakota, such lands to be withheld from private entry, and held by the Government as a great free highway for the especial purpose of a cattle trail. It was assumed that the necessary action would also be taken whereby lands might be set aside for the purpose of such a trail through the Indian Territory and in the State of Texas. But in consequence of action taken by the State of Kansas in the month of February, 1885, inimical to the establishment of the proposed trail within her borders, a matter hereinafter set forth with some degree of particularity, it was deemed best by the advocates and promoters of the trail to locate it in the State of Colorado along the western boundary of the State of Kansas. A bill to this effect was accordingly introduced in Congress during its present session, by Hon. James F. Miller, of Texas. (See Appendix No. 30.)

It is said that the natural water supply along this proposed route is not usually sufficient for the needs of the cattle, but it is believed that by sinking artesian wells at suitable distances apart this objection can be overcome. It is also maintained that there will be much less danger of Texas fever by this route than by the route from Dodge City to Ogalalla, for the reason that the former will be located upon much more elevated ground. On map No. 1, at the end of this report, is delineated the old Texas cattle trail, known as the Fort Griffin and Dodge City trail, and also the route of the proposed trail around the western border of the State of Kansas.

THE COMMERCIAL IMPORTANCE OF THE TEXAS CATTLE TRAIL.

The most concrete and demonstrative expression of the importance of any commercial movement is of course the statistical record of its magnitude during a series of years extending up to the present time. Such a record of the movements of Texas cattle is presented in the annual report of the Board of Trade of Kansas City, as follows:

THE TEXAS CATTLE DRIVE.

Approximate statement of the number of cattle driven north each year from Texas, since the beginning of the movement.

Year.	Number.	Year.	Number.
1866	260, 000	1877	201, 159
1867	35, 000	1878	265, 646
1868	75, 000	1879	257, 927
1869	350, 000	1880	394, 784
1870	300, 000	1881	250, 000
1871	600, 000	1882	250, 000
1872	350, 000	1883	267, 000
1873	405, 000	1884	300, 000
1874	166, 000		
1875	151, 618	Total	5, 201, 132
1876	321, 998		

This statement embraces both beef cattle shipped east from the western cattle markets of Kansas, and young cattle driven north to stock northern ranges. This was more particularly the case during the earlier years, but it is stated by Mr. W. H. Miller, secretary of the Kansas City Board of Trade, Appendix No. 50, that "during the last six or seven years nearly all of the drive has been made up of stock cattle for ranges north of Texas." According to the best estimate which can now be made, there have been about 2,000,000 young cattle driven from Texas to northern ranges during the last seven years, which at $15 a head would amount to $30,000,000. The "drive" of the year 1884 was about 300,000, which at $17 a head amounted to $5,100,000. These figures, the best which can be obtained, are of course only rough approximations. They clearly indicate, however, a large demand at the north for young Texas cattle, and a supply adequate to meet such demand. The movement has been about as regular as commercial movements are generally; the tendency, on the whole, being in the direction of progress. It is asserted, upon apparently good authority, that fully one-half of the blood of all the cattle on the northern ranges to-day is of the Texas strain. Many persons largely engaged in the cattle trade at the north and the cattle raisers of Texas generally, maintain that Texas must in the future hold the position of a breeding ground, and the northern ranges that of a maturing and fattening ground. But that view is controverted by a majority of the herdsmen of the north, and especially by those engaged in the business of raising cattle and of improving the breed of northern range cattle. The question as to the reasonableness and propriety of establishing the proposed cattle trail depends also somewhat upon the—

QUANTITY OF LAND NECESSARY FOR THE PROPOSED TRAIL.

The public lands of Texas belong to that State. The quantity of land which the Government of the United States is asked to donate for the purpose of establishing the proposed trail may therefore be assumed to begin at the southern border line of Colorado, and to extend to the northern border line of the United States. It is proposed that it shall be of variable width, from 200 feet at crossing places for "native cattle," to 6 miles at the widest part. It must of course have sufficient width not only for a line of travel, but also for a feeding ground of cattle "on the trail." Such a trail of an average width of 3 miles, and extending to the Dominion of Canada, as delineated on map No. 1, would be 690 miles in length and have an area of 2,070 square miles, or 1,324,800 acres. If it should be established only from the Southern boundary of Colorado to the parallel of 43° north, which constitutes the northern border line of the State of Nebraska, it would have a length of 420 miles and an area of 1,260 square miles, or 806,400 acres.

The proposed trail would be located chiefly upon "range" land not available for agricultural purposes, other than grazing. The intrinsic value of such lands, which now belong to the Government, cannot be accurately stated, but it is comparatively small.

That the quantity of land which the advocates of the proposed cattle trail ask Congress to set aside for that purpose is not immoderate, comparatively speaking, is clearly indicated by the following table from the annual report of the Commissioner of the General Land Office for the year 1884, showing the number of acres of land conceded by Congress to States and corporations for railroads and for military wagon-roads from the year 1850 to June 30, 1884.

Statement exhibiting land concessions by acts of Congress to States and corporations for railroad and military wagon-road purposes from the year 1850 to June 30, 1884.

States.	Number of acres certified or patented up to June 30, 1884.
FOR RAILROADS.	
Illinois	2, 595, 053. 00
Mississippi	935, 158. 70
Alabama	2, 884, 074. 03
Florida	1, 760, 834. 98
Louisiana	1, 072, 406. 47
Arkansas	2, 516, 525. 96
Missouri	1, 395, 429. 87
Iowa	4, 706, 618. 39
Michigan	3, 229, 010. 84
Wisconsin	2, 874, 088. 79
Minnesota	7, 801, 349. 15
Kansas	4, 638, 210. 67
	36, 408, 760. 85
Corporations	11, 879, 027. 01
Total railroad grants	48, 287, 787. 86
Deduct amount of land declared forfeited by Congress	667, 741. 76
	47, 620, 046. 10
FOR WAGON-ROADS.	
Wisconsin	302, 930. 96
Michigan	221, 013. 35
Oregon	1, 258, 237. 10
	1, 782, 181. 41
	47, 620, 046, 10
Total	49, 402, 227. 51

An idea of the reasonableness of the proposition to establish the proposed trail may be derived from the following statement, showing the quantity of lands granted by the Government in aid of the construction of all of those railroads, which are commonly designated as "Pacific Railroads," and the quantity which would be required for the proposed cattle trail. The quantity of land granted by Congress in aid of so-called Pacific railroads is shown as follows:

Number of acres of land patented to June 30, 1883, by so-called Pacific railroad companies which have received grants of land from the National Government, and the amount of bonds issued to certain of such companies by the United States.

[Corrected by Commissioner of General Land Office to June 30, 1884.]

Name of company now operating the railroads which have been aided by the National Government.	Lands patented.	Bonds issued under grants.
	Acres.	
Northern Pacific Railroad	746, 390	
Union Pacific Railroad (including Denver Pacific and Kansas Pacific)	3, 433, 460	$33, 539, 512
Central Pacific Railroad (including Western Pacific and California and Oregon).	2, 623, 008	27, 855, 680
Atchison, Topeka, and Santa Fé Railroad	2, 935, 163	
Central Branch of Union Pacific Railroad *	187, 448	1, 600, 000
Sioux City and Pacific Railroad	41, 398	1, 628, 320
Southern Pacific Railroad of California (main and branch lines)	1, 192, 702	
Oregon and California Railroad	322, 063	
Atlantic and Pacific Railroad	959, 207	
Missouri, Kansas, and Texas Railroad	984, 106	
Saint Louis, Iron Mountain, and Southern Railroad	1, 382, 410	
Total	14, 807, 355	64, 623, 512

* Now operated by the Missouri Pacific Railway Company.

The comparison which the foregoing tables are intended to present is summarily exhibited thus:

Acres.

Total number of acres granted to States and corporations in aid of railroad construction 47, 620, 046
Total number of acres granted to so-called Pacific railroads 14, 807, 355
Granted to the Union Pacific Railroad Company 3, 433, 460
Granted to the Central Pacific Railroad Company 2, 623, 008
Granted to the Atchison, Topeka and Santa Fé Railroad Company 2,.935, 163
Estimated number of acres required for a cattle trail from Texas to the northern border line of the United States 1, 324, 800
Estimated number of acres required for a cattle trail from Texas to the northern boundary of the State of Nebraska 806, 400

It appears, therefore, that the quantity of land required for a cattle trail of an average width of 3 miles, extending from the southern border of Colorado to the northern boundary line of the United States, would constitute only 2.78 per cent. of the total number of acres granted to and patented by railroad companies, and only 9.35 per cent. of the total number of acres patented by so-called Pacific railroad companies.

It would also be less than one-half the number of acres patented by either the Union Pacific, the Central Pacific, or the Atchison, Topeka and Santa Fé Railroad Companies.

Evidently the driving of young cattle from Texas to the ranges of the north is a commercial movement of great importance. A very large proportion of all the cattle now on the northern ranges came from Texas or are of the Texas breed. The suppression of the movement from Texas by trail would check a legitimate and beneficial competition between the cattle-breeders of the north and of the south, and therefore tend to enhance the price of beef. It would also, in a high degree, operate to the detriment of the enormous cattle interests of the great State of Texas. It appears, therefore, upon purely commercial considerations, greatly to the interest of the whole country that the Texas cattle trail should under proper legislative provisions and safeguards be kept open. Any obstacle to the traffic in cattle between Texas and the northern ranges, other than the restraints imposed by quarantine laws, would of course be in derogation of the provisions of the Constitution of the United States securing the freedom of commerce among the States.

The several trails and Texas cattle markets of Kansas hereinbefore mentioned are delineated on may No. 1, at the end of this report.

The propriety of setting aside even so large a quantity of land as that hereinbefore mentioned for the purposes of a cattle trail also involves a question of policy regarding the disposition of the public domain. That is eminently a question for legislative consideration and determination, and it is one therefore which the chief of the bureau does not consider that he is called upon to discuss. All that he has here attempted to do has been to set forth what appear to him to be the facts of chief importance in this case. He has viewed the subject only from a commercial point of view, and in that light has not hesitated to express his conviction of the importance of maintaining inviolate the principle of the perfect freedom of commercial intercourse among the States and Territories of this country.

OBSTACLES TO THE ESTABLISHMENT OF A NATIONAL CATTLE TRAIL PRESENTED BY THE QUARANTINE LAWS OF KANSAS AND COLORADO.

Since the introduction of the bill in Congress, in February, 1885, for the establishment of a national cattle trail, apparently insuperable obstacles to the consummation of that project have been presented in the quarantine laws recently passed by the States of Kansas and Colorado. Those enactments appear to constitute an absolute embargo against driving or transporting by rail Texas cattle into or across those States.

The alarm caused by the losses incurred in Kansas from Texas fever during the last three or four years gave rise to a pronounced sentiment in favor of quarantining the entire State against Texas cattle. Accordingly, in the month of February, 1885, the Legislature of Kansas, then in session, instructed the United States Senators and requestep the Representatives in Congress from that State to oppose the establishment of a national cattle trail within its borders. This, as before stated, led to the change in the route of the proposed trail, and to the location of it in the State of Colorado, along the Kansas border line. At the same time there was pending in the Kansas Legislature a bill for the purpose of quarantining the entire State against Texas cattle. This bill became a law on the 12th of March, 1885.

THE QUARANTINE LAW OF THE STATE OF KANSAS.

The quarantine law of the State of Kansas provides that—

In the trial of any person charged with the violation of any of the provisions of this act, and in the trial of any civil action brought to recover damages for the communication of Texas, splenic, or Spanish fever, proof that the cattle which such person is charged with driving or keeping in violation of law, or which are claimed to have communicated the said disease, were brought into this State between the first day of March and the first day of December of the year in which the offense was committed, or such cause of action arose, from south of the thirty-seventh parallel of north latitude, shall be taken as *prima facie* evidence that such cattle were capable of communicating and liable to impart Texas, splenic, or Spanish fever, within the meaning of this act, and that the owner or owners, or persons in charge of such cattle had full knowledge and notice thereof at the time of the commission of the alleged offense.

The violation of the act is made a misdemeanor, punishable by a fine of not less than $100, nor more than $2,000, or by imprisonment in the county jail not less than thirty days and not more than one year, or by both such fine and imprisonment.

The thirty-seventh parallel of north latitude is the dividing line between Kansas on the north and Texas and the Indian Territory on the south. This provision, therefore, not only places the whole State of Texas, but also the Indian Territory, under the ban of quarantine, between the first day of March and first day of December, embracing the entire period during which cattle are driven from Texas to the northern ranges. It is not presumable that the great State of Kansas would by any unfair or disingenuous exercise of her undoubted police powers forbid a legitimate commerce in Texas cattle within her borders, or the passage of such cattle across any portion of the State. Whatever differences of opinion may exist as to the expediency of the action of the legislature of Kansas upon this subject, the character of the people of that State and the well-known history of their struggles for the establishment of the principles of popular rights forbid the supposition that such action is induced by any other consideration than a conviction of the necessity of meeting a great emergency of a sanitary nature, and therefore that their quarantine law is designed to protect and not to oppose the public interests. Nor is it presumable that the people of

Kansas will hesitate to modify or abolish such legislation if at any time they shall become convinced that their action in regard to Texas cattle is unnecessary or ill advised. The quarantine law of Kansas may be found in Appendix No. 16.

THE QUARANTINE LAW OF THE STATE· OF COLORADO.

The quarantine act of the State of Colorado, which became a law on March 20, 1885, provides that—

It shall be unlawful for any person, association, or corporation to bring or drive, or cause to be brought or driven, into this State, between the 1st day of April and the 1st day of November, any cattle or horses from a State, Territory, or country south of the thirty-sixth parallel of north latitude, unless said cattle or horses have been held at some place north of the said parallel of latitude for a period of at least ninety days prior to their importation into this State, or unless the person, association, or corporation owning or having charge of such cattle or horses shall procure from the State veterinary board a certificate or bill of health to the effect that said cattle or horses are free from all infectious or contagious diseases, and have not been exposed at any time within ninety days prior thereto to any of said diseases.

It is also provided that—

Any person violating the provisions of this act shall be deemed guilty of a misdemeanor, and shall, on conviction, be punished by a fine of not less than five hundred ($500) or more than five thousand dollars ($5,000), or by imprisonment in the county jail for a term of not less than six months and not exceeding three years, or by both such fine and imprisonment.

The 36th parallel of north latitude is 1 degree, or 69½ statute miles, south of the southern boundary line of the State of Colorado. The quarantine law of Colorado may be found in Appendix No. 17.

THE QUARANTINE LAW OF THE TERRITORY OF WYOMING.

The Territory of Wyoming has, by its stock laws, provided for a territorial veterinarian, with ample authority for the prevention of the spread of disease within her borders. The governor of the Territory is also clothed with ample authority to prevent the introduction of any and all contagious bovine diseases from any other Territory or State, whenever convinced that the conditions exist which render such action necessary. These provisions of law may be found in Appendix No. 18.

QUARANTINE LAW OF NEBRASKA.

The legislature of the State of Nebraska, at its recent session, enacted a quarantine law with respect to the prevention and suppression of cattle diseases quite similar in its general features to that of the Territory of Wyoming. This act, which went into effect March, 1885, provides for the creation of the office of State veterinarian, and of a State live-stock sanitary commission, charged with the duty of attending to all matters relating to cattle diseases. Whenever, in the opinion of the commission, it is necessary to establish quarantine regulations, it is made their duty to notify the governor of the State, who is thereupon required to issue his proclamation announcing the boundaries of the quarantine and all regulations relative to the subject. The enforcement of quarantine against the disease known as Texas, splenic or Spanish fever, differs in no respect from the provisions of law relating to the subject of quarantine generally. The law appears to be carefully guarded against any excessive or unnecessarily injurious exercise of power.

QUARANTINE LAW OF THE TERRITORY OF NEW MEXICO.

The Legislative Assembly of the Territory of New Mexico passed an act, approved March 19, 1884, providing for the appointment at convenient points within the Territory, as near as possible to the frontier, of inspectors of cattle, whose duty it is to inspect all cattle destined for introduction into the Territory. It is also made unlawful for any person or corporation to drive or transport, or cause or procure to be driven or transported, into the Territory of New Mexico any cattle which are, or within twelve months have been, affected with or exposed to any contagious or infectious disease, or which within such period have been driven or transported from or through any district of country where such disease is known to exist at the time of such driving or transporting, or without the certificate of an inspector of cattle.

By an act approved a few days later, namely, April 3, the governor of the Territory was authorized from time to time to suspend by proclamation the operation of the act of March 19, whenever in his judgment the circumstances and public interests warrant and require him to do so, and providing also that the act of March 19 should be suspended in its operation, until such time as the governor might by his proclamation put it into operation and effect. These two acts, therefore, make the whole matter of enforcing quarantine measures in New Mexico as against Texas cattle one of administrative responsibility. The people of Texas appear, however, to regard the action of New Mexico as somewhat inimical to their interests.

REMARKS IN REGARD TO THE QUARANTINE LAWS OF KANSAS, COLORADO, NEBRASKA, WYOMING, AND NEW MEXICO.

The propriety of introducing into a quarantine law positive administrative measures with respect to the conditions of time and space, as has been done by the States of Kansas and Colorado, is of course a debatable question. The State of Nebraska and the Territory of Wyoming have pursued the more usual and cautious policy of throwing upon responsible executive officers the whole duty of administering certain explicit statutory provisions relating to the subject of quarantine. To such officers is also confided the duty of determining when quarantine regulations shall be enforced and when discontinued. They are also empowered to prescribe the particular States or Territories, or parts thereof, which shall be placed under the ban of quarantine. This provision appears to be especially wise and provident, in view of the apparently well-established fact that only Southern Texas cattle are liable to impart the dreaded disease, and that the cattle of Northern and Northwestern Texas are as free of such taint as are the cattle of Kansas and Colorado.

As before stated, the quarantine law of New Mexico throws the whole responsibility of its enforcement upon the governor, as he may, in his judgment, from time to time, deem such action necessary and proper.

FACTS BEARING UPON THE GENERAL QUESTION AS TO THE SHIPMENT OF TEXAS CATTLE TO THE NORTHERN RANGES.

The whole subject of the "Texas cattle drive," and the quarantine laws which have been adopted for restraining it, has here been viewed historically and in its commercial aspects. It is a subject involving antagonisms of interest and differences of opinion upon which it would not be proper in this connection to attempt to pass judgment.

It appears to be a fact beyond all controversy that very many of the present occupants of the northern ranges, constituting probably more than a majority of their total number, are openly and earnestly opposed to the driving of Texas cattle to the northern ranges upon considerations of a purely commercial and economic nature. First, they do not wish to be confronted by the competition of the Texas cattle in their midst. Second, they find that the Texas cattle in very many places "eat out" the grasses upon ranges which for years past they have regarded, as by prescriptive right, their own. Third, the contact of their herds with the Texas herds tends to depreciate the breed of their cattle, owing to the fact that the Texas herds usually contain a certain proportion of Texas bulls. Cows and bulls usually intermingle freely on the ranges. This, of course, interferes with the efforts of the northern herdsmen to improve the breed of their cattle by importing at considera ble expense high-grade bulls. But the fact that the herdsmen of Texas are also making strenuous efforts to improve the breed of their catttle promises in the future to meet that objection.

The fact of the prevalence of a very decided opposition among the northern herdsmen to the continuance of the Texas cattle trade, upon purely commercial grounds, is clearly indicated by the following remarks made before the National Cattlemen's Convention held at Saint Louis in November, 1884, by Mr. A. T. Babbitt, a delegate from Wyoming:

We came from Wyoming objecting to the idea of a trail. Our objection has, to some extent, been misunderstood. We did not object to it on the ground of the liability of infection, or of cattle disease, because cattle driven from the south have never hurt us so far north, and we are not afraid of them. We have objected to the trail simply on the ground of safety of our investments. We have believed that if Government made an appropriation whereby a public highway for cattle was to be established, over which the immense herds of surplus cattle from Texas were to be invited to come and overwhelm us, we were in danger of obliteration and extinction. Now, we have said to our Texas friends, " You favor us in a measure which is very dear to us, and we will favor you with all earnestness and in good part, in favor of every pet scheme from the south." We have made that proposition in good faith, and I say in behalf of my associates from the north, at least from Wyoming Territory Stock-Growers' Association, that we will carry out that in good faith. The idea is, if we can get a fair control of the ranges we desire to occupy, we will not object. We want their cattle. We have made our money on Texas cattle—more than on any others.

This statement is admirable for its candor, but it is in the nature of a proposition to refrain from opposing the prosecution of a legitimate commercial enterprise, upon the condition that the friends of that enterprise would lend their influence in aid of securing for the northern herdsmen the leasing of the public lands, a measure which few besides those personally interested in the adoption of the measure would regard as justifiable upon sound views of public policy.

But, on the other hand, the movement of young Texas cattle to the northern ranges is favored generally by persons engaged in stocking new ranges at the north, or who, from the force of circumstances or of habit, regard that method of replenishing their herds as preferable to the plan of keeping cows and engaging in the breeding of cattle in that section. The people of the State of Texas are, of course, unanimous in favor of the " trail." It is with them a matter of great commercial importance, in view of the fact that Texas is essentially a cattle-breeding State.

Already the quarantine laws of Kansas and Colorado have resulted in serious injury to the State of Texas. Mr. D. W. Hinkle, of San Antonio, states, under date of March 28, 1885, that a year ago more than $1,000,000 worth of cattle had been contracted for in Texas to be driven north, but that $75,000 would cover all the contracts to date for the season of 1885. He adds that bankruptcy threatens many of the herdsmen of Texas. The value of all property in that State has been injuriously affected and values generally disturbed in consequence of the quarantine laws of Kansas and Colorado.

Men engaged in the cattle business in Texas bitterly denounce the quarantine laws of Kansas and Colorado, and do not hesitate to declare their belief that such laws amounted to the suppression of the trail by an indirect and unjustifiable expedient.

It is, of course, to the interest of the great majority of the people of almost every State that they shall be enabled to purchase beef at the cheapest possible rate, and this is of course dependent largely upon the fullest and most unconstrained competition in the cattle trade.

From all the information which this office has been able to collect in regard to Texas fever, it would appear that the dangers to be apprehended from it have been considerably exaggerated, and that the Texas cattle trail might safely be continued under proper sanitary regulations.

CONCLUDING REMARKS IN REGARD TO THE QUARANTINING OF TEXAS CATTLE.

The large and flourishing trade which has existed for many years in the sale of young Texas cattle at the North to stock the ranges of Kansas, Colorado, Wyoming, Montana, Dakota, and Nebraska has, in years past, been highly promotive of the range and ranch cattle interests of those States and Territories, as well as of the State of Texas. No sort of governmental restraint could properly be interposed to the continuance of that business, in order to meet objections of a purely commercial nature, such as those to which allusion has herein before been made. The organic law of the United States establishes throughout all parts of the country absolute freedom of commercial intercourse. Under this beneficent provision, an internal commerce has sprung up many times greater in value than our foreign commerce and there has been a development of industry unparalleled in the history of the world. That the freedom of commercial intercourse should be invaded or even threatened by indirection, through the exercise of the police powers of a State for sanitary purposes, is repugnant to the cherished love of liberty which has from the beginning characterized the people of this country. It is essential to beneficent administration that police powers, like all governmental powers, shall be exercised frugally and with sound wisdom and discretion. Those powers, in their application to sanitation, are designed to meet the exigencies of epidemics and unusual or extraordinary visitations, and not to protect against the ordinary and usual hazards of life. Pushed to the extreme, the exercise of such powers might arrest all enterprise and stop the wheels of commerce. It is inconceivable that the people of any State of the Union would countenance such an unwise and unfair exercise of power, if convinced that it was not abundantly justified by an emergency demanding the interposition of a sanitary rule restrictive of commercial freedom. Any such action would meet the condemnation of the whole country, for it would be opposed to the fundamental principles of our institutions, and it would go in the face of all right, and all justice, and all magnanimity.

THE TRANSPORTATION OF TEXAS CATTLE NORTH BY RAIL WITH SPECIAL REFERENCE TO TEXAS FEVER.

Ever since the completion of the Missouri, Kansas and Texas Pacific Railroad and the Saint Louis, Iron Mountain and Southern Railroad now embraced in the "Missouri Pacific System," the beef cattle of Texas have been transported over those roads to Saint Louis and Chicago, and the evil results of such transportation from Texas fever have not been of any great moment, in a commercial sense. For several years Texas cattle have been allowed freely to mingle with native cattle at the Union Stock Yards of Chicago, the largest cattle market in the world.

and the cases of Texas fever resulting from such contact have been comparatively very few.

During the last two years the Missouri Pacific Railway Company and the Atchison, Topeka and Santa Fé Railroad Company have engaged in the traffic of transporting young Texas cattle to the northern ranges in competition with the movement by trail.

Since April, 1883, about 100,000 young cattle have been brought from Southern Texas over the lines of the Missouri Pacific system to points in Northern Texas and thence driven over the trail to the ranges of the northwestern counties of Texas, and also to the ranges of the northwestern territories. Cattle have also been transported over these lines and their connections as far north as Ogallala, Nebr. The facts in regard to these movements are very clearly set forth in a statement made to this office by Mr. George Olds, general traffic manager of the Missouri Pacific Railroad. (Appendix No. 31.)

The first shipment of Texas cattle over the line of the Atchison, Topeka and Santa Fé Railroad was made in the year 1884. During that year about 30,000 head were moved north over the line of that railroad from Santa Fé and other points in New Mexico. Mr. J. F. Goddard, traffic manager, states that, with no unfavorable legislation, about 75,000 cattle will probably be so transported during the year 1885. (See Appendix No. 33.)

The opinion appears to be quite general that cattle brought north by rail are much more liable to impart the disease than if driven over the trail. This impression prevails throughout Kansas, Nebraska, Dakota, Colorado, and Wyoming.

The prevailing opinion upon the subject in Wyoming is very clearly expressed in the following statement by Hon. J. W. Carey, Delegate to Congress from that Territory and president of the Wyoming Stock-Growers' Association:

In so far as my own experience and that of others in the cattle business in Wyoming go, it has been found to be perfectly safe to admit to our ranges Texas cattle which are driven on the trail. By the time they reach Wyoming and Nebraska, when moved in that way, they appear to lose entirely the liability to impart the so-called Texas fever. We of the northern ranges have not the slightest fear of their introduction among our cattle when driven, but shipments of Texas cattle into Wyoming by rail during the year 1884, taught us by dearly-bought experience that such shipments cannot with safety be permitted. In every instance where the Texas cattle brought by rail came in contact with the northern-range cattle they imparted to them the Texas fever, and even to Texas cattle which had been wintered in Wyoming. The losses in Wyoming, Colorado, and Nebraska amounted to fully one hundred thousand dollars, and would have been much greater but for the enforcement of the quarantine laws of Wyoming Territory, which are very stringent and effective.

This result of bringing Texas cattle north by rail was predicted by two eminent veterinarians, Dr. James D. Hopkins, Territorial veterinarian of Wyoming, and Dr. Law, of New York. These gentlemen affirmed that the cause of Texas fever existed in a latent state in the cattle of Texas, but that during the period of from three to six months required in driving the cattle to northern ranges they became freed of the liability to impart that disease, whatever it may be, the theory being that it passes off in fecal matter. The northern range men were inclined to ridicule this hypothesis, but they learned to their sorrow that it was correct. The same experience in regard to shipments of Texas cattle into northern ranges by rail was had in Colorado, in Kansas, in Nebraska, and in Dakota, and I am informed that in these States and Territories the legislature now, or very recently in session, have been considering the question of stopping such shipments by rail. I am not now informed as to the action which has been taken by those legislatures. The opinion of Dr. Hopkins may be found in Appendix No. 19.

The traffic manager of the Missouri Pacific Railway system, and of the Atchison, Topeka and Santa Fé Railroad appears to be firm in the belief that by means of suitable quarantine grounds they will be able to overcome the present objection to shipments by rail. The enterprise of shipping Texas cattle to the northern ranges by rail must be regarded as in a tentative stage, its feasibility being dependent upon the results of experience.

Evidently the transportation of cattle from Texas to the northern ranges offers certain very marked economic and commercial advantages over the movement by trail. With respect to the consideration of time, it is the difference between 20 miles an hour and 10 miles a day. The trail also has its peculiar advantages in cost. The herdsmen of Texas appear to be of the opinion that their interests would be best subserved by having the option of either mode of moving their cattle north.

THE RANGE AND RANCHE CATTLE BUSINESS IN ITS RELATIONS TO THE PUBLIC DOMAIN.

As before stated, the immense herds of cattle which are now spread over a large part of the Western and Northwestern Territories, graze chiefly upon public lands of the United States, but merely by sufferance and not by virtue of any grant or expressed permission from the Government. The laws of the United States in regard to the disposition of the public lands constitute a barrier to the purchase of such lands in quantities sufficiently large for the conduct of the range and ranche cattle business. This has resulted from the fact that the public sentiment of this country is, and always has been strongly opposed to the disposition of the public lands in large quantities, either to one person or to corporations. The genius of our institutions is in favor of comparatively small holdings, and the result of practical experience under this policy since the first settlement by colonists upon our shores, has caused it to become a cherished feature of our method of disposing of the public lands.

The subject here under consideration suggests a brief reference to the provision of law under which title to the public lands held by the United States has been and may now be acquired.

Formerly, whenever public lands were exposed for sale, the title of pre-emptors was first secured. After that sales were made to any and to all purchasers and to any extent. Under existing laws, however, title to the public lands can be acquired only as follows:

1. Lands which, having been offered at public sale, remain unsold, if not afterward reserved or withdrawn from market, are open to private entry in any quantity at the established price per acre, by legal subdivision.

2. Lands may be purchased at public auction by the highest bidder, when offered pursuant to proclamation of the President or under public notice in accordance with directions from the General Land Office.

3. By pre-emption right or the right of a resident upon public land to purchase within a given time a quantity not exceeding one-quarter section.

4. By homestead entry or the right granted to actual settlers upon the public land, possessing certain qualifications, who comply with prescribed conditions as to residence, cultivation, &c., not to exceed 160 acres, without payment except the fees and commissions required by law.

5. Under the timber-culture laws, by planting and cultivating trees, so that at the end of eight years or at the time of making proof not less than six hundred and seventy-five trees are growing on each acre of 10 acres of a quarter section of land. The fees and commissions prescribed by law are the only charges for this class of entries.

6. Under the provisions of the timber and stone act of June 8, 1878, a person or an association of persons may obtain title to not more than one-quarter section of land that is unfit for cultivation and more valuable for timber or stone, by paying therefor at the rate of $2.50 per acre, after complying with the law as to proof, &c. This method of obtaining title to public lands is limited to the States of California, Oregon, and Nevada, and Washington Territory.

7. By entry under the desert-land act to the extent of 640 acres of land, on which no crops will grow without artificial irrigation. At any time within three years the party making such entry must produce satisfactory evidence that he has introduced water upon each of the smallest legal subdivisions, or portion of 40 acres or less, in sufficient quantities to accomplish the reclamation thereof. Land that will produce a crop of hay without irrigation is not deemed to be desert land.

8. By the provisions of the mining laws a person or association of persons may locate a lode claim not exceeding 600 feet in width by 1,500 feet in length, at $5 per acre. Placer-mining claims may be located to an extent not exceeding 160 acres, subject to certain regulations.

9. An individual may enter not to exceed 160 acres of land under the coal land law, and an association of persons may enter not to exceed 320 acres. An association of not less than four persons who have expended not less than $500 in working and improving a coal mine may enter not to exceed 640 acres. Coal lands within 15 miles of a completed

railroad are sold at $20 an acre and at a distance of more than 15 miles, $10 per acre.

The entering or obtaining of titles to land under the timber and stone act and settlement and mining laws is limited to citizens of the United States, or persons who have declared their intention to become such.

10. In addition to the methods hereinbefore stated, land may be obtained in any quantity by military bounty-land warrant and the various kinds of scrip locations.

At the end of this report may be found the following-described tables, furnished to this office by the Commissioner of the General Land Office:

Statement of the number and area of original and final homestead entries made from the date of the passage of the act May 20, 1862, to June 30, 1884, inclusive, Appendix No. 42. Statement of the number and area of the original and final desert land entries made under the act of March 3, 1877, from July 1, 1877, to June 30, 1884, Appendix No. 43. Statement showing the number of timber-culture entries, with areas, made in the several States and Territories, under the timber-culture acts of March 3, 1873, and June 14, 1878, to June 30, 1884, inclusive, Appendix No. 44. Statement showing the number of acres of land surveyed and unsurveyed in the several States and Territories, to June 30, 1884, Appendix No. 46. Statement of the number of acres certified or patented for railroad purposes up to June 30, 1884, Appendix No. 45.

The State of Texas, after permitting the acquisition of large tracts of her public lands by individuals and companies has finally been brought to see the wisdom of adopting a policy in favor of the settler, similar to that pursued by the Government of the United States. In commenting upon this subject, Mr. George B. Loving, of Fort Worth, Tex., a gentleman employed as an expert by this office, says:

The number of acres anyone can now purchase is limited to two sections, and it is expected that the legislature, now in session, may cut this quantity in two or more fractions, so that the acquisition of large tracts of public land in Texas is a thing of the past. * * * Had Texas lands continued to be disposed of in large tracts they would now be all under fence, and the home-seeker would be compelled to look elsewhere, until such time as the cattle companies found it to their interest to divide and sell their lands.

The wisdom of the land policy of the United States has been abundantly vindicated in the material prosperity and in the intellectual and social development of our Western and Northwestern States. It has also tended to the advancement of the commercial, industrial, and transportation interests of the whole country. It would perhaps have been better if the more restrictive policy of later days in regard to the disposition of public lands had been earlier adopted.

It is, however, a notorious fact that the public land laws now in force, although framed with the special objects of encouraging the settlement of the public domain, of developing its resources, and protecting actual settlers, have been extensively evaded and violated. Individuals and corporations have by purchasing the proved-up claims, or purchases of ostensible settlers, employed by them to make entry, extensively secured the ownership of large bodies of land.

The Commissioner of the General Land Office has several times invited the attention of Congress to such abuses, and to the laxity of the present laws relating to the entry of public lands. The violations referred to are also attributed by him to the insufficiency of the force employed by the Land Office for the purpose of detecting frauds of the character mentioned.

These facts commanded the attention of the Forty-eighth Congress. A bill passed the House of Representatives providing for the repeal of all laws for the pre-emption of the public lands, as well as the laws allowing entries for timber culture and the laws authorizing the sale of desert lands in certain States and Territories. This bill also passed the Senate with an amendment, but too late for final action in the House of Representatives.

It has been asserted, in opposition to the provisions of that bill, that it was conceived in the interest of corporations, and of persons and syndicates desirous of having the public lands sold at auction, whereby they might be enabled to secure the ownership of large quantities of pine lands and other lands which could profitably be used in the prosecution of large enterprises, and particularly the range and ranch cattle business. The subject will undoubtedly receive the attention at the hands of Congress which its importance demands.

As before stated, most of the great range-cattle area of the Northwest is not susceptible of cultivation. Here and there along rivers and small streams of water which flow from the mountain ranges and spurs of those ranges are found meadow lands. Besides, in many localities the soil is of a character which affords the facilities of irrigation and in many instances with astonishing agricultural results. But the proportion of lands so available is small indeed. It is estimated that fully 95 per cent of the lands of Western Dakota, Western Nebraska, Montana, Wyoming, Utah, Arizona, New Mexico, and Colorado, other than the mountain regions, is, on account of the small amount of precipitation of moisture, capable of producing only bunch grass, gramma, buffalo grass, and other nutritious grasses, and sage brush as before mentioned, and therefore is fit only for the pasturage of animals. The limited rain-fall, and the fact that it occurs mainly during the spring and summer months, appear, however, to be essential conditions to the production of these grasses. Hundreds of thousands and even millions of contiguous acres of this vast area are now apparently worthless for ordinary agricultural purposes. No settler would accept such land as a gift, upon the condition that he should depend for a living upon the results of its culture. Its value for pasturage is, besides, dependent upon the condition of reasonable proximity to water. It is found in practice that range cattle can graze to advantage only on lands situated within 6 to 7 miles of water. The result is that throughout the range-cattle area grazing is limited mainly to strips of land from 12 to 14 miles in width along streams of water, while beyond such limits there are, in certain sections, large bodies of land abundantly supplied with nutritious grasses which are available for pasturage only in driving herds from the valley of one stream to that of another.

As already stated, it has been proposed to reclaim large tracts of such lands to the use of the herdsmen by means of artesian wells. The results thus far secured in this way afford grounds to believe that the present capacity of the range-lands in the northern territories can be largely increased.

In certain sections the ownership of lands on both sides of streams has been secured for long distances by persons engaged in the cattle business. By this means they have acquired the use of extensive areas of range or public lands, the same being too far removed from other "water rights" for the grazing of cattle belonging to other persons. During the last eight or ten years a struggle has been going on in certain parts of the range-cattle area between settlers and the owners of great herds for the possession of lands along the streams. In so far as possible the herdsmen, in certain localities, have secured water rights under the homestead and pre-emption laws of the United States, and also by the purchase of the proved-up claims of settlers. It is believed, however, that to a considerable extent such acquisitions have been made in violation both of the letter and of the spirit of our land-laws applicable to the public domain.

But in certain other sections of the range and ranch-cattle area there are very many large herds, the owners of which have secured the title to little if any land through which there are running streams at which cattle can obtain water. Of late years there seems to have been a large increase in the number of herds of this description. So long as the streams are not fenced against them they have had free access to water with the cattle of herdsmen who have secured water rights of their own. Herdsmen of this latter class are, in certain quarters, regarded by the former as intruders upon ranges which for several years they have considered their own for the purpose of grazing cattle, but as such lands belong to the Government they have no recourse against the invaders, who generally come in sufficient force to maintain their rights, not only upon the ranges but also to the privileges and benefits of cattle associations, which are organized with the special view to co-operative work at the semi-annual "round-ups."

This invasion of ranges already stocked and provided through actual ownership of land along streams with the facilities of water, in connection with the gradual encroachments of actual settlers, appears to have led to the practice of fencing in large bodies of range lands, thus converting the so-called "range" cattle business into a ranch-cattle business upon the public lands. The reports of special agents of the General Land Office show that 4,431,980 acres of the public lands have been fenced in for that purpose, and without any shadow of right. During the second session of the Forty-eighth Congress an act was passed forbidding such unlawful occupancy of the public lands, and authorizing the President of the United States to take such measures as may be necessary in order to remove or destroy any such inclosure and to employ civil or military force for that purpose. (Act of February, 1885.)

According to the best and most reliable information which the chief of this Bureau has been able to obtain in regard to the practical results of the present condition of affairs, under which the settler locates where he pleases and enjoys equal rights " on the range " with the great cattle owner, it appears that in certain sections the settlers, by securing locations commanding the water supply, have driven the large herdsmen off. This is said to be quite extensively the case in Montana. In other sections the herdsmen have by securing the ownerships of water privileges under the pre-emption and homestead, and other land laws of the United States, and by the purchase of the proved-up claims of settlers, acquired almost the exclusive right to water supplies, and thus shut out settlers from extensive areas.

FOREIGN OWNERSHIPS OF LAND, WITHIN THE RANGE AND RANCH CATTLE AREA.

To a very considerable extent foreigners of large means, and who indicate no intention whatever of becoming citizens of the United States, have purchased lands within the great range and ranch cattle area, and embarked in the cattle business. Titles to such lands have been secured, not only by individuals, but also by foreign corporations. Certain of these foreigners are titled noblemen of countries in Europe. Some of them have brought over from Europe in considerable numbers, herdsmen and other employés who sustain to them the dependent relationships which characterize the condition of the peasantry on the large landed estates of Europe. The public sentiment of this country appears to be opposed to allowing foreigners to acquire title to large tracts of land in this country. During the second session of the Forty-eighth Congress Hon. William C. Oates, of Alabama, presented a report upon the subject to the House of Representatives, from the Committee on Public Lands, accompanied by the following bill :

A BILL to prohibit aliens and foreigners from acquiring title to or owning lands within the United States of America.

Be it enacted by the Senate and House of Representatives of the United States of America in Congress assembled, That no alien, or foreigner, or persons other than citizens of the United States, and such as have legally declared their intention to become citizens thereof, shall acquire title to or own any lands anywhere within the United States of America and their jurisdiction ; and any deeds or other conveyances acquired by such after the approval of this act shall be void.

The following lists, showing such ownerships, were presented during a discussion on the subject by members of that body :

Number of acres of land purchased by foreigners in the United States within a recent period.

[From a speech of Mr. N. W. Nutting, of New York, in House of Representatives, March 27, 1884.]

Purchaser.	Amount.	Purchaser.	Amount.
	Acres.		*Acres.*
English syndicate No. 1 (in Texas)....	4,500,000	Lord Dunraven	60,000
English syndicate No. 3 (in Texas)...	3,000,000	English Land Company (in Florida).	50,000
Sir Edward Reid, K. C. B. (in Florida).	2,000,000	England Land Company, represented	
English syndicate, headed by S. Philpotts........................	1,800,000	by B. Newgas......................	50,000
		An English capitalist (in Arkasas)...	50,000
C. R. and Land Company of London, Marquis of Tweedale...............	1,750,000	Albert Peel, M. P., Leicestershire, England	10,000
Phillips, Marshall & Co., of London..	1,300,000	Sir John Lester Kaye, Yorkshire,	
German syndicate	1,100,000	England	5,000
Anglo-American syndicate, headed by		George Grant, of London (in Kansas).	100,000
Mr. Rodgers, London	750,000	An English syndicate (represented	
An English company (in Mississippi).	700,000	by Close Bros.) in Wisconsin.......	110,000
Duke of Sutherland...................	425,000	A Scotch company (in California)....	140,000
British Land and Mortgage Company.	320,000	M. Ellerhauser (of Nova Scotia) in	
Captain Whalley, M. P. for Peterboro', England	310,000	West Virginia	600,000
		A Scotch syndicate (in Florida)	500,000
Missouri Land Company, Edinburgh, Scotland	300,000	A. Boyesen, Danish consul, at Milwaukee	50,000
Hon. Robert Tennant, of London.....	230,000	Missouri Land and S. S. Co., of Edinburgh, Scotland....................	165,000
Scotch Land Company, Dundee, Scotland	247,666	English syndicate (in Florida).......	59,000
Lord Dunmore......................	100,000		
Benjamin Newgas, Liverpool, England	100,000	Total......................	20,941,666
Lord Houghton	60,000		

Number of acres of land purchased by foreigners in the United States within a recent period.

[From a speech of Hon. Charles B. Lore, of Delaware, in House of Representatives, June 3, 1884.]

Purchaser.	Amount.	Purchaser.	Amount.
	Acres.		*Acres.*
An English syndicate, No. 3, in Texas.	3,000,000	Lord Dunmore......................	120,000
The Holland Land Company, New Mexico	4,500,000	Benjamin Newgas, Liverpool........	100,000
		Lord Houghton, in Florida..........	60,000
Sir Edward Reid and a syndicate in Florida	2,000,000	Lord Dunraven, in Colorado........	60,000
English syndicate, in Mississippi......	1,800,000	English Land Company, in Florida..	50,000
Marquis of Tweedale	1,750,000	English Land Company, in Arkansas.	50,000
Phillips, Marshall & Co., London.....	1,300,000	Albert Peel, M. P., Leicestershire,	
German syndicate......................	1,100,000	England	10,000
Anglo-American syndicate, Mr. Rogers, president, London	750,000	Sir J. L. Kay, Yorkshire, England...	5,000
		Alexander Grant, of London, in Kansas	35,000
Byran H. Evans, of London, in Mississippi......................	700,000	English syndicate (represented by Close Bros.) Wisconsin	110,000
Duke of Sutherland....................	425,000	M. Ellerhauser, of Halifax, Nova	
British Land Company, in Kansas....	320,000	Scotia, in West Virginia.	600,000
William Whalley, M. P., Peterboro', England	310,000	A Scotch syndicate, in Florida.......	500,000
		A. Boysen, Danish consul, in Milwaukee	50,000
Missouri Land Company, Edinburgh, Scotland	300,000	Missouri Land Company, of Edinburgh, Scotland	165,000
Robert Tennant, of London..........	230,000		
Dundee Land Company, Scotland.....	247,000	Total......................	20,747,000

THE PROPOSITION THAT THE GOVERNMENT SHALL LEASE LARGE BODIES OF THE PUBLIC LANDS TO CATTLEMEN.

In consequence of the difficulties which have arisen from the over-stocking of the ranges by placing herds upon them without at the same time securing for their special use water privileges with adjacent feeding-grounds, and in consequence also, it is believed, of the conflict of interests which, in many localities, have arisen as between the herdsmen and settlers, a majority of the cattlemen appear to have arrived at the conclusion that in order to protect their interests they must, if possible, secure the control of large bodies of range lands by means of long leases from the Government. The attitude of the cattlemen upon this subject appears to be formulated in the following preamble and resolutions, adopted at the National Cattlemen's Convention, held at Saint Louis, November 17 to 22, 1884:

Whereas experience has demonstrated that beef-cattle can be more economically raised in the arid and elevated portions of the country than elsewhere, and that the vast plateau lying between the 98th meridian and the Sierra Nevada mountains, is better adapted for this great industry than any other part of the United States; and

Whereas, under existing laws, the occupants of this region are not able to acquire title to lands in such quantity as to guarantee permanency and security in their business, and to justify such improvements and expenditures as have been profitably made in the more favored States; and

Whereas these lands could be leased for a term of years with profit to the Government, without in any manner conflicting with existing homestead and pre-emption laws, thereby giving greater security to those engaged in this great industry; and

Whereas more than three hundred million dollars have already been invested in ive-stock within the limits specified, although the owners of these herds have been unable to lease or purchase the lands, holding them only by possession and sufferance, their property in constant peril from conflicting claims and unfavorable legislation; and

Whereas the beef raised on these plains has become an important factor in our foreign trade, increasing in greater ratio than any other product, and will, within a few years, if properly protected, become the most important article of food supply sent from our shores; and, under these circumstances, we believe it to be the duty of the Government to aid this great industry in every way consistent with the general welfare; therefore,

Resolved, That it is the sense of this convention that it would be for the best interest of the stock-growers located upon this arid region, and to the entire country, to lease these lands for a term of years, reserving all the rights to actual settlers under the homestead and pre-emption laws: Provided, That the States of California, Nevada, Oregon, and the Territories of Utah and Idaho, be excluded from the contemplation and operation of this resolution.

Resolved further, That a committee of seven be appointed by the chair to prepare a memorial to Congress upon this subject.

This formal expression of opinion, embodying a very large and important public question, addressed to the legislative branch of the National Government, commands, it is believed, the assent of a majority of the large herdsmen. There are many of them, however, who are not in favor of the proposed plan, believing it to be opposed to sound views of public policy, and, besides, likely to work more harm than good to the interests of the cattlemen.   The settlers, and all who favor their interests, are unanimously opposed to it.

In support of this measure it is urged :

First. That such leases would justify the great expense of sinking artesian wells throughout the dry area, and that by such means the possibilities of the dry area for pasturage might be more than doubled. It is asserted that under the present order of things the large cattle owners are discouraged from making such improvements, for the reason that after securing a supply of water settlers might, under existing laws, come in around them and cut them off from the water supplies which they had secured perhaps at great cost.

Second. In favor of the leasing of the public lands as before mentioned, it is maintained that at reasonable rates, the rental of such lands would yield to the National Treasury from $10,000,000 to $50,000,000 annually.   This argument does not appear to be of any great force, in view of the fact that the Government does not at the present time stand in need of an increase of its revenues.   The question as to the advisability of adopting the policy of leasing the extensive range-cattle lands of the interior involves, however, other and exceedingly important considerations, to some of which attention is here invited.

The plan of leasing the public lands would afford to the owner or owners of each herd or to associations of herdsmen, the right to fence extensive areas of the public lands, and would thus debar the homestead settler, the settler engaged in the irrigation of lands under the " desert act," and the settler on lands under the privileges of the timber-culture acts, from allowing his cattle to feed on contiguous ranges which are embraced in the public domain.   But this privilege, now enjoyed alike by the settler and the great herdsman, by the owner of a dozen head of cattle and the owner of thousands, is one of the chief inducements which has led the settler to occupy the lands, of which, under the pre-emption, homestead, and other laws before mentioned, he has been able to acquire the ownership.

Such portions of those lands which the settlers now have under fence are generally, it is believed, rendered susceptible to tillage only by means of irrigation.   As a general rule the soil is cultivated by settlers only to the extent necessary in order to supply their own needs and the needs of their families.   Their only surplus product is cattle.   On account of limited capital but few are kept, and those in many cases are required to be sheltered and fed during stormy weather and periods of extreme cold.   Apparently the effect of allowing the large herdsmen to secure the absolute control of " range lands" through leasing would be to compel very many settlers to abandon their homes and sell them to the large herdsmen at prices which the latter might be able to dictate. But even if the settler should wish to remain, as thus environed, he would, in various ways, be at the mercy of the great herdsmen.

It appears hardly necessary to go further into this subject in the present connection in order to show that the proposition to lease the public lands in large bodies would be in the face of the line of policy regarding the disposition of the public lands which has prevailed from the beginning, and which has wrought beneficially to the commercial and industrial interests of the United States. Evidently it will be much more in harmony with the sentiments and wishes of the people of this country if the National Government shall adhere to its present line of policy regarding the disposition of the public lands and provide additional safeguards and offer new inducements to settlers rather than place any possible barrier to the occupancy of the public lands by them or to their enjoyment of the privileges which they have already secured under existing laws. In a word, it will be much more promotive of the public interests if the lands now held by the Government shall be dedicated to the rearing of men rather than to the rearing of cattle.

Another highly objectionable feature of the proposition to lease the range lands of the great dry area must here be mentioned. The effect, at the present time, of leasing all the available range cattle lands to persons occupying them would be to prevent other owners of herds from engaging in the business. That would, of course, be to shut out competition in a business which has already yielded enormous profits. It is held by some that in certain sections the ranges are now fully stocked; but that is denied. For the Government to take such action as would tend to check competition, and therefore promote a monopoly of the use of its own free lands, would be in the highest degree objectionable. No class of men, much less tenants by sufferance upon the public lands, have reason to expect such protection of their business interests against the hazards of commercial competition. Besides, it is evident that cattlemen would, under the privileges of leasing, combine in great associations, a measure apparently required by the exigencies of the semi-annual "round-ups," and thus be able the more effectually to eliminate competition. In other words, enormous monopolies would be created, having vast territorial sway.

But the people of this country are intolerant of monopoly powers generally. Wherever such powers do exist, apparently of necessity or from the force of circumstances beyond human control, as, for example, in our system of railroad transportation, there is generally a popular demand that the exercise of such powers shall be subjected to a close public scrutiny and to such regulations as experience has proved to be necessary in order to protect the public interests. But it appears to be highly inexpedient to subject the National Government to the duty of supervising or regulating commercial and industrial affairs wherever it can be avoided. The danger also exists that the proposed system of leasing the public lands might become a source of official corruption.

In various ways it would be troublesome, indeed, perhaps even more so than the so-called " Indian problem."

It seems, also, to go without saying that public sentiment in the United States is opposed to allowing unnaturalized foreigners engaged in the cattle business to obtain by the leasing of public lands a more permanent foothold than they have already been able to secure in this country under our land laws now in force.

CONCLUDING REMARKS IN REGARD TO THE OCCUPANCY OF THE PUBLIC LANDS FOR RANGE-CATTLE PURPOSES.

The range and ranch cattle business of the Northwestern States and Territories is one of the most attractive and important commercial and industrial enterprises of the present day, and, as such, is fully entitled to all the encouragement and protection which may be accorded it consistently with the observance of those rules of policy which are fundamental to American institutions, and which have exerted so important an influence upon the course of the social and industrial development of the country.

The range and ranch cattle business of the North has provided an enormous outlet for young cattle from the great State of Texas, the most prolific breeding ground in this country, and it has also provided quite extensively a market for young cattle from the dairy States of the West, and from the State of Oregon and Washington Territory, to be matured and fattened on the northern ranges. It has also added very largely to the beef supply of this country, and thus has exerted a most important influence in placing that very nutritious and desirable article of food within the reach of the laboring classes. It has, besides, afforded a large amount of profitable traffic to transcontinental railroads, and been the means of greatly encouraging railroad construction throughout the Territories, thereby largely increasing their population and wealth. At the same time it has been highly promotive of both the internal and the foreign commerce of the United States.

The northern range-cattle business has also been perhaps the most efficient 'instrumentality in solving the Indian problem, by occupying lands throughout that extensive region over which formerly the Indians roamed, and upon which for centuries the buffalo and other wild animals fed. By this means a vast area, which, but a few years ago, was apparently a barren waste, has been converted into a scene of enterprise and of thrift, and now supplies a large and profitable employment both to capital and to labor. Thus the scope of the national industries has been greatly enlarged and the national wealth increased.

Already the range and ranch cattle industry has passed through two or three successive stages of development, and it appears to be now in a transition state. That in the future it will largely increase, no one who has studied the subject with any degree of care can for a moment doubt.

Evidently it is yet too early to attempt to throw around it the constraints of artificial conditions. Its best and most natural development for the good of the country must come as the result of a growth conformed to its relationships to co-ordinate branches of industry throughout the vast area where now, to a great extent, it occupies the attitude of a pilgrim upon the public lands of the United States. The difficulties of which the cattlemen complain are largely a result of this fact. But the methods of pioneer life are never those of organized society, and it is yet too early to attempt to set bounds to future development.

The conflicts of interests as between the herdsmen themselves and as between herdsmen and settlers, to which allusion has hereinbefore been made, appear to be but the natural and unavoidable result of the interaction of productive forces in the development of the resources of the country, but the history of our race clearly indicates that out of such struggles usually come those adjustments of right and of interest which characterize our civilization and result in the advancement of the commercial and industrial interests of a great and free people.

THE RANGE AND RANCH CATTLE BUSINESS OF NEVADA AND ARIZONA.

The foregoing statements relate more particularly to the range and ranch cattle business of the States and Territories situated east of the Rocky Mountains. The following special statements are therefore presented in regard to the business in Nevada and Arizona.

THE RANGE-CATTLE BUSINESS OF NEVADA.

The range-cattle industry has already attained to considerable magnitude in Nevada. It is estimated that the total number of both range and ranch cattle in the State is about 700,000, During the year 1884, the surplus product was 35,000 head, averaging 700 pounds each when dressed. The chief cattle markets of Nevada are Chicago and San Francisco.

The climate and soil of the ranges and valleys of Nevada and the quality of the natural grasses are especially favorable to the rearing of thoroughbred cattle, both of the milch and beef varieties. Large numbers of high-bred bulls and cows have been imported into the State at great expense.

Much attention has already been paid to irrigation and to the sinking of artesian wells. In this way large tracts of land, formerly arid, have been reclaimed and become productive. There are now about 2,000 miles of ditches in the State, irrigating 150,000 acres of land, and the possibilities of reclaiming large areas of land in this way are very extensive.

Attention is invited to the interesting and instructive statement by Hon. G. W. Merrill, in regard to irrigation and grazing in Nevada. Appendix, No. 26.

THE RANGE-CATTLE BUSINESS OF ARIZONA.

The report for the year 1884, of Hon. H. F. A. Tritle, governor of Arizona, embraces exceedingly interesting and instructive statements in regard to the resources of that Territory, and especially in regard to its capabilities for the raising of cattle. (See Apendix, No. 27.)

There are now in the Territory 300,000 head of cattle, and under existing conditions there is room for 1,000,000 more. With a soil of remarkable fertility the great need is water. The rainfall is sufficient to produce a bountiful supply of highly nutritious natural grasses, but not sufficient for agricultural purposes. The running streams which can be depended upon for supplying the needs of stock are few and far between. As hereinbefore stated, cattle can range only about 6 or 7 miles away from water, therefore vast areas of land beyond such limits, well supplied with grasses, are now unavailable for grazing purposes. The ranges of Arizona embrace 60,000 square miles of good grazing lands, equal to 38,400,000 acres ; a very large part of which cannot now be used for the reason just stated.

A commission appointed to examine and report upon artesian wells in Cochise County, state that " sufficient water has been obtained in this way to water at least thirty thousand cattle, besides affording sufficient irrigation to maintain the gardens that a population attending to this stock would require, and, perhaps, tree plantations for the relief of stock from sun and wind."

Governor Tritle, in his recent report, says, " Should all the grazing land in the Territory be made available in this way it is estimated that there would be ample pasturage for 5,000,000 cattle."

There is also the possibility of largely increasing the area of irrigated lands by the construction of ditches for that purpose, thus utilizing the flow of waters which have their sources in mountain ranges.

Alfalfa, the most nutritious of all the grasses, grows abundantly. It produces five crops annually of from 1½ to 2 tons per acre. It is an excellent food for cattle, and also for hogs.

The climate of Arizona, especially in the northern portions of the Territory, is mild and healthful. No epidemic disease has ever been known among cattle, and the conditions of climate and of soil are favorable to the raising of animals of the higher breeds.

THE RANGE-CATTLE BUSINESS OF THE DOMINION OF CANADA.

The area producing bunch-grass and other nutritious natural grasses extends far north into the British provinces of Assiniboia and Alberta. The fact that the buffalo roams throughout those provinces, and into the province of Saskatchewan, would seem to indicate that cattle may also be fed there, as on the more southerly ranges. It is, however, doubtful as to whether the range-cattle business can be successfully carried on to any great extent in those provinces. Upon this subject Mr. Lorenzo Fagersten, of Chicago, an expert employed by this office, says:

The severity of their winters precludes "range" business in the American sense, and the extra care necessary for the maintenance of a herd equal in quality to our range cattle would add so much to the cost as to completely debar them from our market.

The question as to the raising of cattle "on the range" in the British Northwest is however one yet to be more fully determined by the results of practical experiment. Upon this subject Mr. E. V. Smalley, of Saint Paul, an expert employed by this office, says:

How far north this new cattle district and the comparatively new region in the Valleys of the Bow, the Belly, and the Saskatchewan Rivers east of the mountains will extend, can only be determined by experience. When once stocked the products of this district will go in part to Chicago to swell the enormous cattle movement centering in that city, unless the United States duties on imports stand in the way, and in part to Montreal and Quebec for Canadian consumption, or for shipment to England.

Mr. Smalley adds:

Thus far the beef product of the Canadian ranges has been consumed in the construction camps of the Canadian Pacific Railway, and in the city of Winnipeg.

All the cattle which have thus far been brought over the Canadian Pacific Railway have come from the Montana ranges. Certain of the more northerly Montana ranges are situated nearer to the line of the Canadian Pacific Railway than to that of the Northern Pacific Railroad. This circumstance, and the fact that the supply of grasses in the Province of Assiniboia is abundant during the proper season for marketing, has led to such shipments of Montana cattle by the way of the Canadian Pacific Line. But movements of this sort are sporadic.

The Northern Pacific Railroad constitutes the shortest and cheapest route for the shipment of range cattle to market from at least four-fifths of Montana, and from all parts of Northern Dakota and Northern Idaho.

From all that is now known in regard to the capabilities of the British northwestern provinces for the production of cattle, and in regard to the geographical conditions governing the movement of cattle to market from the northern ranges of the United States, there appear to be no substantial grounds for predicting a cattle movement of any considerable magnitude over the line of the Canadian Pacific Railway.

In British Columbia the climate is generally milder than on the east side of the Rocky Mountain Range, but it is believed that the area there suited to the raising of cattle is not very extensive. The country is said to be broken by an almost uninterrupted succession of mountain ranges and spurs from the Cascade Range, near the Pacific Coast, to the Rocky Mountain range at the east.

THE RANGE AND RANCH CATTLE BUSINESS IN MEXICO.

In a letter addressed to this office under date of April 25, 1885, appendix No. 56, Mr. Levi C. Wade, President of the Mexican Central Railway Company, states that since the opening of that line the number of cattle in Mexico has evidently increased.

Between Paso del Norte and the city of Chihuahua there is a large extent of grazing country, not excelled by any in the United States, with an abundance of nutritious grasses and a plentiful supply of water. It contains many fine lakes and ponds, and on it are pastured vast herds of neat cattle and horses.

Notwithstanding the duties upon cattle imported from Mexico into the United States, the rate being 20 per cent. ad valorem, there is some trade in cattle between Mexico and the United States. During the year ending December 31, 1884, there was transported over the Mexican Central Railroad 2,219 horses and 2,855 head of neat cattle, nearly all of which were shipped from different points in Mexico to the United States. This traffic is constantly increasing. The establishment of a stock-yard at El Paso would promote its development. At the present time the purchase of cattle in Mexico is wholly for the purpose of stocking ranges and ranches in the United States.

GENERAL REMARKS IN REGARD TO THE RANGE AND RANCH CATTLE BUSINESS OF THE UNITED STATES.

The occupancy of the public lands throughout the central and northern portions of the great dry area for range cattle purposes is a legitimate and laudable branch of the national industry. It has subdued and utilized such lands for the production of a cheap and nutritious article of food now brought within the means of purchase by the laboring people of this country, and it has contributed greatly to the foreign commerce of the United States by swelling the volume of our exports. It has also served as an indirect but effectual instrumentality in keeping the Indians upon their reservations, by expelling their game— chiefly the buffalo—from the ranges, and thus removing the main inducement for the Indians to go on hunting expeditions outside of their reservations. Besides, it has supplied in the cow-boys an effective police force, which is ever alert to prevent ostensible hunting excursions by Indians, such excursions in times past having oftentimes been but the pretext to cover schemes for going.‟on the war path.”

It is not a strange thing that a great branch of industry like the range cattle business, which within the space of a few years has assumed gigantic proportion, should in the course of its development have been subject to frictional resistances and embarrassments. But difficulties beset all human enterprises, especially those which are new and have not become fully adjusted to the conditions which constitute their environment.

As hereinbefore stated there are several important features of the range and ranch cattle business which deserve a full and careful investigation by Congress with the view of devising some definite and carefully considered line of policy regarding the disposition of the public land, now so extensively used for the pasturage of cattle "on the range." Such an investigation would, of course, tend to determine the respective rights of cattlemen and of settlers, and it would also embrace incidentally the consideration of the question as to the practicability of increasing the rain fall of the great dry area, and of securing additional supplies of water for cattle and for the purposes of irrigation, by means of artesian wells.

These subjects in their summation constitute one of the largest and most important lines of inquiry which have ever yet commanded the attention of the Government of the United States.

THE GROWTH AND PRESENT MAGNITUDE OF THE CATTLE INTEREST IN THE UITED STATES.

It is impossible to state with any degree of precision the total number of cattle in the United States at the present time. The following table shows the total number for the years 1850, 1860, 1870, 1880, and 1884:

Number of cattle in the United States.

Year.	Milch cows.	Other cattle.	Total.
1850	6, 385, 094	11, 393. 813	17, 778, 907
1860	8, 585. 735	17, 034, 284	25, 620, 019
1870	8, 935, 332	14, 885, 276	23, 820, 608
1880	12, 443, 120	23, 482, 391	35, 925, 511
1884			49, 417, 782

The data in the above table for the years 1850, 1860, 1870, and 1880, are from the Census. The total number for the year 1884 has been compiled as follows: The total number of cattle in the State of Texas is the result of a careful estimate upon the subject by Mr. George B. Loving, of Fort Worth, and Mr. D. W. Hinkle, of San Antonio, Tex. The assessment rolls of the State for 1884 give as the total number 6,517,524 cattle, valued at $81,052,616, but the gentlemen just named agree in the belief that owing to unavoidable errors in the report of the comptroller of public accounts, the total number may be stated at 9,000,000, and their value at $153,000,000. The number of cattle in certain other States and in Territories west of the Mississippi River is taken from a table prepared by Col. R. D. Hunter, president of the National Cattle and Horse Growers' Association, for the national convention of cattlemen, held at Saint Louis, November 17 to 22, 1884. The number of cattle in the remaining States and Territories is from the report of the Department of Agriculture for the months of January and February, 1885. The following table has been compiled from these data:

Total number of cattle and the value thereof in the several States and Territories at the close of the year 1884.

States and Territories.	Number of cattle.	Value of cattle.	States and Territories.	Number of cattle.	Value of cattle.
Maine	350,746	$11,072,378	Ohio	1,801,380	56,149,661
New Hampshire	235,057	7,482,561	Michigan	917,828	28,707,893
Vermont	406,127	10,988,692	Indiana	1,406,929	42,294,540
Massachusetts	270,740	9,173,289	Illinois	2,390,195	74,215,525
Rhode Island	35,125	1,293,524	Wisconsin	1,258,769	34,361,933
Connecticut	229,908	7,940,418	Minnesota	804,393	21,663,589
New York	2,418,303	82,409,227	Iowa	3,664,440	98,451,301
New Jersey	237,804	8,999,468	Missouri	2,572,190	56,492.211
Pennsylvania	1,769,189	57,174,907	Kansas	2,210,000	58,255,536
Delaware	55,004	1,775,058	Nebraska	1,770,181	47,146,932
Maryland	268,085	8,241,044	California	986,600	29,439,385
Virginia	680,259	15,010,541	Oregon	721,861	16,658,440
North Carolina	669,267	9,199,538	Nevada	283,725	5,444,100
South Carolina	358,776	5,002,081	Colorado	918,993	25,341,174
Georgia	955,269	12,594,233	Arizona	233,466	4,486,551
Florida	612,575	5,717,307	Dakota	350,937	9,626,662
Alabama	714,555	8,818,736	Idaho	263,000	6,786,756
Mississippi	688,375	8,933,558	Montana	770,940	22,988,280
Louisiana	406,871	5,973,025	New Mexico	547,113	10,760,073
Texas	9,000,000	153,000,000	Utah	135,087	4,198,727
Arkansas	697,356	10,842,197	Washington	185,625	4,740,573
Tennessee	786,101	14,994,927	Wyoming	1,095,916	19,116,700
West Virginia	454,125	11,539,633	Indian Territory	1,020,000	20,400,000
Kentucky	808,597	23,674,042	Total	49,417,782	1,189,576,926

It is estimated from the best available data that the total number of cattle in the range and ranch cattle area outside of Texas is about 7,500,000. The average value of northern range cattle is, according to the Department of Agriculture, about $25 per head. At this rate the total value of the cattle on the northern range and ranch cattle area may be stated at $187,500,000.

The total number and value of cattle in the United States, in the State of Texas, and in the range and ranch cattle area north of Texas, is therefore as follows:

	Number of cattle.	Value of cattle.
The United States	49,417,782	$1,189,577,000
The State of Texas	9,000,000	153,000,000
The range and ranch cattle area north of Texas	7,500,000	187,500,000

From this it would appear that the total value of the cattle of Texas, and of the range and ranch cattle area north of Texas, is about $340,500,000, which constitutes nearly 28 per cent. of the total value of the cattle in the United States.

The foregoing data are the best which can be procured upon the subject, but they are undoubtedly quite crude.

The number of cattle slaughtered and the value of the annual cattle
product of the country is involved in so much doubt that it is not
deemed advisable to attempt to make any estimate upon the subject.
The annual value of the cattle product of Texas, and of the range and
ranch cattle area north of Texas, may, however, be approximated. According to the best data which can be procured the total number of
beef cattle marketed outside of that State, and mainly at New Orleans,
Chicago, Saint Louis, and Kansas City, was about 625,000, realizing on
the average about $25 per head, or a total sum of $15,625,000.

The number of northern range cattle marketed at Chicago, Saint
Louis, and Kansas City, making proper allowance for duplication, was
about 400,000, and their average value about $40 per head.

The number of beef cattle shipped from Texas, and from the northern
ranges during the year 1884, and their value at shipping points, was
therefore, according to the best available data, as follows:

	Number.	Average value.	Total value.
		Dollars.	*Dollars.*
From Texas	625,000	25 00	15,625,000
From the northern ranges	400,000	40 00	16,000,000
Total	1,025,000		31,625,000

The total value of the exports of cattle and beef products from the
United States during the year ended June 30, 1884, was $41,080,001.
This shows that the value of the cattle products of Texas and of the
northern ranges and ranches was about 75 per cent. of the value of the
exports of cattle and their products from the United States to foreign
countries. It appears, however, from the best estimate which can be
made that the value of the exports of beef from the United States does
not constitute more than 6 per cent. of the total value of the beef product of the country. The fluctuations in the home demand for beef and
beef products, therefore, exert a much more potential influence over
prices than do the changes in the conditions governing the foreign demand. The range and ranch cattle business of the United States also
gives rise to several important internal trade movements, the more important of which will here be mentioned:

First. The driving of young cattle north from Texas to stock the
northern ranges began about the year 1868, and, as before shown, it
has ranged from 100,000 to 450,000 head annually. It is composed
almost entirely of yearling and two-year-old steers with a small proportion of cows and bulls. The total value of cattle constituting this movement amounted, during the year 1884, to about $5,100,000.

Second. Young cattle, both male and female, are also shipped in large
quantities from the States of Iowa, Illinois, Wisconsin, and other States
to the northern ranges to be matured and fattened. This constitutes a

large and valuable adjunct to the dairy business in the States last mentioned, a business found to be more profitable in those States than the
raising of cattle for beef. The female calves are usually kept for dairy
purposes, while the male calves are largely shipped West to stock the
northern ranges. (See Appendix No. 55.) The shipments of this character during the year 1884 over the three principal railroads engaged in
the business were as follows:

Mode of transportation.	Number of cattle.
By Northern Pacific Railroad..	98, 000
By Union Pacific Railroad	26, 180
By Atchison, Topeka and Santa Fé Railroad	31, 000
Total...	155, 180

Estimating the value of these cattle at $27 a head, their total value
was about $4,190,000. (See Appendix No. 54.)

It therefore appears safe to say that the total value of young cattle
shipped into the northern-range area from Texas and from the East,
during the year 1884, was about as follows:

Whence shipped.	Value.
From Texas...	$5, 100, 000
From other States	4, 190, 000
Total...	9, 290, 000

It must be said that these statistics are crude as expressions of the
total movement of young cattle into the northern ranges. They constitute, however, the best available exact data, and are believed to furnish
an approximately correct view of the subject under consideration.

Young cattle were, at an early day in this business, driven from Eastern Oregon and Eastern Washington Territory to stock the ranges of
Montana, Idaho, and Wyoming. Latterly, however, the surplus product
of Eastern Oregon and Eastern Washington Territory has been chiefly
needed for local consumption on the Pacific coast, and for stocking new
ranges in Oregon, Washington Territory, and British Columbia.

There is also another important commercial movement connected with
the range and ranch cattle business of the United States, viz, the shipment of bulls of the finer breeds into all parts of the northern ranges
and also into Texas, for the purpose of improving the breed of the cattle
of those sections. Such high bred bulls are shipped largely from Kentucky, from New York, and other States; to a considerable extent, also,
they are imported from foreign countries. It is impossible accurately
to ascertain the total value of such cattle.

From the best available data it appears probable that the beef product of that portion of the United States which is situated west of the
latitude of Chicago, constitutes about one-half the entire beef product of

the United States. The increase in the beef product of this western portion of the country has been very rapid during the last twenty years. This is clearly shown from the growth of the cattle business of Chicago, Saint Louis, and Kansas City, the principal cattle markets of the West, the city of Chicago being by far the most important of the three.

Number of cattle received at and shipped from Chicago, and the number of cattle slaughtered at that city and sold as fresh, salted, or canned beef, and in the various forms of beef products during the years from 1864 to 1884 :

Year.	Number.			Year.	Number.		
	Received.	Shipped.	Packed.		Received.	Shipped.	Packed.
1864.........	338,840	253,439	70,086	1875.........	920,843	696,534	41,192
1865.........	330,301	301,637	92,459	1876.........	1,096,745	797,724	63,783
1866.........	384,251	268,723	27,172	1877.........	1,033,151	703,402	*324,898
1867.........	329,243	216,982	25,996	1878.........	1,083,068	699,108	*310,456
1868.........	323,514	217,897	35,348	1879.........	1,215,732	726,903	*391,500
1869.........	403,102	294,717	26,950	1880.........	1,382,477	886,614	*486,537
1870.........	532,964	391,709	11,963	1881.........	1,498,550	938,712	*511,711
1871.........	543,050	401,927	21,254	1882.........	1,582,530	921,009	*575,924
1872.........	684,075	510,025	16,080	1883.........	1,878,944	966,758	*697,033
1873.........	761,428	574,181	15,755	1884.........	1,817,697	791,884	*1,182,905
1874.........	843,966	622,929	21,712				

*Indicating city consumption.

It will be observed that there was a falling off in the number of cattle shipped from Chicago during the year 1884 as compared with the shipments during the year 1883; but that the number packed was largely increased.

The total number of cattle slaughtered in Chicago during the year 1884, including those packed and canned and for city trade and shipment in the form of dressed beef, was 1,188,154, as against 1,028,651 during the year 1883.

The growth of the cattle trade at and through Saint Louis is exhibited in the following table :

Number of cattle received at and shipped from Saint Louis during each year from 1865 to 1884, inclusive.

Year.	Number received.	Number shipped.	Year.	Number received.	Number shipped.
1865	94,307	46,712	1875	335,742	216,701
1866	103,259	24,462	1876	349,043	220,430
1867	74,146	26,799	1877	411,969	251,566
1868	115,352	37,277	1878	406,235	261,723
1869	124,565	59,867	1879	420,654	226,255
1870	201,422	129,748	1880	424,720	228,879
1871	199,527	130,018	1881	503,862	293,092
1872	263,404	164,870	1882	443,169	188,486
1873	279,678	180,662	1883	405,090	249,523
1874	360,925	226,678	1884	450,717	315,433

The following table shows the growth of the cattle trade of Kansas City and of the business of slaughtering beef cattle at that point for shipment:

Number of cattle received at and shipped from Kansas City during each year from 1868 to 1884.

Year.	Number received.	Number shipped.	Number slaughtered.	Year.	Number received.	Number shipped.	Number slaughtered.
1868	4,200	....	4,200	1877	215,768	126,570	27,863
1869	4,450	....	4,200	1878	175,344	181,761	18,756
1870	21,000	....	21,000	1879	211,415	155,831	29,141
1871	120,000	100,481	45,543	1880	244,709	194,421	30,922
1872	236,802	206,467	20,500	1881	285,863	223,989	46,356
1873	227,669	182,245	26,549	1882	439,671	359,012	65,119
1874	207,069	166,519	42,226	1883	460,598	387,598	74,314
1875	181,114	126,262	26,372	1884	533,526	463,001	66,250
1876	183,378	120,040	26,765				

The following table shows approximately the movement of cattle through the great primary cattle markets of the West:

Number of " Native," " Range," and " Texan " cattle received at Chicago and Saint Louis during the year 1884.

	Received at Chicago.	Received at Saint Louis.	Total.
Native	1,228,389	90,000	1,318,389
Range	231,734	} 360,717	950,025
Texan	357,574		
Total	1,817,697	450,717	2,268,414

The above statement embraces the great bulk of the cattle received at the great cattle markets of the West. During the year 1884 there were 533,526 cattle received at Kansas City, of which 90,991 were slaughtered at that point for local consumption and for shipment as fresh beef and as packed beef. The total number of cattle shipped from Kansas City was 463,001, but of this number Mr. W. H. Miller, secretary of the Board of Trade, says, "a few extra-fine native cattle are shipped eastward from this city without entering the Saint Louis or Chicago markets, but the general fact is that cattle marketed here are afterwards marketed in one or the other of those cities." (See Appendix No. 50.)

It is said that the short corn crops of the States of Illinois and Iowa during the last two or three years, and the development of the dairy business in those States, have tended to force the beef cattle industry westward to the great range and ranch cattle area.

THE COST OF TRANSPORTING CATTLE TO EASTERN MARKETS BY RAIL.

The cost of transporting cattle from the northern-ranges to Chicago is shown in the following tables of current rates over the Union Pacific Railroad and over the Northern Pacific Railroad.

The rates per car and per head of cattle are given upon the assumption of an average of twenty head of cattle to each car.

Cattle rates from points on the Union Pacific Railroad to Chicago.

From—	Rate per car-load.	Rate per head.
Green River, Wyo	$176 00	$8 80
Bitter Creek, Wyo	166 00	8 30
Rock Creek, Wyo	133 00	6 65
Laramie, Wyo	128 00	6 40
Cheyenne, Wyo	119 00	5 95
Pine Bluffs, Nebr	112 00	5 60
Ogallala, Nebr	95 00	4 75
Plum Creek, Nebr	95 00	4 75

The following table shows the rates per car-load and per head of cattle, loaded and unloaded, by their owners or agents, when shipped from points in Dakota and Montana to Minneapolis and Saint Paul and to Chicago over the lines of the Northern Pacific Railroad:

Cattle rates from points on the Northern Pacific Railroad to Saint Paul or Minneapolis and Chicago.

From—	Saint Paul or Minneapolis.		Chicago.	
	Rate per car-load.	Rate per head.	Rate per car-load.	Rate per head.
Mandan	$60 00	$3 00	$95 00	$4 75
Dickinson, Dak	65 00	3 25	100 00	5 00
Mingersville, Mont	77 00	3 85	112 00	5 60
Glendive, Mont	89 00	4 45	124 00	6 20
Fallon, Mont	91 00	4 55	126 00	6 30
Miles City, Mont	98 00	4 90	133 00	6 65
Rosebud, Mont	106 00	5 30	141 00	7 05
Custer	117 00	5 85	152 00	7 60
Billings, Mont	122 00	6 10	157 00	7 85
Merrill, Mont	129 00	6 45	164 00	8 20
Springdale, Mont	136 00	6 80	171 00	8 55
Livingston, Mont	144 00	7 20	179 00	8 95
Boseman, Mont	155 00	7 75	190 00	9 50
Helena, Mont	160 00	8 00	195 00	9 75

From the foregoing schedule of rates it appears that the freight charges for transporting cattle to Chicago from the meridian passing through the center of the range and ranch-cattle belt is about $6.50. The current rate per head, from Chicago to New York, is about $4.80. The total freight charge for transporting a steer from the cattle belt to New York, may, therefore, be stated at $11.30.

Range cattle are, however, generally slaughtered at Chicago, very few of them being shipped east of that point. The cattle shipped by rail from Chicago to the Atlantic seaboard, and thence by sea to Europe, consist almost entirely of "native cattle" raised in the States of Illinois, Iowa, Missouri, Wisconsin, Minnesota, Nebraska, and Kansas.

The rate of $4.80 per head for cattle from Chicago to New York is equivalent to 53 cents per 100 miles; the rate of $6.40 per head from Laramie on the Union Pacific Railroad to Chicago is at the rate of 60 cents per 100 miles, and the rate of $6.65 per head from Miles City, on the Northern Pacific Railroad to Chicago, is at the rate of 56 cents per 100 miles. In view of the fact that the cattle traffic from Chicago to New York is a regular or "through traffic" of large magnitude and highly competitive, and that the cattle traffic of the Union Pacific Railway, and also of the Northern Pacific Railroad, is a "local" and non-competitive traffic, the rates charged for the transportation of cattle from the northern ranges to Chicago appear to be not only reasonable, but under the circumstances quite low. The managers of the Union Pacific and the Northern Pacific Railroads appear from the beginning to have regarded the cattle traffic as one of great possibilities, and have pursued toward it the liberal and far-sighted policy of imposing such rates as would tend to develop it, instead of imposing upon it the highest rates which it could possibly bear.

THE SHIPMENT OF CATTLE AND DRESSED BEEF.

An important economic change has been inaugurated in the beef-cattle trade of the country, mainly during the last ten years, by slaughtering the animals at the West and transporting the dressed beef to markets at the East and to foreign countries, instead of transporting the cattle themselves. A long controversy has ensued between parties representing cattle interests and the slaughtering or dressed beef interests, in which railroad managers also have taken an active part as to the relative rates which shall be imposed upon these two kinds of freight, which in so far as relates to the traffic interests of the railroads differ widely in their characteristics and incidents. The merits of this controversy cannot be considered here. The question at issue is, however, very fully considered and discussed, in its economic and commercial aspects, in an elaborate report by Mr. Albert Fink, commissioner, to the Trunk Line executive committee, and published in their proceedings of May 31 and June 1, 1883, also in Circulars 614 and 654 of the joint executive committee for the year 1884.

The current rates for transporting cattle and dressed beef from Chicago to the sea-board are respectively as follows :

To—	Rates per 100 pounds.	
	Cattle, net rate.	Dressed beef, minimum weight in car 20,000 pounds.
New York..	$0 40	$0 70
Boston	40	70
Philadelphia...	38	66½
Baltimore..	37	64½

This shows that the dressed beef rate from Chicago to New York is 75 per cent. higher than the cattle rate.   Under these relative rates the dressed-beef traffic has, as hereinafter shown, greatly increased.

The rates charged for the transportation of cattle and dressed beef from Chicago to the sea-board, in comparison with the rates charged for other classes of freight, are indicated as follows :

Current rail rates on the various classes of freight from Chicago to New York.

Class.	Per 100 pounds.	Class.	Per 100 pounds.
First class	$1 00	Ninth class.........................	$0 30
Second class	85	Tenth class.........................	25
Third class	70	Eleventh class.....................	30
Fourth class.......................	60	Twelfth class......................	25
Fifth class.........................	50	Thirteenth class...................	20
Sixth class	45	Cattle (special)	40
Seventh class......................	40	Dressed beef in car-loads of 20,000	
Eighth class.......................	35	pounds minimum weight	70

THE TRANSPORTATION OF CATTLE AND DRESSED BEEF FROM THE WEST TO THE ATLANTIC SEA-BOARD.

An elaborate and very clear statement of facts in regard to the eastward movement of cattle and of dressed beef from the Western and Northwestern States to the Atlantic sea-board is embraced in a letter and accompanying tables prepared by Mr. Albert Fink, commissioner of the East and West Trunk Line Association, in compliance with a request from this Bureau. (See Appendix No. 17.) This movement includes beef and cattle both for consumption in the Atlantic sea-board States and for exportation to foreign countries. The chief cattle and beef markets and shipping points in the West are Chicago, Saint Louis, Indianapolis, and Cincinnati. One of the tables furnished by Mr. Fink shows the shipments from these cities to New York, Philadelphia, and Baltimore, and to the New England States, including the city of Boston. The following statement embraces the data of this sort for the year 1884:

Statement showing the aggregate weight of cattle shipped East from Chicago, Saint Louis, Indianapolis, and Cincinnati to New York, Philadelphia, Baltimore, and the New England States and to other points between the Mississippi River and the Atlantic sea-board during the year 1884:

| To— | Shipped East from— | | | | |
	Chicago.	Saint Louis.	Indianapolis.	Cincinnati.	Total.
	Tons.	*Tons.*	*Tons.*	*Tons.*	*Tons.*
New York	191, 736	57, 227	7, 406	26, 408	282, 777
Philadelphia	15, 759	7, 398		132	23, 289
Baltimore	6, 211	255	20	257	6, 743
New England States	55, 996	7, 532	20	191	63, 739
Interior points	145, 420	82, 228	14, 521	3, 108	245, 277
Total	415, 122	154, 640	21, 967	30, 096	621, 825

From this table it appears that 66.7 per cent. of the entire shipments was from Chicago, and that 30.8 per cent. of such shipments was to New York. It may also be remarked here that a very large proportion of the shipments to "interior points" is to slaughtering establishments whence the dressed beef is shipped east; but to a much greater extent cattle are shipped to points in the States situated between the Mississippi River and the Atlantic sea-board, chiefly in the States of New York and Pennsylvania, to be there matured and fattened, and subsequently shipped chiefly to the great markets of the Atlantic sea-board for local consumption or for exportation to foreign countries.

DRESSED BEEF.

During the last five years the shipment of dressed beef from the West to the Atlantic sea-board, both for domestic consumption and for exportation to foreign countries, has rapidly increased. The following table shows the growth of this movement from 1880 to 1884, inclusive:

Year.	To New York.	To Philadelphia.	To Baltimore.	To New England, including Boston.	Total.
	Tons.	*Tons.*	*Tons.*	*Tons.*	*Tons.*
1880				15, 680	15, 680
1881				75, 259	75, 259
1882	2, 633	448	879	89, 150	93, 110
1883	16, 365	8, 601	4, 158	116, 747	145, 871
1884	34, 955	12, 815	4, 282	121, 015	173, 067

The above table exhibits the fact that the business of shipping dressed beef from the West to the East is comparatively a new business; that during the last five years it has grown rapidly, and that it has attained its largest development in shipments to the New England States. Up to the close of the year 1884 the business of shipping dressed beef East was almost entirely a Chicago enterprise. This is shown as follows with respect to the shipments to New York, Philadelphia, Baltimore, and the New England States during the year 1884 :

Dressed beef shipped East.

	Tons.
From Chicago	172, 824
From Saint Louis	203
From Buffalo	21
From Illinois	10
Total	173, 058

Preparations have been made at Saint Louis for engaging quite largely in the business of shipping dressed beef from that city to the Atlantic sea-board, and it is expected that this movement during the year 1885 will be of considerable magnitude. The relative growth of the shipment of cattle and dressed beef from the West to the East is clearly exhibited in the following table, which shows the number of tons of each shipped from Chicago, Saint Louis, Indianapolis, and Cincinnati to New York, Philadelphia, Baltimore, and the New England States, including Boston, during each year from 1880 to 1884 :

Years.	Shipments of—	
	Cattle.	Dressed beef.
	Tons.	*Tons.*
1880	385, 386	15, 680
1881	511, 828	75, 259
1882	409, 089	92, 978
1883	441, 470	118, 258
1884	337, 187	173, 028

From this data it appears that the shipment of dressed beef from the West to the East has during the last five years increased much more rapidly than that of cattle.

The two conditions essential to the successful transportation of fresh beef from one part of the country to another, and to foreign countries, are a proper degree of refrigeration and proper ventilation. The art of accomplishing these two objects has been carried to a high degree of success. During the last five years fresh beef has been shipped in large quantities from Chicago to Boston, New York, Philadelphia, and Baltimore, and to other Atlantic sea-board cities, and also to Europe. During the year 1884 there were about 19,000 tons of beef shipped direct from Chicago to Europe. It is stated by persons of large practical experience that if fresh beef is kept at the temperature of about 38 degrees Fahrenheit, in a properly ventilated space, it will not deteriorate in quality if so kept for sixty days.

The high degree of success attained in the transportation of fresh beef by sea, as well as by land, is clearly illustrated by the following table, which shows the quantities and values of the imports of fresh beef into Great Britain from each country during the year 1883:

Imports of fresh beef into Great Britain during the year 1883.

Countries from which imported.	Weight.	Value.	
	Pounds.	*£.*	*Dollars.*
Russia	2, 462, 432	54, 434	264, 903
Denmark	61, 040	1, 475	7, 178
Germany	1, 615, 152	42, 902	208, 783
Holland	20, 608	550	2, 677
Channel Islands	51, 968	1, 854	9, 022
France	29, 456	977	4, 754
Portugal	31, 024	736	3, 582
Australasia	170, 464	4, 231	20, 590
British North America	3, 802, 512	94, 221	458, 526
United States of America	81, 868, 192	2, 059, 007	10, 020, 158
Other countries	24, 080	554	2, 696
Total	90, 136, 928	2, 260, 941	11, 0C2, 869

The fact that fresh beef has been successfully transported from Australia to London across the torrid zone, a distance of 13,275 statute miles, via the Suez Canal, and requiring in the passage by steamer forty days, serves strikingly to illustrate the high degree of success which has been attained in the transportation of fresh beef. Such transportation also affords one of the most striking illustrations of the wonderful achievements of modern commerce.

THE SHIPMENT OF FRESH BEEF FROM THE NORTHERN RANGES.

Already the enterprise has been inaugurated of slaughtering range cattle in the Territories at or near railroad stations, and transporting their carcasses East by rail. It is stated by Mr. E. V. Smalley, Appendix, No. 1, that the Marquis de Mores, a French nobleman, has, with the aid of New York capital, established slaughter-houses at several points in Montana. This gentleman has also provided, for the conduct of his enterprise ,refrigerator cars, in which the dressed beef is carried to Duluth, Saint Paul, Chicago, and New York. Cold storage houses have also been established at various points where the meat is kept until marketed.

Mr. Smalley states that " this enterprise, and a few kindred ones of lesser magnitude, have got beyond the experimental stage, and are evidently destined to farther development."

During the year 1884 about 8,000 cattle were slaughtered in Montana, and the dressed beef transported to Eastern markets by rail.

Meat packing has been inaugurated in Texas at Victoria, Dallas, San

Antonia, and Fort Worth, but from the best information which this office has been able to obtain it appears that the business has not as yet been very successfully prosecuted at those points.

In view of the fact already stated, that fresh beef has been successfully transported across the torrid zone from Australasia to London, a distance of 13,275 miles, the passage requiring forty days, there appears to be no good reason to doubt the success of the business of transporting dressed beef from Montana to Europe, as the route lies entirely within the north temperate zone. The distance from Miles City, Mont., to London is only 5,388 miles, and the average time required for such transportation is not over twenty-two days. Practical experience has proved that fresh beef may, under proper conditions as to refrigeration and ventilation, be kept for two months without deterioration.

The success of the transportation of fresh beef from the northern ranges to Eastern markets of course depends largely upon the establishment of somewhat extensive plants for carrying on the business. It is probable also that the lack of the extensive and varied industries for utilizing, in the most profitable manner, the hoofs, hides, horns, blood, and offal renders that aspect of the enterprise less promising in the Territories than slaughtering the cattle at Chicago, where such varied industries exist. Nevertheless the slaughtering of beef cattle at or near the points of railroad shipment appears to be in the line of progress and there is good reason to believe that it will, in the not far distant future, be extensively adopted.

THE EXPORTATION OF CATTLE AND BEEF PRODUCTS TO FOREIGN COUNTRIES.

The exportation of beef salted, or otherwise preserved, has constituted an important branch of the foreign commerce of the United States almost from the time of the organization of the Government. The exportation of canned beef, fresh beef, and of cattle are, however, commercial enterprises of comparatively recent date.

Attention is invited to an interesting communication in regard to the early history of the exportation of cattle and of fresh beef from the United States to Europe by Mr. T. C. Eastman, of New York. (See Appendix No. 39; also to the statement by William Colwell, esq., of Boston, Mass., Appendix No. 53, and statement by Nelson Morris, esq., of Chicago, Appendix No. 54.)

These gentlemen were pioneers in this business, and ever since have been large shippers.

THE EXPORTATION OF PRESERVED MEATS.

The exportation of canned beef is chiefly a Chicago enterprise. It began about the year 1875. Its growth has been mainly a result of the opening up of the facilities of direct railroad transportation from Texas to Kansas City, Saint Louis, and Chicago, the cattle slaughtered for the purpose of canning being chiefly Texas cattle. The exports of preserved meats were first noted in the annual report of this office on foreign commerce in the year 1864.

The growth of the trade since that time is shown as follows :

Value of the exports, from the United States, of preserved meats during the years 1864 to 1884, inclusive.

Year ended June 30—	Value.	Year ended June 30—	Value.	Year ended June 30—	Value.
1864	$936,884	1871	208,362	1878	$5,102,625
1865	142,683	1872	697,067	1879	7,311,408
1866	58,220	1873	575,407	1880	7,877,200
1867	146,992	1874	848,246	1881	5,971,557
1868	75,226	1875	735,112	1882	4,208,608
1869	181,140	1876	998,052	1883	4,578,902
1870	313,757	1877	3,939,977	1884	*3,173,767

* Canned beef only.

The exports of canned beef were first shown separately for the year 1884. Prior to that time such exports were included under the head of " Meats preserved," but have consisted principally of canned beef.

THE EXPORTATION OF CATTLE.

The following table exhibits the number and value of cattle exported from the United States to the several foreign countries during the year ended June 30, 1884 :

Countries.	Number.	Value.	Countries.	Number.	Value.
Great Britain and Ireland	169,257	$17,336,606	Japan	3	$375
Cuba	8,015	145,024	British Guiana	2	150
Mexico	8,093	128,630	Central American States	1	150
British West Indies	1,135	98,968	Dutch Guiana	1	75
British North American Possessions	3,475	96,820	Chili	2	72
Germany	323	30,200	Hayti	1	65
Hawaiian Islands	141	12,785	United States of Colombia	1	40
Brazil	8	1,625	All other islands and ports	2	160
British Honduras	28	1,400			
French West Indies	12	1,320			
French possessions, all other	18	1,030	Total	190,518	17,855,495

From this it will be seen that the total value of exports of cattle from the United States to foreign countries during the year ended June 30, 1884, amounted to $17,855,495, of which the value of the exports to Europe was $17,366,806, or 97 per cent. The exports to Europe were as follows :

Whither exported.	Value.
To Great Britain	$17,336,606
To Germany	30,200
Total	17,366,806

From this it appears that the exports of cattle to Europe were almost exclusively to Great Britain.

Cattle have been exported from the United States to contiguous foreign countries, and to the West Indies for many years, but it was not until the year 1874 that the exportation of beef cattle to Europe was inaugurated.

The number and value of cattle exported from the United States to Great Britain during each year from 1874 to 1884, is shown as follows:

Number and value of cattle exported to Great Britain during each year from 1874 to 1884.

Year ended June 30—	Number.	Values.	Year ended June 30—	Number.	Values.
1874	123	$113,800	1880	125,742	$11,847,642
1875	110	73,000	1881	134,361	12,995,283
1876	244	31,220	1882	68,008	6,960,600
1877	5,091	546,829	1883	76,091	7,602,244
1878	24,982	2,408,843	1884	169,257	17,336,606
1879	71,794	6,616,114			

It is estimated that of the total number of cattle exported from the United States to Europe during the year 1884 about 95 per cent. were from west of the meridian of Chicago.

THE EXPORTATION OF FRESH BEEF.

The exportation of fresh beef from the United States to foreign countries is confined almost exclusively to shipments to Great Britain.

The value of such exports to all foreign countries during the year ended June 30, 1884, was as follows:

To—	Pounds.	Value.
Great Britain	115,601,057	$11,516,369
Dominion of Canada	5,025,253	454,652
British West Indies	150,611	15,423
British Columbia	3,908	351
Cuba	3,194	529
Total	120,784,064	11,987,331

The exportation of fresh beef to Europe began in the year 1875; but it was not until the year ended June 30, 1877, that such exports were separately reported to this Bureau.

The following table gives the exports of fresh beef from the United States to Europe—almost exclusively to Great Britain—during each year from 1877 to 1884:

Exports of fresh beef to Europe.

Year ended June 30—	Quantity.	Value.	Year ended June 30—	Quantity.	Value.
	Pounds.			*Pounds.*	
1877	49,210,990	$4,552,523	1881	103,397,477	$9,657,068
1878	54,034,159	5,008,689	1882	65,372,941	6,329,449
1879	53,832,910	4,873,506	1883	79,070,842	8,160,769
1880	84,454,881	7,425,255	1884	115,601,057	11,516,369

Of the total exports of fresh beef during the last two years about two-thirds were of cattle slaughtered at New York and one-third of cattle slaughtered at Chicago. About 95 per cent. of the entire exports of fresh beef were of western cattle slaughtered at Chicago or transported East by rail and slaughtered at the seaboard.

The following table exhibits the value of the exports of cattle and of beef products of all kinds to each foreign country during the year ended June 30, 1884:

Value of the domestic exports of cattle and beef products from the United States during the year ended June 30, 1884, stated by countries and in the order of magnitude.

Order of magnitude.	Countries to which exported.	Cattle.	Beef products.	Cattle and beef products.
1	Great Britain and Ireland	$17,336,606	$19,118,960	$36,455,556
2	British North American possessions	96,820	1,183,935	1,280,755
3	France		734,001	734,001
4	Germany	30,200	497,694	527,894
5	Netherlands		354,652	354,652
6	Belgium		318,214	318,214
7	British West Indies	98,968	206,122	305,090
8	Mexico	128,630	41,017	169,647
9	Cuba	145,024	14,225	159,249
10	British Guiana	150	81,290	81,440
11	French West Indies	1,320	65,865	67,185
12	Denmark		63,229	63,229
13	Italy		63,137	63,137
14	United States of Colombia	40	61,585	61,625
15	Central American States	150	59,488	59,638
16	Sweden and Norway		40,428	40,420
17	Hawaiian Islands	12,785	25,041	37,826
18	San Domingo		33,250	33,250
19	Hayti	65	28,727	28,792
20	British possessions in Africa and adjacent islands		28,083	28,083
21	Brazil	1,625	23,430	25,055
22	Dutch West Indies		23,910	23,910
23	Dutch Guiana	75	22,749	22,824
24	Hong-Kong		19,991	19,991
25	Venezuela		14,954	14,954
26	Portugal		12,734	12,734
27	Peru		10,881	10,881
28	Chili	72	10,529	10,601
29	British Honduras	1,400	6,397	7,797
30	French possessions, all other	1,030	5,661	6,691
31	Danish West Indies		6,553	6,553
32	Japan	375	5,838	6,213
33	Russia on the Baltic and White Seas		5,337	5,337
34	Azores, Madeira, and Cape Verde Islands		5,011	5,011
35	French Guiana		4,753	4,753
36	Porto Rico		4,366	4,366
37	Russia, Asiatic		4,134	4,134
38	Liberia		3,701	3,701
39	China		2,891	2,891
	All other countries	160	11,751	11,911
	Total	17,855,495	23,224,506	41,080,001

The value of the exports of cattle to England, Scotland, and Ireland, respectively, was:

Whither exported.	Value.
To England..	$15, 476, 661
To Scotland...	1, 859, 945
To Ireland	None.

The value of the exports of beef products to England, Scotland, and Ireland, respectively, was:

Whither exported.	Value.
To England	$15, 057, 142
To Scotland.	4, 060, 203
To Ireland	1, 615

The following tables show the number of cattle exported and the weight of fresh beef exported from Portland, Me., Boston, New York, Philadelphia, and Baltimore for periods of years:

Statement showing the number of cattle of domestic product exported from Portland, Boston, New York, Philadelphia, and Baltimore during each year ended June 30, from 1865 to 1884, inclusive.

Years ended June 30—	Portland.	Boston.	New York.	Philadelphia.	Baltimore.
	Number.	Number.	Number.	Number.	Number.
1865......................................	4				
1866 *.....................................					
1867.......................................		1	1, 144	1	18
1868.......................................		1	1, 071	1	
1869†......................................					
1870.......................................			1, 201	4	11
1871.......................................		4	1, 070		2
1872.......................................		1	1, 037	1	36
1873.......................................		6	990	1	40
1874.......................................		1	1, 267	10	66
1875.......................................		3	1, 564	2	74
1876.......................................		144	1, 589	5	18
1877.......................................		1 566	4, 863	700	12
1878.......................................	130	13, 887	13, 387	1, 007	504
1879.......................................	2, 783	35, 593	27, 210	7, 005	3, 361
1880.......................................	1, 894	52, 482	65, 151	4, 334	8, 457
1881.......................................	4, 613	70, 072	56, 921	652	7, 502
1882.......................................		32, 568	38, 412		3, 688
1883.......................................	2, 027	37, 613	29, 584	7	8, 714
1884.......................................	1, 332	78, 080	73, 161	721	17, 486

* Not reported by districts.   † Animals not reported in detail.

Statement showing the quantities of fresh beef, of domestic product, exported from Portland, Boston New York, Philadelphia, and Baltimore, during each year ended June 30, from 1877 to 1884, inclusive.

Year ended June 30—	Portland.	Boston.	New York.	Philadelphia.	Baltimore.
	Pounds.	Pounds.	Pounds.	Pounds.	Pounds.
1877	3, 330	81, 000	39, 230, 400	9, 896, 260	
1878		727, 025	43, 926, 387	9, 392, 150	
1879		987, 158	44, 414, 227	8, 436, 945	
1880	544, 949	13, 668, 587	60, 689, 725	9, 599, 561	
1881	4, 327, 704	31, 829, 692	63, 819, 659	3, 430, 850	
1882	1, 067, 229	17, 241, 767	47, 097, 217		
1883	1, 706, 270	17, 999, 586	59, 652, 419		
1884	383, 325	21, 622, 840	93, 557, 738		190, 000

Appendix No. 36 shows the value of the exports of Indian corn, wheat, and wheat flour, hogs and pork products, and of cattle and beef products during each year from 1875 to 1884. Appendix No. 37 shows the value of the exports of cattle and their products in detail from 1875 to 1884, and appendix No. 38 shows the value of the exports of cattle and beef products of all kinds to each foreign country during the year ended June 30, 1884.

INFORMATION FURNISHED BY EXPERTS AND OTHERS IN AID OF THE PREPARATION OF THIS REPORT.

A large amount of valuable information has been furnished in aid of the preparation of this report by the following-named gentlemen, who have been employed as experts: (1) Mr. E. V. Smalley, editor of The Northwest, Saint Paul, Minn.; (2) Mr. Lorenzo Fagersten, Chicago, Ill.; (3) Mr. Theodore J. McMinn, Saint Louis, Mo.; (4) Mr. George B. Loving, Fort Worth, Tex.; (5) Mr. D. W. Hinkle, San Antonio, Tex.; (6) Hon. G. W. Merrill, of Nevada; (7) Mr. Morris Marcus, secretary of the Chamber of Commerce of San Francisco.

The reports of these gentlemen may be found in the Appendix to this report.

The following-named gentlemen have, also, by courtesy, furnished valuable information, referred to in the body of this report, and printed in full in the Appendix: Prof. Elias Loomis, LL.D., of Yale College, New Haven, Conn.; Mr. Silas Bent, Saint Louis, Mo.; General William B. Hazen, Chief Signal Officer United States Army; Capt. Samuel M. Mills, Acting Chief Signal Officer United States Army; Mr. Franklin B. Hough, Lowville, N. Y.; Mr. Albert Fink, chairman of the joint executive committee of the east and west trunk lines; Hon. James F. Miller, M. C., of Texas; Hon. Samuel R. Peters, M. C., of Kansas; Mr. George Olds, general traffic manager of the Missouri Pacific Railway system; Mr. J. F. Goddard, traffic manager, and Mr. A. A. Robinson, general freight agent of the Atchison, Topeka and Sante Fé

Railroad; Mr. W. H. Miller, secretary of the board of trade, Kansas City, Mo.; Mr. Thomas C. Eastman, New York; Hon. Noah C. McFarland, Commissioner of the General Land Office; Maj. A. W. Edwards, editor of the Daily Argus, Fargo, Dak.; Hon. John Hailey, Delegate in Congress from the Territory of Idaho; Hon. Joseph K. Toole, Delegate in Congress from the Territory of Montana; Hon. Morton E. Post, late Delegate in Congress from the Territory of Wyoming; Hon. Joseph M. Carey, Delegate in Congress from the Territory of Wyoming; Mr. Thomas L. Kimball, general traffic manager of the Union Pacific Railway; Mr. T. F. Oakes, vice-president of the Northern Pacific Railroad; Mr. James W. Bell, secretary of the Continental Cattle Company, Saint Louis, Mo.; Col. R. D. Hunter, president of the National Cattlemen's and Horse Growers' Association, Saint Louis, Mo.; Mr. George T. Williams, secretary of the Union Stock-Yards, Chicago, Ill.; Mr. W. B. Farr, secretary of the National Stock-Yards, East Saint Louis, Ill.; Mr. J. M. Hannaford, general freight agent of the Northern Pacific Railroad Company; Messrs. Armour & Co., Chicago, Ill.; Messrs. Swift Brothers & Co., Chicago, Ill.; Mr. George H. Morgan, secretary of the Merchants' Exchange, Saint Louis, Mo.; Mr. H. V. Poor, editor of Poor's Railroad Manual, New York; Mr. J. P. Galloway, Bedrock, Colo.; Hon. Thomas M. Bowen, United States Senator from Colorado; Mr. T. M. Baldwin, chief of division, General Land Office; the Commissioner of Indian Affairs; Mr. Charles A. Maxwell, chief of division, Office of Indian Affairs; Hon. E. P. Roggen, secretary of State of Nebraska; Hon. Richard Coke, Senator of the United States from Texas; Mr. N. J. Wilson, Denver, Colo.; Mr. Paul Clendenin, Fort Verde, Ariz.; Mr. Levi C. Wade, president of the Mexican Central Railway Company; Mr. W. W. Nevin, secretary of the Mexican National Construction Company, New York; Mr. Thomas Sturgis, secretary of the Wyoming Stock-Growers' Association, Cheyenne, Wyo., and Mr. A. T. Atwater, secretary of the National Cattlemen's and Horse-Growers' Association, Saint Louis, Mo.

APPENDICES.

APPENDIX No. 1.

STATEMENT PREPARED BY MR. E. V. SMALLEY, OF SAINT PAUL, MINN., IN REGARD TO THE RANGE AND RANCH CATTLE BUSINESS OF THE UNITED STATES.

THE CATTLE INDUSTRY OF THE NORTHWEST.

The business of raising cattle in the Northwestern States and Territories of the United States has developed with remarkable rapidity during the past few years, and has now attained such proportions as to entitle it to rank among important national industries. If it can be said to be based originally upon a theory, that theory was that the native grasses of the plains and valleys which had formerly supported vast herds of buffalos would support vast herds of cattle when the buffalos ceased to graze upon them, and that as the wild animal had managed to exist through the severe winters in the dry herbage, the domestic steer would learn the same method of self-preservation. The cattle industry, beginning in the country convenient to the Union Pacific Railroad in Western Nebraska, Colorado, Wyoming, and Southern Idaho, spread northward into Montana and Western Dakota, until it has reached the northwest territory of Canada. It received a powerful stimulus from the building of the Northern Pacific Railroad, which was completed through Montana in 1882 and 1883, and opened the way to the stocking of new ranges with young cattle shipped in from Iowa, Illinois, and Minnesota, besides furnishing a convenient outlet for sending beef cattle to eastern markets. Previous to the building of this highway Montana cattle were either driven southward to the Union Pacific line, or shipped down the Missouri River by steamboats from Fort Benton and Bismarck. The shipments began in 1874 with about 3,000 head, and increased during the five following years, respectively, to 5,000, 6,000, 10,000, 20,000, and 25,000. The subsequent increase was less rapid until 1884. In 1883 the shipments were 30,418 head, and in 1884 85,300 head, an increase of 180 per cent. This remarkable increase was caused, in part, by the fact that the new herds shipped in by rail or driven in across the plains from the older and better-stocked ranges of Wyoming, Kansas, Nebraska, and Colorado, and in some instances from distant Texas, had become productive. Some allowance must also be made for cattle shipped at points on the Northern Pacific Railroad from ranches in Wyoming, which had previously been shipped by the Union Pacific. The best measure of the increase of stock on the Wyoming and Western Nebraska ranges is furnished by the receipts of cattle at Omaha via the Union Pacific, which increased from 48,220 in 1876, to 121,554 in 1883.

THE GREAT RANGES.

The great cattle ranges of the Northwest occupy the flanks and valleys of the Rocky Mountain system and stretch eastward across rolling plains broken by low ranges of mountains or by "bad land" formations into western Dakota. Roughly speaking, their width may be said to be about 700 miles, their eastern boundary being the prairies of Dakota, where agriculture without irrigation is feasible, and their western boundary the main divide of the Rockies, though in some places they lap over the divide upon the western slope. Still farther west there is another cattle region of considerable extent, lying beyond the Bitter Root Mountains, and occupying portions of the Great Plain of the Columbia and the valleys of the Snake, the Spokane, the Yakimo, and other tributaries of that river. In much of this region, however, the wheat farmers are crowding the cattle off the rolling bunch-grass plains. The beef cattle sold go westward to supply the local markets of Portland, Oregon, and of the towns on Puget Sound and in British Columbia. As yet there has been no eastern movement from these remote western ranges, but there probably will be in the near future, as the beef product will soon exceed the home demand.

In Montana and Dakota less than one per cent. of the acreage occupied as range territory is valuable for agriculture; in Wyoming scarcely any. The rainfall is insufficient for the growth of crops, and agriculture is only practicable in narrow strips of ground along the borders of the streams where irrigating ditches can economically be taken out. The broad plateaux between the water courses and the slopes of the hills and mountain spurs and ranges must remain for all time what they are to-day, vast natural pasturages, where the native grasses furnish abundant food for cattle and sheep. Cattle-raising in this region owes its notable success, first, to the dryness of the climate, which causes the snow to be blown off the slopes of the hills so as to expose the dried grass; second, to the broken nature of the country, affording shelter in "conlees," and ravines to the animals during severe storms, and lessening the violence of the north wind; and, third, to the admirable qualities of the bunch-grass which covers the ranges. This grass (*Boutelona oligostachya*) affords in its cured state the properties of both hay and grain. It grows in small bunches, which average from six inches to a foot in height, and it shoots from the root in spring before the frost disappears. Its verdant period is very short, for about the first of July it begins to turn yellow, curing itself into firm nutritious hay where it stands. The stalk is solid, unlike that of tame grass, and the head is well filled with small hard seeds, which are retained throughout the winter. Usually the tufts stand from 2 to 4 inches apart. In some districts the intervals are filled with the short, fine, curly buffalo grass; in others the ground is bare between the bunches. From the sparse manner of growth of the bunch-grass a large area of surface is required for the pasture of a comparatively small herd, and it is a common estimate among stock-raisers that thirty acres are needed for each animal. Where a range is pretty well stocked a portion of its area is generally preserved for winter pasturage, the cattle being kept off it during the summer and fall.

THE CANADIAN RANGES.

In the Northwest Territory of the Dominion of Canada, a region lying directly north of Montana, the country is similar in character to that on our own side of the boundary east of the Rocky Mountains, much of the surface being covered with bunch-grass. In spite of the high latitude and the severe cold of the winter season stock-raising is successfully carried on, but thus far the beef product has been consumed in the construction camps of the Canadian Pacific Railroad and in the local markets of the city of Winnepeg. All the cattle brought over the Canadian Pacific to eastern markets have come from the Montana ranges. At no distant day, however, the Canadian Northwest is destined to produce a large beef surplus west of the Rocky Mountains. In the region drained by the Upper Columbia River there are extensive grass tracts unoccupied by herds. The climate is much milder than that of the country east of the Rockies, and will undoubtedly afford a profitable field for stock-raisers when the completion of the Canadian Pacific gives a direct outlet to markets. How far north this new cattle district and the comparatively new region in the valleys of the Bow, the Belly, and the Saskatchewan Rivers east of the mountains will extend can only be determined by experience. When once stocked the products of these districts will go in part to Chicago to swell the enormous cattle movement centering in that city, unless the tariff stands in the way, and in part to Montreal and Quebec for Canadian consumption or for shipment to England.

QUALITY OF RANGE BEEF.

Montana and Wyoming range cattle make excellent beef. The steers grow to an average weight of about 1,100 pounds. Texas cattle, driven as yearlings and two-year-olds to the northern ranges will weigh when four years old about 950 to 1,050—at least an average of 1,000 pounds. A Montana steer is worth, at a shipping point on the Northern Pacific Railroad, from $10 to $15 more than a Texas steer. The Texas stock steadily improves on the bunch-grass feed of the north, and in two generations gains weight and firmness of flesh and assumes the general character of the northern stock. It is now well settled among cattlemen that the climatic conditions adapted for securing the best results in range cattle are a cold, dry winter, free from storms of sleet and wet snow, and a short, warm summer, without excessive or long-continued heat. The plateaux and valleys of the northern portion of the Rocky Mountain system and the elevated plains stretching eastward from the mountains, broken by many spurs and by the fantastic Bad Lands formation, appear to fulfill these conditions admirably. The northern herds are not as prolific, however, as those of more southern ranges, and the driving of Texas young cattle to Wyoming or Montana ranges to mature into beeves is proving to be a profitable enterprise.

LIFE ON THE RANGES.

The large profits realized in the stock business have attracted during the last decade considerable capital from the eastern States and from Great Britain. Adventurous Englishmen, often the younger sons of noble families, find in this industry a congenial pursuit. It is impossible to obtain statistics of the amount of English capital embarked in stock-raising, or the number of Englishmen personally concerned in the ownership or management of cattle ranches; but English participation in joint stock companies and English individual ownership of herds is a notable feature of the business in the entire grazing belt, and especially in Colorado and Wyoming. A recent English writer, Mr. William A. Baillie-Grohman, in a volume entitled "Camps among the Rockies," says on this subject: "The stockman's life out west is one offering certain attractive inducements to the English character, for not only does his vocation bring with it an infinite amount of exercise on the bright breezy plains in a temperate zone in the most delightfully bracing climate in the world, but it is a life where manly sport is an ever-present element. The cowboy and his horse are one. The interest he takes in his equine friends is not of the vicious nature to which our natural attachment to the equine race has been degraded in our own native land; it is healthier in all respects. If the young settler goes far enough west, shooting of the best kind can be combined with the duties of life. Wapiti and Bighorn are often found in either a day's or a two days' ride, and an encounter with the dreaded grizzly roaming freely over the uplands will test his nerves It is a rough life, indeed, coming straight from his English club existence. It will at first perhaps repel him; but the roughness has its good sides, a short experience generally sufficing to weed out the effeminate and unmanly. With the exception of Australia, which I do not know, I opine that in no country will the traveler see in the most out-of-the-way nooks and corners such happy faces, such sterling manliness, as among stockmen in districts where they are often several months without seeing a human being."

It is not uncommon for young English university graduates of high social position to lead for a year or two the rough life of a hired cowboy on a ranch, to learn the cattle business and be competent to manage a large herd to be purchased with the capital of friends at home when they have fitted themselves for the responsible undertaking.

Cattle owners frequently live in the towns and only visit their ranges during the round-up season, leaving the management of their herds to foremen. Many instances are related of men who have grown rich from a small investment in stock made years ago, they meantime pursuing their ordinary avocations in the settlements.

Two antagonistic tendencies are now at work in the cattle country, one in the direction of the growth of powerful corporations, controlling large capital and monopolizing extensive ranges with their herds; the other in that of the steady encroachment on these ranges by small herdsmen who select the best sites on the streams, obtain title to land by pre-emption and homesteading, and perhaps also under the desert act, which gives a mile square of territory for bringing water upon each quarter section, and then pursue the mixed avocation of farming and stock-raising, having no membership in the stock associations which claim the right to the ranges on which they have settled, but looking sharply after their own cattle. Careful observers of these two tendencies believe that unless some provision is made by law for leasing large tracts of public land to stock companies the small herdsmen will gradually push the large herds off from the more desirable ranges. The result would doubtless be a larger total cattle product, for winter losses would be lessened by greater care, and the ranges would be more fully utilized. There must always remain, however, extensive tracts of territory scantily grassed and poorly watered, which will offer no attractions to the settler and upon which only large herds, ranging over hundreds of square miles, can profitably be maintained.

The improvements on a cattle ranch are usually of the rudest character. A log house or "shack," to shelter the men, is erected near a stream, and a rude stable built near by for the ponies and saddles.

If possible, a location is selected near a natural meadow where hay can be cut for the few ponies kept for riding in winter. Most of the horses pick up their feed on the ranges the year round, like the cattle. Sometimes, but not often, an irrigated field of oats or barley will be found near the ranch building. Some of the rich cattle companies have built good structures, but as a general thing the entire expenditure for buildings on a ranch is not more than $400 or $500. The foreman or the owner, with his cowboys, live in a rude fashion without beds or furniture, sleeping in their blankets on the earth floor of their cabins and rarely tasting such luxuries as milk, butter, or fresh vegetables.

DRIVING CATTLE ON TRAILS.

Originally the northwestern ranges were stocked with cattle driven from Texas or Oregon. Texas from an early day has been a great cattle reservoir, and has produced a large annual surplus from the stock first brought into the country from Mexico.

The cattle of the Oregon pioneers driven across the plains from Missouri, became the progenitors of great herds, which, on account of the limited local market of the Pacific coast towns, were sold cheaply to drivers to drive eastward to the ranges beyond the Rocky Mountains.

The drive from Texas or Oregon to Northwestern Wyoming or Eastern Montana occupied from four to six months. Now the railroad has almost entirely superseded the overland trail, save for Texas cattle driven through the Indian Territory to shipping points in Kansas, or to fatten on new ranges in the northwest.

Cattle driving, or "riding on trail" as it is called by the stockmen, is an undertaking requiring hardihood, skillful horsemanship, and a knowledge of the character of the wild country to be traversed. There are mountain ranges to climb, vast barren plains to cross, where the soil seems to be a mixture of sand and ashes and no water is found for long distances, and where the only vegetation is sage-brush and grease-wood, and rivers to ford, liable to dangerous freshets. To conduct a herd of wild cattle across a wild country for hundreds of miles without loss from straying and stampeding is no light task.

A trail party driving a herd of four thousand cattle will usually consist of a captain and six or eight cowboys. They will have one or two wagons for blankets and provisions, a cook, and from forty to sixty ponies for riding.

A day's drive will not average more than 15 miles. The animals "drift" rather than travel, feeding as they go. A stampede, scattering the herd over wide expanses of broken country, is what is most dreaded by the cowboys. Such an occurrence is thus described by Mr. Baillie-Grohman:

"Thunder-storms, though by no means frequent, are a source of danger in summer and are very terrifying to wild cattle. On the approach of one of these violent outbursts the whole force is ordered on duty; the spare horses—of which each man has always three, and often as many as eight or ten—are carefully fed and tethered, and the herd is 'rounded up;' that is, collected into as small a space as possible, while the men continue to ride around the densely massed herd. Like horses, cattle derive courage from the close proximity of man. The thunder peals, and the vivid lightning flashes with amazing brilliancy, as with lowered heads the herd eagerly watch the slow steady pace of the cow-ponies, and no doubt derive from it a comforting sense of protection. Sometimes, however, a wild steer will be unable to control his terror and will make a dash through a convenient opening.

"The crisis is at hand, for the example will surely be followed, and in two minutes the whole herd of four thousand head will have broken through the line of horsemen and be away, one surging bellowing mass of terrified beasts. As an American writer on the origin of these ponies very correctly remarks, stampedes may arise from any cause. Sometimes an inexperienced cowboy may startle the herd by an unusual shout. Sometimes the war-whoop of Indians may alarm it. Sometimes a stampede may result from some uncommon sight, which, frightening the leaders, will take off the whole herd. Fancy a pitch dark night, a pouring torrent of rain, the ground not only entirely strange to the men but very broken and full of dangerously steep water-courses and hollows, and you will have a picture of cowboy duty. They must head off the leaders. Once fairly off they will stampede 20, 30, and even 40 miles at a stretch, and many branches will stray from the main herd. Not alone the reckless rider, rushing headlong at breakneck pace over dangerous ground in dense darkness, but also the horses—small, insignificant beasts, but matchless for hardy endurance and willingness—are perfectly aware how much depends upon their speed that night, if it kills them. Unused, till the last moment, remains the heavy cowhide 'quirt' or whip and the powerful spurs with rowels the size of 5-shilling pieces. Urged on by a shout the horses speed alongside the terrified steers until they manage to reach the leaders, when swinging around and fearless of horns, they press back the bellowing brutes till they turn them. All the men pursuing this maneuver, the headlong rush is at last checked, and the leaders, panting and lashing their sides with their tails, are brought to a stand, and the whole herd is again rounded up."

After a stampede a count is made of the herd to find how many head have strayed, and some of the men are sent out on fresh horses to scour the country and hunt up the lost animals. Single animals on such occasions have been known to stray a hundred miles.

The railroad, as we have said, is supplanting the trail. To what an extent this is the case may be judged from the statistics of a single road traversing the cattle belt. During 1884 the Northern Pacific Railroad carried into Dakota and Montana ninety thousand head of young Eastern cattle to stock new ranches, and also brought from Washington and Oregon eighty thousand five hundred head for the same purpose. Railroads now penetrate all parts of the cattle country except the Pan Handle of Texas. The stockmen of Texas recently advocated, in the national convention held in Saint Louis, the establishment by the Government of a national trail, 6 miles wide, leading from the northern boundary of Texas to the British territory, but this plan was earnestly opposed by the men from the northern ranges, who naturally want to preserve their bunch-grass country for the increase of their own herds, and do not at all approve of the driving of Texas cattle upon them to fatten for market. To some extent young cattle are still driven from Texas to the northern ranges to stock new ranches, but this feature of the stock industry is diminishing year by year. The recently-occupied ranges of Western Dakota were stocked with cattle driven from 'Texas, and ten thousand head have been contracted for in that State, to be delivered next summer in the Bad Lands of the Little Missouri.

The railroads have not only greatly stimulated the cattle industry, but have done much towards improving the quality of the stock on the ranges by the facilities they afford for shipping in blooded bulls and Eastern cattle of good breeds. A marked improvement in the character of the range cattle coming to market is noticeable in recent years. Gradually the long-horned Texan type is disappearing from the northern ranges, supplanted by the Short-horn, the Hereford and the Polled Angus. Stock brought from the East is called "Pilgrim cattle." Usually these cattle suffer more the first winter than the natives, but they soon become acclimated.

DISTRICT ASSOCIATIONS AND BRANDS.

The stockmen on the ranges assume an ownership of the country occupied by their herds without having any title whatever to the soil, unless it be to a few quarter sections near the streams where their buildings stand. According to their ethics the original occupants of a given region alone have the right to pasture cattle upon it and to exercise the privilege of determining whether they will share their range with new comers. They divide the country into round-up districts, in each of which there is an association, with officers and by-laws. The boundaries of a district are usually a stream or a mountain range which forms an obstacle to the cattle "drifting." These districts vary greatly in size. Perhaps a fair estimate of their average area would be 2,000 square miles. The members of an association make an annual contribution to pay "round-up" expenses, including the building of corrals and the maintenance of the round-up parties. This fund is augmented by the sale of "mavericks." A maverick is an animal which has escaped branding when a calf following its mother, and the ownership of which, when found later, cannot therefore be determined. It is sold at auction, and branded with the purchaser's brand, the price being turned into the association's treasury. Every cattle owner devises for his use a brand, and records it in the office of the clerk of the county where his range is located. It then becomes his property, like a trade-mark, and he is entitled to claim all animals marked with it. He does not depend wholly upon the brand, however, but adopts also a peculiar method of slitting or punching the ear of the calf. The brands or ear-marks are explained in a pamphlet issued by the association, and are sometimes advertised in the local newspapers. The cowboys in any round-up district know all the brands in that and the adjoining districts. When a herd changes ownership, the purchaser acquires the right to the brand as well as to the animals, and advertises it as his own. He brands the calves, however, with his original mark, so that in time, as the older cattle are sold, his whole herd will be uniformly branded. So numerous are the brands of the large cattle companies which have absorbed the herds and ranges of small stockmen that entire columns in newspapers devoted to stock interests are occupied with cuts explaining them. Branding injures the hide, and the tanners and leather dealers are beginning to protest against it. At the Saint Louis cattle convention, held in 1884, they made an exhibit showing that side branding took from 2 to 6 cents per pound from the value of the hide. They recommended that branding should be limited to a single mark on the hip. Experiments are now being made at the University of Colorado to ascertain if a durable mark can be made with chemicals. If these experiments are successful the whole barbarous practice of punching red-hot irons into the flesh of the animals and gashing their ears and dewlaps with knives may be abolished.

Membership of an association is obtained by buying the herd of an old member or negotiating with the association as a body for admission. On some ranges new men bringing in cattle have little difficulty in being admitted to the association, but on others the occupants have passed resolutions declaring that the range is fully stocked and that no new herds will be admitted. Of course there is no legal power to keep out new men who may wish to bring in cattle, but such men would be boycotted by not being allowed to participate in the round-ups, by having their mavericks taken as the property of the association, and by being annoyed in many ways by the cowboys of the old occupants of the Territory. It is not often that a stockman will attempt to put a herd into a round-up district without the consent of the association. Trouble sometimes arises, however, between the owners of large herds and settlers who take up land for farming along the streams, fence in the water, and keep a few herds of cattle to graze near by. The stockman dislikes the settler. He wants the whole country kept as an open range, and has a hearty detestation of fenced fields. In the best grazing districts, such as the Judith Basin and the Tongue River Valley, Montana, the tendency is more and more towards the occupancy of the land by ranchmen who raise crops and keep small herds, and whose fences obstruct the freedom of the great ranges. In Wyoming and Colorado and also in the more southern regions stock companies controlling large capital have in many instances attempted to hold vast areas of pasturage by inclosing them with barbed wire fences without any right of ownership to the soil. In some instances these fences have surrounded the homestead improvements of farmers, and conflicts have arisen between the two classes. In Texas at one time there was found a Fence Cutters' Society, whose members rode about, equipped with big shears, and cut every wire that obstructed their way. Legislation authorizing the leasing of public lands for grazing purposes was urged upon Congress by the cattle convention lately held at Saint Louis. Such legislation is opposed by most of the newspapers in the West on the ground that it would hinder the development of the country by preventing the settlement by farmers of the arable valleys lying within the bounds of the extensive regions which are claimed as a whole to be strictly pastoral districts. It seems desirable, however, that Congress should, by some well-guarded measure, provide for the ownership of grazing lands in larger tracts than the homestead and pre-emption laws authorize. Otherwise the rule of the strongest will prevail and powerful companies will monopolize large tracts of country capable of supporting a considerable population. It is to the interests of owners of large herds to hold as much territory as possible that they may have ample range for the increase of their cattle, but public policy opposes this system of monopolizing the public domain and looks to the occupancy of the grazing belt by actual settlers owning small herds and farming wherever agriculture is practicable. In this way the resources of the immense areas, where cattle and sheep raising will always be the chief industries, can most fully be developed.

TERRITORIAL ASSOCIATION WORK.

The district associations are united into territorial associations. Of these larger associations whose affairs are conducted by delegates from the districts, the typical and best organized one is that of Wyoming Territory, which has 335 members. A leading feature of its work is a system of inspection of brands, carried on by salaried agents at the various shipping points. The object of this system is to identify stray cattle and restore them to owners. In an article on the work of the association for 1884, which recently appeared in the Northwestern Live Stock Journal, published at Cheyenne, Wyo., the following facts are given :

A number of inspectors have been employed during the shipping season at various points on the railroads, the more important stations being Council Bluffs, Saint Paul, Valentine, and Pacific Junction, with inspectors this season also at Miles City, Dickinson, and Mandan, the latter points acting as a check upon Saint Paul, or, in other words, a double inspection on Northern Pacific points, thus making the work in that quarter almost perfect. The total number of cattle shipped from the Territory embraced within the operations of the association have been 223,107 head for the season, of which it is estimated that about 166,000 in round numbers were from Wyoming alone. Of this very large shipment Messrs. Wyatt and Hartman inspected 109,677 head at Council Bluffs, among which they found 1,126 estrays; Thaddeus Cole, at Saint Paul, inspected 94,249 head, finding 453 estrays; at Valentine, Nebr., 24,762 head were passed upon by inspector Murray, who discovered 25 estrays, and F. E. Brainard, at Pacific Junction, inspected 14,429 head, finding 123 estrays among them. This work of inspection this season alone has saved to the stock-growers within the jurisdiction of the association a total of 1,727 estrays, returned to the owners or held in trust for them, representing a value of at least $60,465; and all this involving an outlay of a trifle more than $4,000.

Under the new law a total of 2,033 mavericks were discovered and disposed of by the round-up foremen. Heretofore the custom was, attended with more or less dispute, to brand mavericks with the brands of the owners of that portion of the range upon which they were found. This year all such stock was branded with the mark of the association, and sold at auction as required by law. The prices received for mavericks varied from $1.50 to $30.50 per head, according to competition in bidding, but we are informed that those who paid the very low prices have expressed a willingness to settle with the association at a reasonable figure.

" Rustling " under the new law has been greatly curtailed, and it is estimated that the number of cases of illegal branding have not amounted to more than one-twentieth of what they numbered in former years. In all cases where errors have occurred, or where the foremen have placed the association's brand upon the flesh-marked mavericks, remuneration has been allowed for such animals where proper proofs of ownership have been presented.

The work accomplished through the employment of a competent veterinarian, in conjunction with the territorial government, has been of a successful nature. Prompt action in this department of the service has doubtless saved much loss to the members of the association as well as to all stock-raisers in the Territory. It has served to make the quarantine laws of value and done much to prevent irregularities among the stock throughout this section of country.

The detective service, too, has been successfully conducted. The officers of the association have been constantly upon the alert until cattle-stealing in Wyoming is now virtually one of the "lost arts." A number of cases have been prosecuted to a successful termination, others are still in the courts, where they are being vigorously pushed, and a few new cases will doubtless be instituted; but the day is not far distant when, under the present mode of dealing with crookedness in this direction, cases for cattle-stealing will be few. The business is now attended with so much risk that few men dare to embark in it, while matters have been made so lively for old offenders that they do not care to further pursue this vocation.

As a general rule no care whatever is given to cattle on a range, and the owners do not see them save at the semi annual round-ups. Some of the more prudent stockmen send cowboys out on the ranges after severe winter storms to succor animals likely to die by driving them to sheltered places, where grass can be found, but this is not commonly done. In a comparatively few instances owners of small herds separate them in winter from the mass of cattle on their range and feed them on hay after deep snow falls. The general practice, however, is to let the cattle shift for themselves the year round and to accept a winter loss of from 3 to 5 per cent. from starvation and exposure as an incident of the business. Only when the losses are higher than 5 per cent. do the stockmen grumble. Extremely cold weather is not fatal to cattle if they can get food. The dangerous weather is after a snow-fall moister than usual covers the grass, gets crusted and lies solidly upon slopes usually swept bare by the wind. Cattle will endure very low temperatures if their vitality is kept up by sufficient food. Stock-raising, as we have remarked, is successfully carried on in the British Northwest Territory, which lies west of Manitoba and north of Montana, although the mercury sometimes falls as low as 55° below zero. It is a remarkable fact that the winter losses in Northern Montana are no greater than in Kansas and Colorado, although the difference in latitude is ten degrees. Even as far south as Texas such losses have in some seasons of severe northers been heavier than on the ranges on the Sun and Teton Rivers, north of the Upper Missouri.

Two "round-ups" take place every year, the spring or calf round-up, and the fall or beef round-up.

Each association appoints a round-up captain, who gives notice of the place and time of assembly and superintends the work. The cattle owners send each a number of cowboys proportioned to the size of their respective herds, and each cowboy brings four or five good horses. Tents, wagons, camp equipage, and a cook are provided. A central camp, the principal corral, is established. The force is then divided into small parties and the whole district is thoroughly scoured from end to end by the mounted cowboys, who search every ravine and hollow, every *coulee* and wooded slope, and drive in the stock. Two or three men are dispatched to each of the adjoining districts to take part in the round-ups and claim stray cattle belonging to their home association. Near the central corral the great herd is held together night and day by riders who circle around them. In the spring the only work is to drive the cows with their calves into the corrals and mark the calves by branding and ear-slitting. In the fall late dropped calves are cut out of the herd for the drive to the shipping station on the railroad. Each owner or his agent is present to indicate the number of animals he wishes to ship. The drive is a joint affair, but on arriving at the railroad the cattle are separated into different pens according to their ownership, and the transportation to market and sale are matters which each owner arranges for himself.

SHIPMENTS TO MARKET.

The Montana cattle shipments are mainly by way of the Northern Pacific Railroad, that line having moved 3,447 cars, containing 76,560 head, during 1884, and the Canadian Pacific 432 cars, containig 8,740 head. The cattle shipped by the Canadian Pacific come from ranges on the Upper Missouri and its tributaries near Fort Benton, where the distance is nearly equal to points on the two roads. They are driven northward because of the better feed on that route. This movement was somewhat restricted last fall by the action of the Canadian Government in putting, for a time, an embargo on American cattle, because of the prevalence of pleuro-pnuemonia in regions far south of Montana, and the quarantine obstacles were not removed until the shipping season was pretty well advanced.

From the Wyoming ranges, including those of Western Nebraska and Southwestern Dakota, the shipments during 1884 are reported to have reached to the total of 166,000 head. Entire reliance, however, cannot be placed on figures giving a division of the shipments by territorial lines, from the fact that the ranges overlap these lines and there is no agreement as to what number of cattle shipped at points in one Territory should be assigned to the product of another. Thus, many Wyoming cattle are shipped in Montana and *vice versa.* A better method of arriving at the total beef product of the ranges is to take the shipping statements of the railroads which traverse them. The figures of these roads for 1884 are as follows:

```
Union Pacific.............................................................. 109,666
Northern Pacific..........................................................  76,560
Sioux City and Pacific....................................................  24,762
Burlington and Missouri River Railroad in Nebraska........................  14,429

    Total ................................................................ 225,417
```

To this should be added the shipments of Montana cattle over the Canadian Pacific and the shipments (of no great magnitude on lines other than the Northern Pacific) penetrating Dakota; also the number of animals slaughtered and shipped as dressed beef, which was about 8,000. With proper allowances due these items we may place the grand total of the beef product of the Northwestern range for 1884 at 250,000 head.

The Union Pacific Railway Company furnishes the following statement of the receipts of cattle at Omaha over its lines and at Kansas City over all lines;

Year.	Receipts at Omaha.	Receipts at Kansas City.
1876..	48,220	183,378
1877..	81,900	215,768
1878..	95,600	175,344
1879..	115,686	211,415
1880..	121,860	244,709
1881..	149,490	285,863
1882..	123,286	439,761
1883..	121,554	460,780
Total	857,596	2,217,018

The Kansas City receipts represent in great part the product of the Southwestern ranges in Texas, New Mexico, and the Indian Territory, but include, however, the cattle from Western Kansas and Colorado.

The annual movement of beef-cattle from Northwestern ranges to Eastern markets begins in September and ends about the 1st of December. Chicago is the objective point of all the moving trains, and is the great central cattle market of the continent. A project is on foot to establish a route to the East by the way of Duluth and the Great Lakes, and ship live cattle from Montreal by this route and from thence to England, to be fattened on English farms; but this movement has not yet got beyond the stage of interesting theory. The water route to the sea-board has thus far made no figure in the business of cattle transportation.

The current cattle rates over the Union Pacific Railway to Chicago are as follows:

From whence shipped.	Per car.	From whence shipped.	Per car.
Green River, Wyo.....................	$176	Cheyenne, Wyo	$119
Bitter Creek, Wyo	166	Pine Bluffs, Nebr	121
Rock Creek, Wyo	133	Ogallala, Nebr.........................	95
Laramie, Wyo.........................	128	Plum Creek, Nebr......................	95

The following table shows the rate per car-load upon cattle loaded and unloaded by the owners or their agents and shipped from points on the Northern Pacific line in Dakota and Montana:

Shipped from—	To Saint Paul or Minneapolis.	To Chicago.
Mandan, Dak	$60 00	$95 00
Dickinson, Dak	65 00	100 00
Mingusville, Mont	77 00	112 00
Glendive, Mont	89 00	124 00
Fallon, Mont	91 00	126 00
Miles City, Mont	98 00	133 00
Rosebud, Mont	106 00	144 00
Custer, Mont	117 00	152 00
Billings, Mont	122 00	157 00
Merrill, Mont	129 00	164 00
Springdale, Mont	136 00	171 00
Livingston, Mont	144 00	179 00
Bozeman, Mont	155 00	190 00
Helena, Mont	160 00	195 00

A car contains from twenty to twenty-two head, and twenty-one head is the average load. It appears from the above table that the cost of transportation of a steer from a point about midway across the cattle belt (Miles City, Mont.) to Chicago is $6.33. To this must be added the cost of feeding en route, and the expense of the men sent with the cattle. Cattle trains run with the speed of from 15 to 18 miles an hour, and about once in twenty-four hours a lay-over is made to feed and water the stock, of from twelve to twenty-four hours. For this purpose the yards are provided at points at which hay can be procured at a cheap price. In the methods of transporting stock for market the chief improvements in recent years have been in increasing the speed of stock-trains and making more frequent stops for feed and water. There have been numerous inventions in cattle cars, but they have come into very limited use. A so-called "parlor cattle car" has a passage along one side for supplying hay and water to the animals without unloading. A suspension truck, lessening the jarring of the car body is meeting with some favor from railroad companies and shippers. It is evident, however, that the only important practicable improvements in the beef transportation system lies in the direction of shipping the carcass instead of the live animal, and thus at the same time saving the expense of hauling the waste matter in the steer and bringing the meat to the consumers in as good a condition as when the creature is driven from the range. A noteworthy beginning in this direction has been made during the past two years by a French nobleman, the Marquis de Mores, who with the aid of New York capital has established slaughter houses at several points in Montana and runs refrigerator cars to Duluth, Saint Paul, Chicago, and New York, having erected cold storage houses at numerous places to keep the meat until it is marketed. This enterprise and a few kindred ones of lesser magnitude operating in other portions of the cattle belt have got beyond the experimental stage, and are evidently destined to further development. They encounter the opposition of a large interest engaged in the handling of live-stock in transit, and especially of those vested in extensive stock yards in Chicago, and they need more cordial co-operation of the railroads than they now receive. The railroad companies being fully equipped with cattle cars naturally take a conservative view of and are disposed to look with small favor on a change that will make this equipment useless and would require the construction of expensive refrigerator cars.

EXPENSES AND PROFITS.

Profits in the cattle business vary too much from year to year to be definitely stated. The usual figures given at long established ranches in Wyoming and Montana range from 20 to 30 per cent. per year on the capital invested. The variable factors in the problem of the profits are the size of the calf crop, the extent of the depredations of wolves on the young calves, and the amount of winter losses. The productiveness of a herd is not a fixed figure. The rule is to count on calf crop equal to 70 per cent. of the number of cows. As the number of cattle on the ranges has increased, so it appears that the number of wolves "a bunch" of cattle will defend the calves against the attack of the marauders, when a cow and her calf stray away from the "bunch" the calf falls an easy victim to a famished pack. Of late the stockmen have begun to make vigorous measures to destroy these enemies of their herds. Bounties are offered for wolf scalp by the county authorities, and the stock association frequently offers additional sums for killing them. Poison is the common method of destruction, the animals being much too watchful and fleet-footed to be hunted successfully with guns and dogs. Winter losses may wipe out the profits of years. In one exceptionally severe winter nearly one-third of the stock in Yakima County, in Eastern Washington, perished. In the winter of 1880 and 1881 the losses in Wyoming and Colorado were very heavy.

The "breaking-up storms" occurring about the end of March are most dreaded by the stockmen, the cattle, enfeebled by their long exposure, being in poor condition to resist their rigors and live for two or three days without food. The snow falling during the storm is moist and consequently does not drift and leave portions of the ground bare, like the dry snow of the winter months.

The average cost of raising a steer on the ranges, not including interest on capital and investment, is usually estimated by the large stock owners from 75 cents to $1.25 a year. Thus a steer four years old ready for market has cost the owner $4 or $5 to raise. When driven to the railroad he is worth from $25 to $45. A recent estimate, approved by a number of Wyoming ranchmen, placed the profit at the end of the third year on a herd consisting of 3,000 cows, 1,000 yearlings, and 35 short-horned bulls, representing in all, with ranch improvements and horses, on an investment of about $70,000 dollars at $40,000.

A writer in Harper's Magazine gives the following statement of profits on a herd of Texas yearlings (steers) driven to a range in Wyoming and pastured there until old enough for market:

Purchase.

1,000 head of yearling Texas steers, to be delivered on a northern range, at
$15 each... $15,000
1,000 head of two-year-olds, at $18 each.................................... 18,000
Branding the same, say.. 250
Two years' herding, at $1 each per year..................................... 4,000
                                                                              ——————
                                                                              37,250

At the end of the second year sell 750 head of the older lot, which
will then be four years old, to be delivered at the railroad shipping station, at $33 per head.. $24,750
1,250 will then be left to be herded one year, at $1 each............... 1,250
                                                                              ——————
                                                                              38,500

At the end of the third year sell the balance of first lot, which will
then be five years old, viz, 200 head (allowing 5 per cent. for losses),
at $36 per head.. 7,200
Also 500 head of the youngest lot, then four years old, at $33....... 16,500
Cost of herding the balance one year................................. 500
At the end of the fourth year sell remainder of herd, which will then
be five years old, after deducting 10 per cent. for missing and losses
will leave 400 head, at $36 per head.............................. 14,400
Add to cost for taxes and incidentals................................ 850
                                                                      ——————
      Total product of sales....................................... 62,850
      Total cost and expenses..................................... 39,850
Profit at end of four years nearly 60 per cent.................... 23,000
                                                                      ——————
                                                                      62,850

The drawback to investments of this character is the fact that constant renewals must be made by purchase or the business will soon run itself out.

The same writer gives the following figures as written out by an experienced cattleman in one of our eastern counting-houses during the winter of 1880–'81, the object being to show what would be the result of an investment of about $50,000 at prices as they stood at that time:

Put on the range 1881, 2,000 cows, 140 bulls, and 1,000 one and two year old steers, cost $57,000; 1882, will brand 250 steer calves and 250 heifer calves; 1883, 700 steer calves and 700 heifer calves; 1884, 700 steer calves and 700 heifer calves; 1885, 800 steer calves and 800 heifer calves; 1886, 1,000 steer calves and 1,000 heifer calves; 1887, 1,300 steer calves and 1,300 heifer calves; total increase, 4,750 head each of steers and heifers, the heifer calves of 1882, and 1884 raising progeny during the three following years.

Inventory at the end of six years.

1,650 three, four, and five year old steers, average value, $30 each	$49,500
800 two years old, at $22 each	17,600
1,000 one year old, at $15 each	15,000
1,300 calves, at $10 each	13,000
2,450 cows and heifers, at $20 each	49,000
1,000 yearling heifers, at $15 each	15,000
1,300 calves (heifers), at $10 each	13,000
1,000 steers (original purchase), at $30 each	30,000
2,000 cows (original purchase)	40,000
140 bulls	5,600
	247,700
Ranch expenses first two years $6,000	
Ranch expenses third and fourth years 8,000	
Ranch expenses fifth and sixth years 10,000	
Add 20 per cent. of the gross amount for losses during six years 49,540	
	73,540
Net value of herd at the end of six years	174,160

Experienced herdsmen on the northern ranges usually estimate the annual profit on capital invested at from 20 to 30 per cent. for years when the winter losses are no greater than 5 per cent. When much larger profits are reported it will generally be found on investigation that they are in part derived from the increase in the value of herds bought at the low prices prevailing a few years ago in regions then remote from railroads. When the roads advanced into the Northwest the demand for cattle to stock new ranges caused a sudden and considerable rise in prices, and fortunes were realized in the sale of old herds. The cost of managing a large herd is less per head than that of managing a small one, and this fact has led to the consolidation of herds and the formation of stock companies with large capital. These companies buy the herds of small ranchmen and they get possession not only of the cattle but of the country on which they range. A single cattle company in Wyoming advertises its ownership of ninety different brands, each of which represents a herd formerly a separate property. In other words this company has swallowed up ninety different ranches with their herds.

NUMBER OF CATTLE ON THE RANGES.

There is no accurate data as to the number of cattle on the Northwestern ranges. Range cattle are subject to local taxation and owners are required by law to make annual returns to the assessors, but, as may well be supposed, a species of property that escapes in part even the diligent search of its proprietors at the semi-annual round-up and must be sought for in the breaks of the prairies, the gorges of "bad lands," and the lonely defiles of mountain spurs, is never fully listed. The assessors have no way of verifying the returns of the cattlemen and the cattlemen themselves do not know, with any degree of exactness, how many animals carrying their brands may be roaming over the ranges. The assessors' reports for Montana for the year 1884 show a total of 855,963 head, with an estimated selling value, at $35 per head, of $30,340,850. Probably the actual number if an accurate count were possible, would be found to be not far from 1,100,000.

The following shows an estimate of the number of cattle in all the Northwestern ranges in the United States at the close of the year 1884:

Wyoming	1,500,000
Nebraska	500,000
Dakota	250,000
Montana	1,100,000
Idaho	300,000
Oregon	250,000
Washington	200,000
Total	4,100,000

FURTHER DEVELOPMENTS OF THE CATTLE INDUSTRY.

In nearly every section of the Northwestern cattle country the new-comer, seeking for a good opportunity to put in a herd, will be assured by the old stockmen that the range is already overstocked. Whether this is true or not he will only be able to ascertain by careful personal investigation. Self-interest naturally leads the present occupants of the Territory to discourage the bringing in of more cattle. They wish to preserve ample room for the increase of their herds.

The individual who owns a thousand head looks forward to the time when by selling only the steers and keeping the heifers for breeding, they will increase to five thousand ; the company owning five thousand expects in a few years to own twenty thousand or more. If the grass land now occupied is taken up by new herds the present owners of stock must be content to see their business soon limited to sale of the annual increase of their cattle. It is the opinion of competent observers who have traveled extensively in the grazing districts that the ranges will sustain four or five times as many cattle as are now upon them. Large areas which formerly sustained enormous herds of buffalo are entirely vacant ; other large areas are but partially occupied ; others, however, are pretty fully stocked, and here and there may be found a district, as, for example, some of the older-settled valleys of Montana, where the grass has been "eaten out" by overstocking.

Considerable new territory will be thrown open to the stock industry by the reduction of the large Indian reservations in Dakota and Montana. The Great Sioux Reservation, in Western Dakota, could be reduced to one-third of its present dimensions without any injury to the interests of the Indians. Measures are already in progress for cutting down about one-half of the area of the Crow Reservation, in Montana, which is now about as large as the State of Connecticut. The portion to be released from Indian control is nearly all excellent bunch-grass range. The largest of all the existing reservations is that of the Blackfeet Piegans, River Crows, and other tribes lying between the Upper Missouri and the British boundary, which covers an area about equal to that of the State of Ohio. It is proposed by the Indian Commission to establish three small reservations within this territory and to restore the remainder of the old reservation to the public domain. Nearly all the area which will be thus thrown open to white settlement consists of good grazing land. The Milk River Valley, which now lies wholly within the reservation, is especially valuable for range purposes, combined with farming by irrigation on the bottom lands near the river and its tributaries. In Washington Territory much good grass land has lately been added to the open range country by the reduction of the Moses Reservation. To confine the Indians in smaller areas than were assigned to them when they lived by hunting is to put them in the way of becoming civilized. The game which once furnished them with food and clothing·is now gone, and the nomadic life encouraged by the possession of enormous reservations is not favorable to the formation of habits of industry.

With the opening of new ranges by the reduction of Indian reservations and the better stocking of the existing ranges, the cattle industry has a large field for further development. The local and territorial associations are performing an important work in systematizing the business and reducing the losses by straying and by theft. Indian depredations, once a serious matter, have been so far restrained as to be no longer important. Economy is introduced in the care and handling of cattle, and efforts are constant to improve the breeds. The stockman is no longer a lawless semi-savage adventurer, but is a practical man of business, and often an educated gentleman, who spends his winters in Eastern cities. In a word, the whole industry of raising range cattle is becoming established and well ordered. At the same time its profits are no doubt diminishing, but they are still large enough to attract fresh capital and enterprise, and to insure its expansion up to the full limit of the capacity of the grazing belt.

EUGENE V. SMALLEY,

SAINT PAUL, MINN., *January* 15, 1885.

APPENDIX No. 2.

STATEMENT PREPARED BY MR. LORENZO FAGERSTEN, OF CHICAGO, ILL., IN REGARD TO THE RANGE AND RANCH CATTLE BUSINESS OF THE UNITED STATES.

When ten years ago the first shipment of dressed beef was successfully landed in England, everybody connected with the cattle trade of this country hailed that event as the dawn of a new era in the profitable utilization of the vast public domain west of the Mississippi. At any rate it induced eastern and foreign capitalists to engage in cattle raising as a regular business. It soon became apparent that our primitive herds of Texas were unsuitable for the markets; that only the better class of our natives, *i. e.*, the cattle of the East of higher grade, which, originally from Europe, had by the mixture of the blood of the various breeds, lost the identity of any particular race, could compete with the stall-fed animals of England. The remedy was near at hand. The vast herds of Texas cattle were crossed with natives, and a distinct breed of American cattle, designated as range cattle, was gradually established. All commercial cattle at the western markets are now classified as Texas, native, or range cattle. The shipments of dressed beef to England continued without interruption, but subject to too many contingencies to be considered more than a speculative venture, instead of a legitimate business. The expansion of our foreign dressed-beef trade was evidently limited. Only the well-to-do demanded beef of an unexceptional quality, and their wants once filled the market became glutted to such an extent that American beef in England sold below the price in New York City. Our cheese, canned goods, and pork products furnished subsistence to the laboring classes at a cost even below the price of the beef of an inferior quality, which we might have sent. Finally, it was difficult to overcome the prejudice of the public at large. Not wholly without reason was American dressed beef at that time looked upon with suspicion. The cattle were slaughtered at our eastern seaboard, immediately on arrival from a journey of some thousands of miles from their shipping point. In transit, deprived of water and feed, in over-crowded cars, they reached the slaughter houses in the East in a reduced and unhealthy condition. The beef was cooled by ice, a reprehensible method, wrong in principle, the refrigerator method by cold and dry air being practically unknown at that time. What was true then holds good now.

Meantime the population of our cities was steadily increasing. The country was prosperous. The workingmen of America transformed themselves into beef-eaters, an important epoch in the history of our national economy. We discovered that there was a domestic demand adequate to the supply of range cattle, the common-sense breed of America. We knew that Chicago, the great mart for Western produce and the center of the most extensive railroad system of the continent, was equal to any new distributive enterprise, but unlimited capital was needed, with energy, perseverance, and business experience, to successfully combat prejudice and the jealousy of a class of men who always, from personal motives of gain, are opposed to any scheme that may threaten to curtail their enormous profits. At this stage prominent Chicago firms entered the market. The domestic dressed-beef trade was methodically arranged, daily quotations of dressed beef were posted as regularly as the prices of any other commodity ; the incidental features of the trade disappeared, and the vital question of an equitable distribution of our abundant meat supply was solved.

THE ORIGIN OF AMERICAN CATTLE.

Native cattle.

Although at that early date no statistical record was kept, we know that the early settlers of the Eastern States brought from their trans-atlantic homes, among their chattel, live-stock of all kinds. That the immigrants, whenever they had the choice, selected only the best of their stock is a natural supposition. Then, as now, England and Holland were noted for their excellent cattle. As the Dutch and English emigrants predominated, we may omit the less numerous stragglers of other nationalities, and consider the cattle of to-day the direct descendants of English and Dutch stock.

With the superior natural resources of the New World, and the constant influx of a good class of cattle from Europe, it became an easy matter for the Eastern farmer to keep the breed up to the European standard. By the intermixture of the various grades of cattle the specific character of any particular breed was so modified as to necessitate the adoption of a new name for this new variety, and by common usage "Native" was selected. It is from this class that the exporter of live cattle or dressed beef makes his selections.

Texas cattle.

As the European cattle followed the emigrant from his old home, so the native cattle accompanied the Eastern pioneer on his western progress.'

In the far Southwest, beyond the Mississippi, this advance guard of civilization encountered intractable herds of half wild cattle, descendants of French and Spanish stock of only common quality.

They had to a degree degenerated by adapting themselves to natural conditions and surroundings of their habitation, Texas.

This class of cattle became known as "Texans."

As there was no market for these herds, there was no incentive to care for their proper maintenance until the impetus imparted to cattle-raising in general by the first shipment of dressed beef to England led to the crossing of the two breeds.

Since that time an improvement is noticeable, car-loads of native bulls being shipped from Chicago and Eastern markets to Texas ranges every year.

The cross between the original "Texan" and the high bred "native" is classed as

Range cattle.

In this class is included a considerable number of original "Texans," which, from one to two years old, are yearly brought to the ranges lying north of Texas.

It is a remarkable fact, proved by statistics and figures obtained from practical men in the trade, that these "Texans," owing to changed conditions and external circumstances, show a decided improvement when mature for the market over the cross-bred cattle on a Texas range.

It may be truly stated that this grade, i. e., range cattle proper, or the cross between native bulls and Texas cows, is *the breed* for the domestic market.

Admirably adapted to the range, this class is as profitable to the grower and butcher as satisfactory to the consumer.

Cattle statistics.

It is evident that any report of the number of cattle in the Western States and Territories must be very incomplete and unreliable, and any estimate based on such reports only approximately correct.

After allowing for unintentional errors there remains an unknown quantity, which may be expressed as the willful misstatement of the informant, so much the more liable to occur in this case, where the unit represents a considerable sum of taxable property.

Besides, the geographical distribution of this vast aggregation of cattle is so disturbed by local influences—weather and crops—that any estimate as to number and quality of any particular location holds good only for a limited period.

Assessors' returns not being obtainable, we submit the census of 1880, which may prove interesting in the new form we have adopted.

Comparative number of cattle, 1880, and quality as indicated by local prices.

Rank.	State.	Number.	State.	Quality.
1	Texas	1,000	Illinois	100
2	Missouri	432	Nebraska	99
3	Iowa	416	Kansas	93
4	Illinois	385	Indiana	91
5	Colorado and Territories	308	Wisconsin	85
6	Indiana	236	Minnesota	81
7	Kansas	198	Colorado and Territories	80
8	Wisconsin	195	Missouri	77
9	Minnesota	124	Iowa	65
10	Nebraska	113	Arkansas	50
11	Arkansas	113	Texas	40

COMMENTS.

The Indian Territory, Wyoming, Montana, and Dakota have since that time absorbed a large proportion of the natural increase of Texas and other States west of the Mississippi River, but the intentional errors and omissions of young cattle in the aggregate estimate of 1880 were probably large enough to balance, with the remaining portion of the natural increase, the number marketed for beef up to 1885.

The dairy interest of some of the States increases their rates of comparative quality. The assessors' returns of the last few years, if properly analyzed, would show the effect of the deficient corn crop upon the distribution of cattle during that time.

CONCLUSION.

The supply of cattle in the West at the beginning of 1885 was probably equal to the total of census 1880 plus the largest portion of the natural increase, but the numerical center has changed since that time, owing to successive failures of the corn crop in Iowa, Missouri, Illinois, and Kansas on one hand and the increasing demand from northern ranges on the other.

Receipts and shipments, as reported by the secretaries of the principal stock-yards of the West for year 1884:

Chicago.

Receipts, 1,816,500; shipments, 791,000; city use and Chicago packing-houses 1,025,500.

Specification of receipts and shipments by railroads.

Railroads.	Receipts.	Shipments.
Baltimore and Ohio	1,800	19,400
Chicago and Alton	258,000	17,000
Chicago and Atlantic	2,500	68,300
Chicago, Burlington and Quincy	480,000	12,600
Chicago and Eastern Illinois	23,000	5,700
Chicago and Grand Trunk	2,900	1,800
Chicago, Milwaukee and Saint Paul	202,000	7,100
Chicago and Northwestern	269,000	13,700
Chicago, Rock Island and Pacific	232,500	19,800
Chicago, Saint Louis and Pittsburgh	4,200	70,600
Illinois Central	89,000	10,200
Lake Shore and Michigan Southern	2,700	200,000
Louisville, New Albany and Chicago	8,000	1,800
Michigan Central	2,800	180,100
New York, Chicago and Saint Louis	1,100	35,000
Pittsburgh, Fort Wayne and Chicago	2,000	117,800
Wabash, Saint Louis and Pacific	230,000	10,100
Driven into yards	5,000	
Total	1,816,509	791,000

Calves.—Receipts, 52,300; shipments, 31,000; city use and Chicago packing-houses, 21,300.

Analysis—approximate estimates.

Receipts.	Cattle.	Shipments.	Slaughtered.
Natives	1,000,000	720,000	280,000
Range cattle	400,000	71,000	329,000
Texas cattle	416,500	None.	416,500

Remarks.—Of the 720,000 natives shipped, 65,000 were probably exported to England direct from Chicago, alive and 20,000 exported as dressed beef. An appreciable number of the rest were shipped West with 20,000 native calves. The balance went East.

Saint Louis.

No specified returns being furnished, we record the total number reported as 390,000 Texans received and 304,000 shipped.

Kansas City.

	Receipts.	Shipments.	Slaughtered.
Natives	100, 000	80, 000	} 100, 000
Texans	430, 000	350, 000	

As the Western exodus of Texas cattle is here met by the Eastern influx of natives, the analysis is approximated, but the total aggregate is correct.

Council Bluffs.

No report from this very important transfer station. Correctly interpreted, such a report would illustrate the interchangeable nature of the cattle trade without materially changing the aggregate supply.

Minnesota transfer station.

	Receipts.		Shipments.
Range cattle from Montana	75, 000	Natives and Texans to Montana	74, 000
Texas cattle	74, 000	Montana range cattle to Chicago	75, 000
Not specified	14, 000	Not specified	3, 000
		Slaughtered	11, 000
Total	163, 000	Total	163, 000

Remarks.—As very few cattle are shipped direct east from points west of Chicago, where all shipments are ultimately disposed of, except a considerable number of Texas cattle directed to northern ranges and shipments for local consumption to interior points, the difference between receipts and shipments at the above-mentioned stock-yards should be added to Chicago returns in order to get at, approximately, the number of cattle that are yearly marketed for beef.

The figures furnished by Mr. S. M. Sullivan, at the Minneapolis transfer station, are particularly interesting as showing the circuitous channels of cattle migration.

Of the 74,000 shipped to Montana no doubt a goodly number were Texans, direct from their far-off home, to be reshipped after two or three years to the Chicago market as range cattle.

Slaughter-house statistics furnished by leading houses.

	Average weight of cattle.
	Pounds.
Natives	900 to 1, 400
Range cattle	1, 100 to 1, 350
Texans	800 to 1, 050

Comparative value of different grades of cattle of 1,000 pounds live weight for the dressed beef trade, as ascertained by practical experience :

	Pounds.
The dressed carcass of a native steer	530 to 550
Cured hide	57½ to 60
Texas steer	570
Cured hide	70
Range steer	575 to 590
Cured hide	62½ to 65

	Pounds dressed.
1,200 pounds live native	670 to 685
1,300 pounds live native	750
1,400 pounds live native	810 to 840

These are startling figures at first sight, but they admit of a rational explanation. A native steer of 1,000 pounds live weight must not be compared with a Texan of the same heft. The latter, to attain this weight, is matured, while the former is in the lowest stage in the progress of his grade. The large intestines and the well-developed digestive organs of the native steer, inherited from ancestors and developed during generations of feeding on succulent grasses, with water *ad libitum*, counts against him, especially after having had his fill of feed and water before being driven to the slaughter-house. This disproportion disappears by the time he has reached maturity, when he has added 300 pounds of flesh and fat to his carcass.

The Texan, raised under different conditions, fed on the dry though nutritious grasses of his clime, where water is rather a luxury, and confined to his own resources for obtaining a draft, has no use for a large paunch, and nature does not provide it. At 1,000 pounds live weight he has reached the maximum of his development as a Texan. The crowded condition of Texas ranges, where 17 acres of grazing are needed for the proper support of every head of cattle per year, and the mixed composition of the herds, steers grazing among cows, restrains his development beyond that point.

On the other hand, the range steer, the happy medium between the two, better cared for than the Texan, with plenty of room on new ranges and no cows to distract him, hardier than the native, but with qualifications for a flesh producer inherited from his native progenitor, covers himself with fat instead of a thick hide like the Texan, for protection against the inclemency of the weather.

When ready for market he "figures out" to the satisfaction of all parties concerned, being evidently destined to become the cheap and nutritious staple beef of this continent.

GENERAL REMARKS.

Texas and the Indian Territory are breeding grounds of this country, 80 to 90 per cent. of calves are raised there, whereas 46 per cent. from an equal number of cows is considered a fair average on a northern range.

From 350,000 to 400,000 one to two years' old Texans are driven or shipped by rail to northern ranges every year, and it verily looks as if a national trail from Texas north, through the adjacent States and Territories, was desirable from economical reasons as well as sanitary

A large proportion of the number of Texas cattle reported as slaughtered at Kansas City, Saint Louis, and Chicago, is absorbed by the canned-goods trade.

The value of all cattle in general has increased with the improved quality, but the advance in the prices of dressed beef does not correspond to the increased demand and higher prices of cattle.

The price of cattle is to some extent enhanced by speculation among range owners, but prices of dressed beef are kept in check by the adoption of the more economical way of supplying the East with dressed beef from Chicago direct.

This result, so much the more desirable at this time, when the purchasing power of the people is at low ebb, goes to prove that "the greatest good to the greatest number of people" is the reward of improved husbandry.

CHICAGO, *January*, 1885.

APPENDIX No. 3.

STATEMENT PREPARED BY MR. THEODORE J. M'MINN, IN REGARD TO THE RANGE AND RANCH CATTLE BUSINESS OF THE UNITED STATES.

THE CATTLE DRIVE OF 1884.

During the year 1884, about five hundred thousand cattle were driven northwest over the old trail to the Northern Territories or shipped by rail. The year last past was noteworthy as that during which a larger number of cattle were shipped by rail than ever before. The average weight was, approximately, 600 pounds, and the value on the trail at points of shipment about $3 per hundred, or $18 per head, or $9,000,000 in the aggregate.

The drive mentioned was mostly sold at Caldwell and Dodge City, Kans., and at Ogalalla, Nebr. At the first-named place a comparatively small proportion was sold for distribution in the Indian Territory; at Dodge City a large proportion was sold for distribution in Colorado and New Mexico; at Ogalalla, in Nebraska, the balance was sold to ranchmen in Wyoming or Montana, or shipped East over the Union Pacific. Most of the cattle driven were steers. It has been estimated that the drive of 1885 would aggregate seven hundred thousand head, but the losses during the winter of 1884–'5 and hindrances to the drive are likely to be so serious as to abridge this estimate considerably.

Of the annual drive, a very small number, an insignificant but unascertained proportion, is sold to farmers; but, practically, the entire drive goes north for the replenishing of northern ranches or ranges.

QUALITIES OF BEEF.

So far as the different qualities of beef offered at Saint Louis, Chicago, and Kansas City are concerned there would be some variance, but to what extent it would be impossible to determine accurately. The cattle from Montana, Wyoming, and the northern territory tributary to Chicago disclose, when killed, a maturity and weight not found in cattle from more southern latitudes. Range cattle from the Indian Territory, and from other localities tributary to Saint Louis, kill to good advantage and have been favorite purchases with dressed-beef buyers, and also with buyers for live shipment to Eastern markets. The Western cattle sold at Saint Louis and Kansas City are practically of one grade, and lighter and less mature than the Wyoming and Montana cattle sold at Chicago. The native butcher steer, when suitable for the block, will weigh from 900 to 1,200 pounds, while the Texan steers, in approximate or relative condition, will only weigh 750 to 1,000 pounds; with this difference in weight remembered, the difference in price would be about $1 per hundred; that is to say, if the native would sell at $4.50 to $5.25, the Texan would sell at $3.50 to $4.25. But if the Texan and native were of equal weight the price would be almost identical. And as the Texas cattle gradually improve by breeding, the native and Texas prices come more nearly together. The Texas animal has small bones, and there is proportionally more beef to the weight for that reason. But the Texas steer, ungraded and unimproved, would be kept free from the influence of better blood if his percentage of good yield were seriously impaired by the infusion of any of the strains of imported stock. True, the Texas steer has more beef in his body than in his legs; if he had not, he would net an unprofitable amount of meat, as the original Texas leg was designed more for celerity than for yield. A Texas steer of 900 pounds average would net more than a native of the same weight, because the Texas of that weight is comparatively fat and would grade "good," while the native steer of that weight would grade "common." A good Texan will kill, as stockmen say, more to the hundred than a common or medium native; but a "good" native or well-graded half-breed will kill as much to the hundred as a "good" Texan. The Texas steer is expected to yield from 54 to 57 per cent., but in prime condition will "kill out," as it is phrased, 60 per cent. of meat. The Texas tenderloin is but little if any heavier than the loin of a good native steer.

90

FRESH, SALTED, AND CANNED BEEF.

Of the Texas cattle slaughtered at Saint Louis and Kansas City, about five-eighths at the latter place are sold as fresh beef, one-eighth is packed as salt beef, and one-fourth canned. In Saint Louis, seven-eighths of the cattle slaughtered are sold as fresh beef, and the remainder is packed or salted. The best of the killings at both points is sold as fresh meat,·the next or second grade meat is packed in barrels, and the poorest quality is canned.

Saint Louis in 1884 received 450,717 cattle, as follows:

By Chicago and Alton Railroad	21,051
By Missouri Pacific	190,578
By Saint Louis and San Francisco	100,119
By Saint Louis, Wabash and Pacific	61,374
By Missouri Pacific (Kansas and Texas Division)	917
By Saint Louis and Iron Mountain	32,268
By Cairo Short Line	6,905
By Louisville and Nashville	5,359
By Saint Louis and Cairo	700
By Ohio and Mississippi	3,534
By Indianapolis and Saint Louis	2,955
By Vandalia	5,332
By Toledo, Cincinnati and Saint Louis	469
By Chicago, Burlington and Quincy	2,414
By Keokuk and Saint Louis	1,094
By river	15,748
Total	450,717

Of the cattle received over the Missouri Pacific 60 per cent. were range cattle; over the San Francisco, 85 per cent.; over the Wabash, 10 per cent.; over the Chicago and Alton, 10 per cent.; over the Iron Mountain, 90 per cent.; and these leading lines brought in most of the stock.

WESTERN KILLING AND EASTERN SHIPMENTS.

The Western killing has not been uniform. Freight rates frequently changed, have made shipments of live stock to the East, first profitable then disastrous, and again remunerative; so that during a single year there would be such variance that no correct trace could be kept of the comparative magnitude of the dressed beef and live-stock shipments; but there are a few well-ascertained facts from which useful, if not conclusive, inferences may be drawn. The number of cattle annually slaughtered in the United States is over 6,000,000 head, and the weight 3,000,000,000 pounds. Ten years ago the Boston meat supply came from New England, and Western beef was comparatively unknown; now about 75 per cent. of the New England demand is supplied from the Western plains. In 1883 New England received 40,000 tons of live cattle and 106,894 tons of dressed cattle.

A late number of Bradstreet's contains an interesting article on the beef supply of New England, from which the following is taken:

"The books of the trunk-line commissioner show the number of tons of cattle and dressed beef respectively forwarded, all rail, to Boston and New England in each of the years 1878–'83 and the first nine months of 1884, as follows:

Tons of cattle and dressed beef.

Year.	Cattle.	Beef.	Cattle.	Beef.	Cattle.	Beef.
1878	95,256	2,870	58,340	2,223	153,590	5,102
1879	92,480	12,975	51,480	10,543	143,900	23,518
1880	124,674	22,305	56,049	20,465	180,733	42,770
1881	106,303	29,718	34,378	45,541	140,680	75,259
1882	62,548	29,830	13,862	59,318	76,410	89,145
1883	88,451	43,711	12,448	73,036	100,899	116,747
1884*	54,852	35,316	7,277	54,321	62,129	82,637

*Nine months.

The growth and dimensions of the exports of cattle and beef from Boston and Portland since 1876 appear as follows:

Tons exported, Boston and Portland.

Year.	Live cattle.-	Dressed beef.
1877	1,096	42
1878	9,812	363
1879	26,863	493
1880	38,063	7,106
1881	52,271	18,079
1882	22,797	9,155
1883	27,808	9,853

The beef in cattle of the better grade is estimated at 55 per cent. of the live weight. Subtracting the exports from the receipts and reducing the cattle to beef at this ratio the following statement shows approximately the amount of Western beef received alive and dressed, respectively, for New England consumption since 1877:

Western beef eaten in New England.

Year.	Received alive.	Received dressed.	Total.
	Tons.	*Tons.*	*Tons.*
1878	79,077	4,470	83,817
1879	54,403	23,025	87,428
1880	78,468	35,664	114,132
1881	48,625	57,180	105,805
1882	29,487	79,993	109,480
1883	40,200	106,894	147,094

It appears accordingly that the New England consumption of Chicago dressed beef has risen regularly and very steadily from 4,740 tons in 1878 to 106,894 tons in 1883; while the consumption of Western beef received on the hoof has fallen from 79,077 tons to 40,200 tons, and that the former kind last year amounted to 72 per cent. of the whole. The most remarkable growth in the cattle trade has been the advancement of the dressed-beef business.

The following gives an idea of the extent of the purchases of that kind of stock:

Swift Bros. & Co 331,550
Armour & Co 253,000
G. H. Hammond & Co 140,000
Libby, McNeil & Libby 113,987
Fairbank Canning Company 120,000

Total number of head 958,537

The number of cattle slaughtered for canning purposes was 300,000 head more than in the previous year.

Regarding dressed beef, greater strides are making in the business than are generally realized. Dressed beef is not only prepared at Chicago, but in the far west, in sight of the cattle ranges themselves, a thousand miles or more west of Chicago. This was an innovation. In Montana there was especial activity in this direction. The meat-preserving establishments beyond the Mississippi are becoming numerous. The first venture was the Continental Meat Company, at Victoria, Tex. The next one was at Dallas, and others followed at San Antonio and Fort Worth in the same State. At Cheyenne, Wyo., and at other places that might be mentioned has the process of dressing and shipping meat been established, and with great success. The increased facilities for making dressed beef and increased sales of the article show conclusively that there is an increasing demand for it. When dressed beef was first introduced it met with considerable opposition, especially on the part of shippers of cattle on foot to the Eastern markets; but experience has shown that the meat reaches the consumer, when slaughtered and dressed and put in refrigerator cars, in a much better condition than if sent on the hoof. Regular trains of dressed beef are now sent to the sea-board and intermediate points laden with dressed beef every day, notwithstanding the considerable advances from time to time in freight charges, and the submission of the shippers to what has appeared to them to be an arbitrary proceeding instigated at the suggestion of those shipping beef on the hoof.

The increase in the refrigerator-car business is just equal to the increase in the total receipts of cattle at the starting place of those cars, which shows that the new way is steadily encroaching upon the ground of the old, and despite the vast amount of capital arrayed against it.

Prices for range cattle were higher last year than in 1881, but lower than in 1882.

TEXAS FEVER.

There is no subject connected with the cattle business, in any of its forms or phases, about which there is such a diversity of opinion as there is about the Texas fever. Experts differ as to its cause, its effect, and its transmissibility. Concerning it, however, the following facts seem to be well established and indisputable : Texas cattle affected will communicate the disease to natives that cross their range or trail. Ailing Texas cattle will impart the disease to half-breeds or to other Texas cattle that have been " wintered " or away from the Texas range and acclimated in territory north of the South Platte; this latter proposition, however, has been questioned. The fever was never very destructive north of the South Platte until 1884. when Texas cattle were extensively carried to the north by rail. Whether the disease is transmitted by saliva, excretion, by ticks, or the hoof, or by all of these means, is not settled to the satisfaction of all interested inquirers and students. It has been said that the Texas cattle proper do not suffer from the disease, but this involves the apparent paradox that they can impart what they do not possess. Texas cattle over-heated, over-driven, taken rapidly into new and contrasting climates, or continuously confined and excited do suffer from the Texas fever, and will communicate their ailment to northern stock, whether it be half-breed, wintered or (acclimated) Texans, or native cattle, but the pure Texan will not communicate it to his fellow. This transmission of the disease occurs whenever the northern cattle cross the trail or invade the range of affected cattle. Gradual driving or the following of the spring northward by easy stages over the old trail acclimates the Texas cattle as they progress, and the disease does not appear. A leading cause of the spread of the disease along the line of the trail is the fact that the route has been varied and indefinite. No contiguous farmer or ranchman could tell certainly when his cattle were ranging upon the trail; he was caught innocently and unawares, and, once affected, his herd was liable to melt away. Thrifty young northern cattle may recover; two-year-olds and over usually die. The establishment of a fixed, and particularly of a fenced, route, would greatly lessen if it did not wholly remove the danger of infection. Whether it be determined to take the cattle north by rail or trail, the establishment of quarantine grounds at distances of 150 or 200 miles, would seem to be advisable for the seclusion and resting and acclimating of the affected herds.

OBJECTIONS TO TEXAS CATTLE TRAVEL.

Farmers living along railroads over which Texas cattle are shipped object, to the extent of their ability and opportunity, to the transportation of that class of stock if it be stopped in transit; and the people of Kansas and Nebraska object, with all the vigor consistent with forbearance and magnanimity of the Western character, to the driving of the same cattle over an extended and indefinite trail; but which is the more urgent in opposition cannot be determined. A difficulty often spoken of as attendant upon the Western cattle business is the handling of affected cattle at the market yards. Several years of observation have demonstrated to me that this difficulty is but slight and easily obviated. Separated alleys for ingress and egress and separate pens and scales for feeding and weighing in Saint Louis make a case of infection the exception, and it need not occur at all. The yards at Chicago and Kansas City are nearly, if not quite, as well arranged, so that infection, if it occur, can usually be traced to carelessness.

PUBLIC SENTIMENT.

The people in Kansas and Nebraska are divided in sentiment upon the matter of the cattle trail; a majority of the inhabitants, however, are opposed to it, regarding its establishment of doubtful expediency or safety. There can be no doubt but that farmers and buyers of stockers and feeders in Missouri and neighboring States are not disposed to risk the purchase of Texas cattle during the dangerous season; that is to say from April 1st to November 1st.

As to whether the Texas cattle are considered helpful or hurtful to the northern Territories, at this time, the trade opinion is perhaps in a state of transition, certainly not of settled conviction, owing to the new conditions and problematical result of the agitation concerning leases, public land, and the trail. Under the old order of things, the Texas cattle were considered tributary and promotive of the cattle interests of the northern Territories, as the prolific breeding in the south afforded fresh and needed supplies to the fattening ranchman who had more grass than cattle in the north. Besides, Texas cattle sent to market from the western plains did not compete with the northern range cattle, being of an entirely different grade and weight. But the incoming settler at the north has appropriated small sections or bodies of watered land in the midst of vast ranges and so controlled the indispensable water privileges, thus abridging greatly the grazing area. Such ranges as have been secured and are now held by large herdsmen are becoming overstocked and further supplies of southern cattle, if the area is not protected, are sure to impoverish the remaining range. Again, the southern cattle were considered tributary and promotive of the northern industry so long as the increasing supplies brought no disease; but, as noted above, an indefinite and unknown trail afforded an opportunity for infection, which could not be guarded against, and the shipments by rail and the careless and indiscriminate driving from different points on the railroad across the country in 1884 resulted in losses that have spread an excessive and almost unreasonable apprehension throughout the north.

Railroad transportation would take cattle to the northern pasture grounds more rapidly than the drive by trail; but the new arrivals would have to be quarantined during the dangerous season, which would be about the time occupied by the drive, and the trail would have the advantage of adding weight, saving freight, and so acclimating the cattle as to remove danger of infection.

Artesian wells have been sunk on or near the Sand Hill Plains of Texas, and the yield of water has been all and more than was anticipated, and quite sufficient for the purpose originally contemplated; but the want of title, either by lease or purchase, is an insuperable obstacle to the further or extensive sinking of an adequate number of wells for use on the great regions yet unappropriated and as yet unwatered.

The closing of the old or the failure to establish a new and better trail will doubtless lead to the abandonment of the cattle business by a large number of Texans; to the indiscriminate shipment to market of cattle suitable and unsuitable; to a great glut in market supplies, and to a decline in value, to be followed in a year or eighteen months by reaction, scarcity, inadequacy, high prices, and ultimately by the fixing of such prices that meat to the laborer will become a luxury enjoyed, as in the old countries, but thrice or twice a week. Cheap meat must necessarily mean large herds, large grazing areas, and large capital. The capitalist is an inevitable incident; and the capitalist cannot be exterminated with any greater propriety or impunity than the owner of the small farm, but he can be governed and fostered and controlled in the interest of the meat consumers. Western grazing lands, those in particular proposed to be devoted to the trail, are not suitable for small agricultural uses; the capitalist in some localities could raise beeves for the feeding of a multitude, where the farmer could not support his own family, and, in his feeble attempt, would only hold ground capable of feeding hundreds in the hands of capital. The lands best or even well suited to agriculture are too valuable for grazing, and the capitalist would not care to put them to a use less profitable than the best use to which they could be adapted; but a small holder with nothing to lose and all to gain could well afford to go upon untillable land and get in the way of capital, if his relinquishment were to be the result of lucrative inducement. The question has two sides, and all meat-eaters are interested in a just and impartial determination.

Receipts of cattle at Chicago, Saint Louis, and Kansas City.

Chicago:

Baltimore and Ohio Railroad	1,841
Chicago and Alton	257,913
Chicago and Atlantic	2,562
Chicago, Burlington and Quincy	480,481

Chicago and Eastern Illinois	23,016
Chicago and Grand Trunk	2,944
Chicago, Milwaukee and Saint Paul	201,844
Chicago and Northwestern	269,173
Chicago, Rock Island and Pacific	232,457
Chicago, Saint Louis and Pittsburgh	4,189
Illinois Central	89,208
Lake Shore and Michigan Southern	2,711
Louisville, New Albany and Chicago	8,119
Michigan Central	2,834
New York, Chicago and Saint Louis	1,096
Pittsburgh, Fort Wayne and Chicago	2,034
Wabash, Saint Louis and Pacific	230,303
Driven into yards	4,972
Total for year	1,817,697

Saint Louis, 1884:	
Chicago and Alton Railroad	21,051
Missouri Pacific	190,578
Saint Louis and San Francisco	100,119
Saint Louis, Wabash and Pacific	61,374
Missouri Pacific (Kansas and Texas Division)	917
Saint Louis and Iron Mountain	32,268
Cairo Short Line	6,905
Louisville and Nashville	5,359
Saint Louis and Cairo	700
Ohio and Mississippi	3,534
Indianapolis and Saint Louis	2,955
Vandalia	5,332
Toledo, Cincinnati and Saint Louis	469
Chicago, Burlington and Quincy	2,414
Keokuk and Saint Louis	1,094
By river and driven in	15,784
Total	450,717

Kansas City, 1884:	
Hannibal and Saint Joseph Railroad	4,399
Wabash, Saint Louis and Pacific	4,721
Missouri Pacific	56,909
Union Pacific	63,253
Southern Kansas	88,343
Kansas City, Fort Scott and Gulf	33,469
Kansas City and Saint Joseph	10,546
Atchison, Topeka and Santa Fé	24,561
Chicago and Alton	6,625
Chicago, Rock Island and Pacific	6,776
Driven in	15,124
	533,526

Chicago	1,817,697
Saint Louis	450,717
Kansas City	533,526
Grand total	2,801,940

NORTHERN GRAZING.

Concerning the origin of the northwestern grazing there are different accounts. There has been a common supposition that the fact of the thrift of the buffalo in former years, during the inclement season, suggested the feasibility of pasturing cattle on the wild range. But whatever might have been inferred from the habits of the buffalo, the first demonstration of the fattening effects of winter feeding in the north seems to have been an accidental discovery. In the winter of 1864–'65, just twenty years ago, Mr. E. S. Newman, who was conducting a train of supplies overland to Camp Douglas, was snowed up on the Laramie Plains. Arranging the train in habitable shape he turned the oxen out to die in the neighboring waste places. But the fatigued cattle began to improve from the start, and in March were gathered up in better condition than when they were set adrift to starve and feed the wolves. This discovery led to the purchase of stock cattle for fattening in the north, and the trade has steadily grown to its present proportions, accel-erated greatly during the past fifteen years by the building of the various roads in the north and west. The bunch-grass is perhaps the leading food of the north-ern range, but the gramma and the buffalo grasses also abound, and when the snows fall so deep that grass is not obtainable, cattle eat the white sage-brush, which retains its greenness all the winter; and in cases where this too fails, the black sage-brush is eaten, and all are nutritious. But cattle prefer the grasses, and will paw about the brush to secure it. But the light snows blow away as a rule and leave the grasses exposed. The white sage is second choice, and the black sage is the last resort. It seems to an extent true that the northern grass is more nutritious than the southern, but the fact that the cattle mature better in the North is perhaps at-tributable as much to the climate as to the food. But the best grass in all the graz-ing country is the alfalfa or lucerne. It has been known for centuries; the first trace of it being in Media ; it was taken to Greece in the time of Darius, five hundred years before Christ, thence to Rome, thence to France, thence to South America. It is cultivated in Chili and came thence to our country, where it has proven to be of incalculable value to the feeders who are situated to make it available. This grass requires sunshine and well-mellowed and permeable ground. It is vigorous, perennial, and abundant as clover, is relished by cattle either green or dry, and will fatten swine. It ameliorates and enriches instead of exhausting the ground, because leguminous and broad leaved. It draws nourishment from the atmosphere, and the shedding of the foliage enriches the earth that bears it. It is no sooner mown than it pushes out fresh shoots, and under the best conditions will yield three crops per annum. In the dryest and most sultry weather, once well set and growing, it will send its roots 2, 10, or 15 feet to find moisture. In Wyoming two large crops per annum have been gathered. The stem grows from 2 to 4 feet high, and the yield is from 3 to 4 tons per acre. It needs, in most cases, careful cultivation, not being indigenous, but plains and valleys, before barren and useless, have been made fruitful and capable of sustaining thousands of cattle and hogs. And the cultivation necessary to the growing of alfalfa assures a large growth of timothy, the two making beeves that rival the corn-fed native in weight and quality. Cattle in Wyoming (on the Beckwith-Quinn ranch) which were rejected by a purchaser in the fall of 1883 as "tailings," were fed on the mixed timothy and alfalfa during the winter of 1883-'84, turned on the range during the summer of 1884, and last October weighed from 1,600 to 1,800 pounds, and were in no way distinguish-able from the corn-fed natives of equal weight.

THE FUTURE OF GRAZING.

The future of grazing is full of problems and of possibilities. In the United States the annual consumption of meat is about 120 pounds per capita; in England, 105 pounds ; in France, 74 pounds, and in Germany, 69 pounds per capita.

In 1864 the beeves imported into England sold for $65 each; in 1883 the price had gone up to $95 each.

In Prussia the increase since 1873 was a fraction over 1 per cent., while the increase in the population was over 8 per cent.

Ten years ago stock cattle in Texas cost $4 per head; now they cost from $15 to $18 per head.

The grazing area is becoming circumscribed ; the people, the meat consumers, are rapidly increasing in numbers. Populous countries do not raise enough meat for their own consumption. State and national legislation in this country favors the small holder, and thus a population ultimately for which it will become impossible for the lands divided and subdivided into small holdings to furnish an adequate meat supply. Mexico, in course of time, seems likely to become the breeding-ground in place of Texas. The old Spanish land grants which have come down for hundreds of years unimpaired offer unbroken tracts in large areas suitable for breeding and feed-ing, and already American capitalists are inspecting and buying the best grounds.

But if that country becomes a new Texas the trail and transportation will become even more important problems than now; and quarantine, as now, an incident.

In any event, meat must gradually advance, whether rapidly or not depends upon the wisdom of the legislation.

The expediency of the trail, of leasing, of irrigation, and the profitableness of graz-ing depend largely upon the meteorological condition of the Northwest, which is ably discussed by Capt. Silas Bent, of Saint Louis, in the following paper :

METEOROLOGY OF THE MOUNTAINS AND PLAINS OF NORTH AMERICA, AS AFFECTING THE CATTLE-GROWING INDUSTRIES OF THE UNITED STATES.

Mr. President and gentlemen of the Cattle-Growers' Convention :

Congress, by its laws regulating the sale of public lands, recognizes three classes or grades of land, to each of which it has prescribed the maximum quantity that may be sold to the same person in any one locality, as follows:

" Six hundred by 1,500 superficial feet of mineral lands, 160 acres of agricultural lands, and 640 acres of barren or desert lands."

These have hitherto been thought to cover all the purposes for which the public lands would be required.

Since those laws have been enacted, however, and only within a few years past, another industry has been developed which requires the use of much larger areas of land to make it at all possible of economical and successful prosecution, and that is cattle growing. But it so happens that the lands required for this industry are by no means the best for agriculture or mining, and are often, on the contrary, quite unfit for either of these purposes, but are known and characterized as the grazing or "Buffalo Plains" of the West, from the fact that they were infested by these and other herds of wild browsing animals, who preferred the scanty tufts of the wiry but succulent and nutritious grasses that were found upon the plains to the more rank and abundant growth of the surrounding regions. This untrained instinct of these wild herds is nature's testimony of the special fitness of these plains for pastoral purposes, and we, as intelligent people, cannot do better than to follow nature's promptings in the utilization of these lands.

These plains extend from Texas to Canada, about 1,200 miles in length, and with a width easterly from the base of the Rocky Mountains of about 300 miles, making an area of 360,000 square miles, or upwards of 250,000,000 of acres of land, which, with rare and limited exceptions, are fit only for grazing and can never be profitably used for any other purposes. The laws should, therefore, be amended by adding another or pastoral grade to the public land schedule, and with authority for leases alone to be made to persons wanting such lands in tracts of not less than 20,000 nor more than 300,000 acres to each lessee for terms of twenty years, which would prevent these lands being monopolized by a few persons to the detriment of others, and would yet give to the tenant security in those proprietary rights necessary to prevent trespassing by others or disturbance from Government agents or officials.

As I have before intimated, these lands can never be converted into agricultural lands, notwithstanding the various schemes proposed from time to time for their irrigation and reclamation from agricultural sterility; for there are physical causes for that sterility which neither the power nor the ingenuity of man can change, and it has been thought that a brief discussion of these causes might not be uninteresting to the members of this convention, and I have been asked to give you my views in regard to them.

To do this will, of course, involve a wider range of investigation than if the simple facts and conditions of the problem were accepted without going back to their origin or cause, through the meteorological processes by which these facts and conditions are brought about.

I will first call your attention to this skeleton map of North America, where only the main ranges of mountains, chief lakes, and principal rivers are laid down, other details being omitted so as to prevent confusion. The principal range of mountains extending through Central America into Mexico is a continuation of the Andes of South America. In Mexico, however, these mountains are known as the "Sierra Madre," or "Mother Range," and which throws off two branches, one to the northwest, along the Pacific coast, into California, where it is known as the "Sierra Nevada" or "Snow Range," and which runs thence up into Oregon, where, with a lower altitude to the range, it assumes the name of the Cascade Mountains, and where it is broken into a number of detached, isolated, but majestic peaks, such as Mounts Jefferson, Hood, Adams, Ranier, Saint Helen's, &c., which stand as hoary sentinels surpliced in eternal snow to mark the great ways through which the moisture-laden winds from the Pacific Ocean gain access to the heart of the continent.

The other and in many respects the grander branch from the Sierra Madre is the Rocky Mountain range, which running almost due north, about the 110th and 120th meridians of longitude, until the parallel of 45° north latitude is reached, where this range sinks to an elevated "divide" of from 6,000 to 8,000 feet above the level of the sea.

Lying between these ranges and extending from the Sierra Madre to the Yellowstone Park, lies a plateau or plain of comparative sterility and barrenness, comprising much of the Territories of Utah, Arizona, and Nevada.

With this preliminary description of the map I shall now proceed to discuss some of the meteorological phenomena that have a direct bearing upon the question before us. It is generally believed that the sun is a direct evaporater of humidity and especially of the ocean waters, and that the evaporation from the ocean is mostly from the equatorial regions of the earth, that the vapor from this evaporation is transported by the winds through the upper regions of the atmosphere, directly north and south, to its points of distribution in the temperate and frigid zones.

This, however, I think is a fallacy, and that in reality, notwithstanding the enormous evaporation that does undoubtedly take place in equatorial regions, by far the greater part of that evaporation is precipitated back to the earth's surface within the tropics, and that by quite a different process are the regions of the earth beyond the tropics supplied with the water from the heavens.

The sun's rays being more nearly vertical within the tropics, have so much the more heating power, and the surface waters of the ocean there are thus brought up to the general temperature of 88° F., from whence this heated water is carried north and south to the earth's extremities by grand ocean streams, which are the life-giving arteries of the oceanic and interoceanic circulation. Of these streams there are four, the two grandest and greatest of which are thrown off to the southward from the equatorial currents of the Pacific and Indian Oceans, whilst the remaining two are thrown off northwardly from the tropics into the North Atlantic and Pacific Oceans. The first of these latter is the Gulf Stream, whose general character is familiar to us all. The other is the Kuro-Siwo, of more recent discovery, which starts from the southeast coast of China and running northeastwardly, with a velocity of from 30 to 80 miles a day, and losing only 1° of warmth for every 300 miles that it travels, washes the south coast of Japan, and spreading a mantle of tepid water of upwards of 70° of temperature over the surface of the North Pacific, it envelopes the whole west coast of our continent from Behring's Straits to the equator with its genial warmth, and gives to that region the delicious climate, which is now becoming so well known to us all.

Now, whilst the sun by its heat in the tropics has prepared these waters for rapid evaporation, by giving to them their high temperature, yet the sun itself cannot and does not evaporate any portion of them, except through the medium of the atmosphere. And the power of the atmosphere to produce this evaporation is in exact proportion to its low temperature and its dryness as compared with the water at the time of its contact with these tepid waters from the equator.

The prevailing winds in the temperate zone are from the westward. The west winds which come to the North Pacific from the plains of Central Asia and Siberia are cold, contracted, and dry, with a temperature frequently below the freezing point, so that when they reach the tepid waters of the Kuro-Siwo they at once respond to the warm and expanding influence, and as they expand drink up by evaporation prodigous quantities of the latter, which, as invisible vapor or fogs, are borne eastwardly across the surface of the ocean to the west coast of our continent.

That portion of these winds that reaches our coast about the mouth of the Columbia River, is chilled by the Cascade Mountains, and made to yield such quantities of rain as to have produced a forest growth of vegetation so rank and majestic as to be unrivaled by any other forests of North America ; and just north of the Cascades, from the open gateways through the mountain ranges, guarded only by the detached and hoary peaks before named, between which these west winds carry their burden of warmth and moisture to gladden and fatten the face of the interior of the continent, but which on their way pay such tribute to these majestic sentinels as to clothe and crown them in the purity of everlasting snow, and then reach the elevated region of the Yellowstone Park with still abundant moisture, which is dealt out from their hitherto invisible treasures with such royal profusion as to give birth to and keep in perennial flow the grandest system of rivers on the face of the globe, viz, the Columbia, McKenzie, Saskatchawan, Assinaboine, Yellowstone, Missouri, and Colorado, which, radiating north, east, south, and west from this immediate region, and with courses of thousands of miles each, distribute their waters into all the oceans surrounding the continent. This may therefore be not inaptly called the "Water dome of North America."

Stretching eastwardly from this "dome" to the mouth of the Saint Lawrence River, on the Atlantic coast, lies a declining ridge from which waters run north into the Hudson Bay and south, by the Mississippi, Illinois, and Ohio Rivers and their tributaries, into the Gulf of Mexico, and east of the Alleghanies, by the Potomac, Delaware, Hudson, Connecticut, and other rivers, into the Atlantic Ocean.

But all these mighty rivers that have their genesis in the direct pathway of these west winds across the continent are cradled upon the crest of the ridge just described by the great lakes of Superior, Michigan, Huron, Erie, and Ontario, which alone are estimated to contain one half of all the fresh water resting upon the face of the earth, and which, notwithstanding necessary enormous drain from them by evaporation, yet have always such a surplus of water as to keep an unvarying flow from the majestic Saint Lawrence River. Now the waters which supply the rivers radiating from what I have termed the "water dome" all come from this west wind from the Pacific, as I believe do also those which supply the other rivers in the Mississippi Basin, west of the Alleghany Mountains, together with those waters that fall into and make the great lakes.

Whether or not the waters that go into the rivers east of the Alleghanies come from the same source is doubtful. I think, however, that through local agencies they come from the Gulf Stream of the Atlantic. Yet it is not unreasonable to believe and affirm that by reason of the waters that do come from the prevailing west winds from the Pacific that it is the Kuro-Siwo of the Pacific that irrigates and fructifies the heart of the continent of North America.

Now, it may be asked, what has all this to do with the aridity of the alkali plains of Colorado and New Mexico? Very much, as I shall endeavor to show by first calling your attention again to the water supply that is carried under the wings of this west wind from the Pacific Ocean and distributed nearly, if not quite, across the continent (when not interrupted by the condensing power of intervening mountain ranges), since that is the gauge by which the quantity of water carried by these winds can be measured; and if found in one portion of these winds it is not unreasonable to believe that other portions of these same winds carry a corresponding quantity. But let us now see what becomes of that supply from that portion of these winds which strike the land south of Oregon, and which, being slightly chilled by the coast range of mountains and hills, give out moisture enough to envelop the coast with fogs and clouds during many months of the year. Passing thence into the interior these winds are thrown upward against the cold flanks and peaks of the Sierra Nevada, where, being condensed, they crown the latter with their coronets of eternal snow. Descending the eastern slope of the Sierra Nevada range, these winds reach the plateau of Utah and Arizona before described, so robbed of moisture that the earth's sterility is but the evidence of its unslaked thirst.

Continuing eastwardly these west winds then climb the western slope of the Rocky Mountains, but without moisture enough in them to clothe with vegetation the rock-ribbed walls whose somber and rugged nakedness attest the infrequency of rains upon them. Still the altitude of these mountains is so great, and therefore so cold, that their supreme peaks wring from the shrinking winds what little moisture remains in them to add sparkling coronets of snow also to their majestic heads. But these winds, pitching thence down the eastern slope of the Rocky Mountains, reach the plains of Colorado and New Mexico so completely dry as to be unable to give forth even a morning dew, and hence the alkaline sterility of these plains, which no human intervention can change or alleviate.

Now, I hope it has been made apparent that these plains, as well as the plateau of Utah, Nevada, and Arizona, owe their sterility to no accidental nor remediable cause, but to the immutable laws of nature, which are not to be changed by man; that these lands, as they stand and will forever stand, are not fit for agricultural cultivation, except in rare localities along the water courses, but are especially fitted for grazing and cattle growing, and which, in my judgment, should as a whole be set aside by the Government for the encouragement of that industry alone, since the water courses and the water privileges are imperatively required by the ranchmen, and without which all the rest of the grazing plains are practically worthless. Nor is this a hardship to the farmer, for agriculture has had and is still having more lavish and unpaid for favors conferred upon it by the Government than any other industry among our people, and the farmer should not complain if the laws are so modified—in justice to a great and valuable interest—as to require the farmers not to interfere with that interest by taking the kernal of the land for their own use and leaving naught but the husks for herdsmen.

If you ask wherein has agriculture been so favored by the Government, I will say that ever since Mr. Jefferson began to attract immigration to this country by proclaiming to the world that he would give to the agriculturist all the land he wanted in fee simple forever upon the payment of the mere cost of its survey, $1.25 per acre, while farmers in Europe are paying an annual ground rent of $20 per acre, agriculture has been and is subsidized to the annual amount of not less than $18.75 per acre, less the cost of transportation of that acre's products to the competing markets of Europe.

But not only that, agriculture is further subsidized by the hundreds of millions of dollars paid by the Government for the building of railroads to open up and make these lands of easy access and lessen the cost of transportation to and from; that the Government has been subsidizing agriculture for nearly one hundred years; has paid out upwards of $150,000,000 in the purchase of lands from foreign powers, in addition to that acquired by conquest, all of which have been and are being wisely bestowed in subsidies as an encouragement to agriculture, and which subsidies have been the means of building up the population and wealth of the country as nothing else could have done.

It is nothing but right, therefore, that now, when a sister branch of industry asks to be protected from influences that must be fatal to its success, though that protection should require the exclusion of a comparatively few farmers from certain regions of the public domain that are better suited for that industry than for agriculture, the Government and Congress will I am assure grant that protection.

Agriculture has already $13,000,000,000 invested in its industries, with thousands of millions of acres of land of the public domain still open and free to its occupancy, outside of these grazing lands, which the cattle-growers must have in undisturbed control.

It is not the purpose of this convention to antagonize the agricultural, nor any other element of the community, against the industry you represent. But when an industry of the magnitude and rapidity of growth such as yours wants recognition and protection from Congressional laws, so that those engaged in it may know what they have to look to and depend upon before putting more money into that industry, I think there need be no hesitancy on the part of the representatives at this convention to appear before Congress and frankly and fully state their case, and ask its favorable consideration; for I feel sure an equally frank response will be accorded to their just demands, and no other, I am sure, will be asked.

You don't ask the Government to give you anything without fair compensation for the same; nor do you ask for any privileges superior to those given to other interests in the community.

Certain parts of the public domain are already set apart for mining, as others are set apart for agricultural cultivation from which cattle-grazing is excluded, not by the words of the law, it is true, but by the operations of that law which forbids those lands being sold in any other than such small lots and tracts as to entirely exclude from them cattle-raising upon a scale at all profitable for beef supply to our people and those of Europe. Then, as a matter of justice, let these certain ridges or plains, which nature intended for grazing ground, and the most of which can be used for no other purpose, be set apart, as a whole, to be called "pastoral lands," which the Government shall not alienate in fee simple to any one, but hold them open for leasing for terms of twenty years, in large tracts, and thus protect them from monopolies and at the same time preserve them under control for the use of the cattle-growers and the beef-makers for not only America, but for the rest of the civilized world.

SILAS BENT,
Las Animas County Cattle Growers' Association.

Texas fever was discussed by Professor Waterhouse before the members of the first national convention of cattlemen, and the following is taken from his address:

"The Texas fever perplexes the pathologist with mysteries that elude explanation. Facts which a costly experience has made familiar to many members of this body may not be so well known to men unacquainted with the business of grazing. It is surpassingly strange that only cattle in apparently perfect health transmit the disease, while animals sick with the fever do not spread the contagion. Cows dying of the complaint do not communicate the disorder to their sucking calves. In uninfected pastures, northern herds, though separated from Texas cattle only by a wire fence, do not catch the fever. Migration seems to be an especial source of danger. Cattle born in the infected districts are not usually liable to attack, but sometimes, when healthy southern animals are driven in the hot season only a short distance from their native pastures, they fall victims to the malady. The losses of stockmen are aggravated by the fact that the contagion selects the most valuable animals for destruction. Fat cattle are peculiarly subject to the distemper. The pestilence is most prevalent and fatal in the months of July and August. The germs of the disease, which may have lain nourished in the system, are developed into deadly activity by the heats of summer."

Upon the same subject, Mr. James D. Hopkins, veterinary surgeon of the Wyoming Stock Growers' Association, said to the convention:

"What is Texas fever? This question has been asked of me many times lately by those whose cattle were sick and dying. Veterinary science has much to learn in regard to this plague. We know how it is carried into healthy herds, and we know how to avoid it. We can tell you of the morbid lesions found after death, and we can describe to you its symptoms during life.

"It is to be hoped that the people of Texas will some day awake to the importance of this subject, and create the necessary laws that will enable them to employ an expert veterinarian whose duty it shall be to solve the problem of its causation, and give to the world a remedy for this pestilence. Experience and observation of experts has demonstrated that all cattle inhabiting the low, swampy region of the States bordering on the Gulf, as far north as Virginia, have this disease in a latent or mild form; that this disease is probably due to certain food upon which southern cattle subsist, whereby the system of these animals becomes charged with deleterious principles that are afterwards propagated and dispersed by the excreta of apparently healthy animals.

"This explanation would seem to be proved by the fact that when herds are trailed from Texas, the cattle of Indian Territory and Kansas suffer, if allowed to graze on the Texas trail. The Texas herds continuing north on changed food and water, become in sixty days free from the germs of disease, and are safe to mingle in any herd.

"Again, all cattle brought north by railroad, whether for beef or breeding purposes, leave the germs of Texas fever in all yards, cars, and pastures through which they may pass, and their virulence continues until after frost. Very fortunately northern cattle sick with this disease cannot transmit it to other cattle.

"Stock-growers of Texas have considered the subject of transportation of their stock to the north, and earnestly desire that they may have an outlet for their surplus stock in any way that it can be done with safety to northern herds, and believe that the solution of this problem is in the establishment of a national trail by the United States from the Gulf of Mexico to the British possessions.

"In the transportation of Texas cattle for beef purposes to Chicago and the Eastern States, I should suggest that this convention use every effort to induce railroads carrying such cattle to provide separate yards, shutes, and cars, and thereby prevent the infection of regular feeding places, which in the past have proved to be just so many centers of contagion, spreading Texas fever to many herds of cattle being transported for breeding and feeding purposes. It is unnecessary for me to cite instances of contagion from this cause. The public press during the past summer has made you only too familiar with accounts of disease traced to this great neglect.

"You may be assured that the experience of the northern stock-growers during the past summer in handling Texas cattle by railroad has not been so pleasant or profitable as to induce them to engage in it next year, unless under proper sanitary safeguards."

THEODORE J. McMINN.

SAINT LOUIS, *January* 31, 1885.

SAINT LOUIS, *February* 16, 1885.

DEAR SIR: In answer to your inquiry I have to say that the number of people employed in the cattle business in the Indian Territory, New Mexico, Colorado, Wyoming, Kansas, Nebraska, Dakota, and Montana can only be rather remotely approximated.

Since the formation of cattle companies, the distribution of shares has increased the number of persons interested beyond all discovery. One company represents at least 2,000 shareholders, another over 700, and in each case the company is represented by two or three names. But in the actual management and "employment," an estimate more or less accurate may be made.

In handling range cattle, two cowboys at least are required for every 3,000 cattle, and in States where agriculture is pursued and many of the cattle are found on farms the number of persons represented by every thousand cattle would be greater, so that at the least calculation there would be employed in the cattle business the following:

State or Territory.	Number of men employed.	State or Territory.	Number of men employed.
Kansas	2,299	New Mexico	520
Nebraska	1,669	Utah	198
Colorado	1,186	Washington	297
Arizona	203	Wyoming	781
Dakota	309	Indian	731
Idaho	286		
Montana	642	Total	9,121

Allowing for overseers, and other help this would make the aggregate something over 10,000, of which cowboys constitute not less than 9,000.

But the "cowboy" as formerly known is becoming daily a less and less important factor and comparatively infrequent personage.

Leasing, fencing, and the management of great herds by companies on strictly business principles, have gradually eliminated the old-time cowboy, who kept all the cattle he had, secured all he could by fair means or foul and a branding iron; who gambled at every opportunity, fought and shot without cause, and drank without stint. The ruffian of the plain is disappearing. Fewer cowboys are needed and a better class is employed.

Allowing for persons employed in the cattle business in connection with agriculture in some of the States named, 15,000 in the aggregate would not be far out of the way.

Very respectfully,

T. J. McMINN.

JOSEPH NIMMO, Jr.,
  Chief Bureau of Statistics.

APPENDIX No. 4.

STATEMENT PREPARED BY MR. GEORGE B. LOVING, OF FORT WORTH, TEX., IN REGARD TO THE RANGE AND RANCH CATTLE BUSINESS OF THE UNITED STATES.

FORT WORTH, TEXAS, *January* 20, 1885.

DEAR SIR: In compliance with your telegram of the 5th and letters of the 3d and 7th instant, I herewith respectfully submit the following information (as near as I have been able to prepare it within the short space of time allowed) in regard to the Texas cattle trade in its present condition, and covering as near as I have been able to all matters of moment affecting the general interests of the United States in this particular line. I trust it will be sufficient for the purposes desired. The assessment rolls of the State of Texas, according to the comptroller's report, show that there were at least 7,000,000 cattle in the State on January 1, 1884. The extent of the whole area of Texas is 172,600,000 acres; each head of cattle, according to the comptroller's report, using on an average 25 acres. The actual number of cattle is about 9,000,000 head; the discrepancy in the comptroller's report arising from the fact that but few, if any, of our largest ranchmen render the full number of cattle owned by them for taxation.

After deducting land used by horses and sheep and land totally unfit for grazing, together with the land in cultivation, the average of grazing land to each head of cattle would probably be about 15 acres. These are not exact figures, but are near enough in the consideration of the live stock interests of Texas.

In round figures the stock are worth on an average about $17 per head. In Eastern Texas the price of cattle is about $13 per head; in Central Texas $15 per head; in Western Texas and the Panhandle from $20 to $25 per head, according to the grade and quality. This makes the cattle interests of the State amount in value to $153,-000,000. I believe it to be an underestimate as to number, as there is quite a year's increase to be added since January, 1884; and there is a certain latitude permitted in giving in the number for assessment, which will offset any possible overestimate as to value. I have not the slightest doubt but that you will have figures presented to you as being more exact; in fact I am satisfied that from the south the figures will be amply represented in the report from the party delegated to furnish same from the southern part of the State. I shall, therefore, confine myself to a more general reply to the different subjects touched upon in your letters of instructions.

In classifying the cattle of the northern half of Texas, I should divide them three times: all east of Tarrant County being called Eastern Texas cattle; all west of Tarrant, Western Texas cattle, and those located in the Panhandle part of the State Panhandle cattle. In the Panhandle there are twenty-six counties of 16,500,000 acres. In this piece of country there are certainly no more than 500,000 cattle. In the western block, which consists of twenty-seven counties, 17,000,000 acres, there are a few less than 1,000,000 cattle. There is no way of arriving at the exact figures, as most of the counties are unorganized, although attached for legal purposes to other settled counties.

The movement of stock into unorganized counties has a tendency to permit the owner to escape taxation until permanently located, and will account for meager returns from the western country.

The next tier of counties eastward, called Northwest Texas, comprise 17,000,000 acres, and contain 1,500,000 cattle. Then the eastern section, of equal size, contains 1,250,000 cattle, as near as data at hand will show. The county of Greer, containing 1,678,080 acres, furnishes ample pasturage for 1,200,000 cattle. The title to this county is now the subject of Congressional action. It is the only absolute range county without fence in Texas; and, considering the abundance of water and good grasses, and natural protection to stock, is possibly the best grazing field for range stock. It is the only county where lands are not secured to any marked extent. The county of Tom Green, which furnishes a range for 250,000 cattle, does not belong to the territory embraced in my report, and can only be written up in detail by some one resident there. It is an empire in itself, the eastern portion being thoroughly stocked with cattle, horses, and sheep. This county embraces 12,579 square miles of grazing land. The ranges in the eastern portion have been stocked to their range capacity several years, the west and the northwest receiving the surplus; then as the territory became occupied, the ranges were developed in the west and in the Panhandle, a steady movement going onward from east to west, while at the same time the movement from southern ranges to the north and west was equally steady.

In Eastern Texas the average stock owned by each person does not exceed 100 head; in the west the average is about 600 head, and in the Panhandle 1,000 head. I arrived at these figures last year by a long and careful calculation; and while somewhat disappointing to a lover of great averages, the fact remains that the larger stocks of individual owners and corporations are offset by the greater number of middle sized and small stocks. It was but natural that the larger stocks should first move west. As the eastern ranges became overstocked, the question as to who should first move was always answered by the owners of the greater numbers, as they could afford to run outfits strong enough to be a defense in case of necessity.

Range cattle are not fed or sheltered in any portion of the State, except the eastern part, only as nature provides. In the last-named part of the State it is generally found necessary, during the winter season, to feed for a few months—the feed used generally being cotton-seed, prairie hay, or millet, but only in sufficient quantity to carry them through the winter, until the rising of the grass in the spring. Many ranges capable of carrying thousands of cattle are wasted for want of water, and much ground is virtually lost for want of some protection in the shape of timber or brakes in the land formation. It accounts for the stockmen taking risks from Indian depredations, in order to stock up lands on the edge of the plains, while a great territory between the settlements and the plains was not carrying cattle, except in most favorable localities. It also accounts for the scarcity of stock on 8,000,000 acres of the plains of Texas, which are amply grassed, but which afford very little protection and very little water. If taken as a range country, without further improvement, very few more cattle can be carried within the State without loss; but there is not the slightest doubt in my mind that by a system of improvements which owners can afford to institute, the carrying capacity of the range can be almost doubled.

The capacity of different parts of the State varies very materially, according to the quality of the grass grown and the nature of the soil. In the central portion of the State, where the prairies are covered with a thick coat of what is generally termed sage-grass, it is estimated that 5 acres to the animal is quite sufficient to furnish grazing the entire season; while in the western and Panhandle part of the State, where a great portion of the grass is devoured by prairie dogs and a considerable amount of the land is rendered worthless by "scalds" or bald places, it is generally estimated that it will require on an average 10 acres of land to each animal. In fact, there are places where I doubt if less than 15 to 20 acres would be found sufficient to furnish grass the entire season, one year with another. That part of the State known as the "Staked Plains," being almost entirely free from prairie dogs, is covered with a very thick growth of fine mesquite grass, which furnishes splendid grazing the entire season, and would, in my opinion, readily carry one animal to every 5 acres, and keep them in fine condition the year round.

In many counties along the line of the Texas and Pacific Railway, between Callahan County and the eastern edge of the Staked Plains, and as far north as the Panhandle, it is estimated that more range is eaten and destroyed by prairie dogs than by the cattle; in other words, if the dogs were destroyed that part of the State would furnish grazing to twice as many cattle as it ever can do as long as the dogs are permitted to remain.

Water (the first necessity) can be obtained in any portion of the State at less than $1 per acre, which amount is usually the difference in price between watered and unwatered land. The best is the artesian well, which will furnish water at different depths between 100 and 500 feet. Tanks can easily be constructed at a reasonable outlay, even if an artificial bottom should become necessary, in order to hold the rainfall, which is quite improbable, as, so far as the experiment has been made, no difficulty has been found in constructing tanks built in the ground, so as to hold water the entire season.

If a better water supply be obtained, vast areas of unused ranges which are not pastured in summer and which bear summer grass, would become available. The common sage-grass grows in abundance over tracts, which are almost bare of cattle, during the time it is at its best as feed. The first frost kills it, rendering the pasturage of little value during the winter months.

Up to late years nearly all ranges have been held by possession rather than by legal title, and the purchase or lease of solid bodies of land being general only during the last few years.

The improvements, outside of fencing, amount to but very little; not one-tenth of the western half of the State is fenced.

Last year Texas marketed as beef in the home markets at New Orleans, Chicago, Saint Louis, and Kansas City fully 1,000,000 beef cattle, realizing an average of about $25 per head. Panhandle and Western beef cattle averaged $35, but the lighter and less mature steers from the eastern section and from the southwest cut down the average. Texas sent up the trail 450,000 young cattle which did not realize over $17 per head. These cattle consisted of one and two year old steers and heifers. The number of beef marketed was excessive, and the low average in price is due to the marketing of immature cattle and dry cows, in order that the ranchmen might be able to meet the demands, owing to the withdrawal of money by Eastern capitalists, a consequence of the depression existing throughout the States.

Properly speaking, the whole of Texas produces range cattle, and I am unable to mark upon a map the territory which does not produce stock raised strictly upon the range, unless I except the eastern part of the State above referred to, where it is generally found necessary to feed to some extent during two or three of the winter months. The trail herds are furnished principally from the southeast, southern, and southwestern part of the State. The cattle used in stocking the ranches of the northwestern and Panhandle part of the State are generally taken from the central and eastern part, as there is no risk of loss on the new ranges by reason of the introduction of stock from these sections. The north line of Tom Green County, leading east to Eastland, and straight east to include Ellis County, and thence north as indicated on the map, is the line I should specify as the boundary of cattle liable to the so-called Texas fever. All cattle north and west of this line are subject to the disease from the passage of southern or coast cattle. It is not that cattle of the north are liable to disease from the passage of cattle from ranges immediately south of the line, but south of that line I have never heard of a case of so-called Texas fever, whereas immediately upon the line specified I have known ranchmen complain of losses by reason of the trail herds passing over the ranges.

I know of no good reason why Northwest Texas should be debarred from driving cattle to any range in or out of the State. I consider it of the utmost importance to the State that a trail should be established over which Texas cattle can safely move without risk to other stock; believe it to be necessary for the security of northern herds and believe it to be but justice to Texas. Any law preventing the movement of Texas cattle out of the State is manifestly unjust, because it is acknowledged that the cattle of the upper or northern ranges have not been charged with infecting any range; and even if our cattle were all diseased to the extent charged against the coast or Southern Texas cattle, there should be a privilege granted so far as a right of way over the common property of the United States, there being no hindrance to the movement of cattle from any portion of Texas to the crossing of Red River in Wilbarger County. All that is absolutely necessary is the right of way through the Indian Territory, which will not interfere with any vested right; then through Western Kansas and Nebraska. Beyond there is no opposition to the movement of trail cattle to any of the open ranges, which is based on any reliable grounds or complaint which is founded on truth. Whatever may be the disease it is no longer malignant after so long a drive, yet it may have been contracted by cattle further north through the agency of coast Texas stock, which have been quickly transported by rail to Nebraska and driven from points on the Union Pacific Railroad. The trail is necessary to Texas stock to offset any possible overcharge for a rail transit. Without an outlet for Texas cattle the range would soon become greatly overstocked, so much so that the beef would not mature, and, in fact, I very much doubt if after a few years there would be sufficient range to support the number of cattle that would be on it, much less to fatten and mature the beef. By such overproduction the business of cattle-raising would be entirely ruined, and the United States deprived of the million of fat cattle that are now being furnished annually from the ranges of Texas.

Allowing that no impediment existed by reason of any law, or any disease, or any antagonism by reason of the drive or rail transit, and while the railroads continue their liberal policy towards the stockmen, there is very much more in favor of rail transit than there is in favor of the old method; and in advance of placing these advantages before you, in detail, I would submit that the movement of one hundred and fifty thousand head of young stock from southern points in Texas to Wichita Falls, the terminus of the Fort Worth and Denver City Railroad (all of which might have been driven had the owners been so disposed) is an indication of the feeling of stockmen, which would be more marked this year if the certainty of a northern outlet would permit the transportation to be engaged at once. The use of the trail has been simply to remove the young stock from the southern portion of Texas to the markets of Northern Texas, the Indian Territory, Kansas, Colorado, Nebraska, Wyoming, Montana, and Dakota, as each market called for them. The stocking of these ranges has been a gradual process. Where the drive begins and where it ends, to-day, no man can tell; and it becomes defined now only a little south of Fort Griffin, in Texas, where most herds cross the Clearfork of the Brazos and end at Dodge, Kans.; whereas it used to be at 'Ogallala, Nebr., where the herds left the trail for their new destination. The latter-named place was formerly the selling point for all herds which were driven on speculation; whereas now nearly all the stock driven for sale on the open market are disposed of at Fort Dodge, Kans.

There were three recognized trails, one passing Fort Worth and entering the Indian Territory at Salt Creek, Montague County; one, the present Fort Griffin trail, and another through the Panhandle, west of Fort Elliott. The latter was last established and first abandoned. Before the settlement of Central Texas, the stocking up the Panhandle, the use of the Indian Territory as a grazing ground, and while the northern ranges were but scantily supplied with stock, the movement of cattle was unobstructed, either by fences or dead lines. Every foot of ground being open, it was an easy matter to select a good route and move the cattle over it at the good will and pleasure of the owner, and the abundance of grass enabled the cattle to gain flesh from the time they became reconciled to being under trail. Time was no particular object, because the trail stock required no time for recuperation, after reaching their destination as they could make the journey, even so far as Montana, while the grass was still green. After reaching their destination a month of close herding or line-riding sufficed to locate the stock and reconcile them to their new surroundings. In those times (even five years ago) a railroad built alongside the trail and carrying at low rates would not have carried a hoof. The open country afforded grass and water and proper driving was simply herding; a stockman could not herd cattle on his own range cheaper or keep them in better condition than he could on the trail. Then, as the country was not so heavily stocked as now, trail stock (and all stock, for that matter) gained flesh quicker. were ready for the drive earlier, had plenty to eat on the drive, and plenty to eat and ample room after the drive, and every stockman had the choice of several different routes. To-day all these conditions are changed. In Texas the western trail has been closed up and no stock pass directly through the Panhandle. The eastern trail has been closed up by farm fences three years, leaving in Texas, as before stated, only one that can properly be called a trail, which is the one leading by Fort Griffin to the crossing of Red River, at Doan's store, in Wilbarger County. This trail is simply established, because more stock travel over it than reach the Red River by any other route. There is no law to prevent Southern cattle from moving in open ground in Texas, nor has any such law ever been proposed. Still, the purchase and settlement of Texas lands, together with the State carrying so many more stock, has changed the aspect of the trail, and stockmen are more willing to pay freight charges, even from Southern to Northern Texas, and then fit up for the northern drive by trail rather than risk driving in, around, and between the farms and pastures, where, the driving limits being so much more contracted than in former years, the grazing is often inferior and the water supply often scant.

The drive through the Indian Territory is over a route none too well watered, and, in fact, the same may be said in reference to the grazing, even as far north as Dodge, Kans., where so many cattle are held during the summer season awaiting sale.

The conclusion is that the ranges of Texas do not put the young cattle in as good condition as they should be for the drive. There is not so much grazing on the available routes, and time is now an object, because trail cattle need to gain more flesh after arriving at the winter ranges before the winter sets in, as not so much flesh is gained as heretofore (if any) by the drive.

Now, the movement of cattle from Southern Texas to Northern Texas by rail is a success; and if the trail can be kept open from the northern part of Texas (say near Wichita Falls) to the northern ranges, it will afford one very satisfactory outlet for Texas cattle, as they can be shipped from any and all parts of the State to Wichita Falls, and then be driven from there to the northern ranges, while other railroad lines will furnish an outlet for those who prefer to make the entire journey by rail, provided they are permitted to unload the cattle after reaching their destination, which can only be satisfactorily arranged by providing ample quarantine grounds for the cattle to be held upon until a sufficient time has elapsed to insure safety to the native cattle from contact with the immigrant herds.

The Nebraska people have decided that all Texas cattle arriving by rail are diseased and all arriving on foot are free from disease; consequently, in the absence of any measures to protect him the Texas stockman is absolutely forced to claim as a right the way out of Texas by the way of the Indian Territory, Western Kansas, Colorado, and Nebraska. Before leaving the subject of rail transit, it may be as well to state that the trail movement has the advantage over rail transit as to cost of transportation and delivery; but stockmen would be willing to pay more for quick transit if the charges be regulated somewhat; and they fear, should entire dependence be on the railroads, the business would be squeezed dry of any possible profit by excessive charges on the part of the railroad company. There being no assurance of fixed and equitable transportation charges, stockmen cling to the trail as affording an alternative and safeguard against extortion. There is nothing to prevent young stock from being driven from even the southern part of Texas to the extreme northern ranges, and making the entire journey by rail in good condition, provided, they have proper attention while en route and are unloaded, watered, and fed as often as every twenty-four hours; and provided further, that the water and hay furnished them are of good quality and such as range cattle can use. Prior to the meeting of the stock men at Saint Louis, but after it was found that any movement of cattle to northern points by rail would be antagonized by all the northern cattle associations, I was informed that it was contemplated to inclose as a quarantine ground some large piece of railroad ground on the line of the Union Pacific Railroad, and use it as grazing land for all through stock, until competent veterinarians would pass them out with a clean bill of health, and I was somewhat surprised that the railroad men failed to submit the plan for the consideration of the assembled stockmen. I am satisfied it would have received their favorable indorsement as the solution of a vexatious and difficult problem, that is to say, the removal of Texas cattle to the northern ranges without danger to the native herds with which they come in contact.

The number of calves dropped on Texas ranges is considerably greater in proportion to the number of females than in the Northern Territories; and there is some difference in the calf crop in the northern and southern ranges of Texas. In the north the percentage of two-year-old heifers giving calves can be placed at 20 per cent.; in the southern portion I have had it placed at above 50 per cent., while the percentage from grown cows in either section would be about the same—from 85 to 90 per cent. Further north there is some difference, which I attribute to the climate, as the two-year olds do not (and certainly ought not to) bring many calves. Then, again, many of the northern-range calves die. With few exceptions the bulls run with the cattle all the year round, and there are quite a number of February and March calves dropped. Certainly a great number of these calves coming at this season of the year die, and quite frequently the mothers die also. February and March find all range cattle very weak, and the cow about to give birth to a calf is in no condition to do so. How they manage to raise any early calves in the northern part of Texas or in the ranges further north is a mystery; still there is no organized effort to prevent loss, which could easily be done by the ranchmen keeping the bulls from the cows until the proper season, say June or July, which would cause the calves to come after the winter was over, and the mother had begun to improve, and consequently there would be but little risk of either dying. In Southern Texas the two-year-old heifer with a calf by her side has a better chance of bringing a calf as a three-year-old than in the more northern ranges. In the latter, if a heifer brings a calf at two years old, she almost invariable fails to bring one at three years, which is not the case in the southern part of the State. In the northern ranges it would be much better if none of the heifers would bring calves until they are three years old, as the young heifers cannot or do not wean their calves, and have become so weakened from the continual drain on their system that the spring not unfrequently finds a fat yearling at the side of a dead cow, and the cow just coming three years old. This applies only to range cattle, as there is very little difference, if any, in the increase of small bunches of fed cattle, either in the north or south. Probably there is more certainty in the northern part of the State in the number of calves from matured cows, and more in the south from young stock. In this connection I may add that the further north, after leaving Texas, the smaller the percentage of calves, and that the percentage might be largely increased in any part of the grazing country by a larger supply of bulls and more careful handling during the rounding-up season. As stated above, Texas produces already more calves than she can mature, while it is doubtful if the Northern Territories show such an increase in stock cattle as will prove that females can be run on a profitable basis. This does not apply to the Indian Territory, Colorado or Kansas, nor (except to a less extent) to Wyoming, Montana, and Dakota.

That steer cattle mature better on the more abundant grasses of the North is too well known to require any evidence to support the statement. This is the whole life of the Texas drive. Three-fourths of the cattle driven are steers; and if steers were not to be had, the drive would be very much curtailed. A Nebraska-Texan, by which I mean a steer produced in Texas, but removed to Nebraska (one or two years old), on the Chicago market at four years old, should average from 1,100 to 1,300 pounds. At the same age, if matured in the Panhandle or northwestern part of Texas, would weigh from 1,000 to 1,100 pounds; if matured in the eastern or southern part of the State, would weigh from 850 to 950 pounds; if matured at three years old (as many of them are), would weigh, respectively, from 100 to 200 pounds less. The northern ranges furnish grazing at a profit on the first cost of yearling and two-year-old cattle, and gain the additional weight over the Texas average. In further proof of the additional profit to be derived from producing steers in Texas and removing them at one or two years old to the northern ranges to be there matured, I might mention that quite a number of our largest and most practical stockmen of Texas have steer ranges in the Northern Territories, where they have for several years and hope to continue, to remove their young stock. Although the difference between Texas and Nebraska is greater, there is a very marked difference in the weight of steers from the southern and northern ranges of Texas. A steer raised and matured in the Panhandle of Texas will weigh, at four years old, 300 pounds more than if matured in the southern part of the State. This is due to the climate, to a larger acreage, to better grass, and to a more regular improvement in blood. The range system of Texas will never produce as large and well-developed steers as will the ranges in the Northern Territories. Hence it may be considered that a drive of 400,000 head adds at least 80,000,000 pounds of beef to the supply of the United States the second year after their removal; and the stoppage of this emigration would cause a corresponding loss from the present supply, which would be felt in 1887. It is not possible that this loss can be made up from the alleged breeding-grounds of the north; nor would the Texas ranges, which are already stocked, be able to mature the surplus. The consequence, as I view the outlook, would be a surplus of light Texas cattle on the butchers' market for a year, and then a great falling off in the supply from every range section in the United States. In other words, if Texas were required to mature all her steer cattle and only allowed an outlet for them when they were ready to go to the butchers, she would soon find herself overstocked, and with more cattle than could possibly subsist on the range.

The land system of Texas differs very much from that of the United States. The State was very liberal to the early settlers and those who fought for independence against Mexico; also, to the railroad companies, to the public schools, universities, and asylums. A couple of years since all unsurveyed lands could be bought for 50 cents per acre, and surveyed school lands could be obtained in seven-section alternate tracts at $1 for dry, and $2 for watered lands; so that millions of acres were disposed of. The State donated 3,000,000 acres for a capitol building. Finally, by enactment of the legislature, all the lands not otherwise disposed of were transferred to the public schools; and of these there are 25,000,000 acres left, which are principally in the Panhandle, the west and southwest; so that there is but a remnant available for settlement, and these only by purchase.

The number of acres any one can purchase is now limited to two sections; and it is expected that the legislature now in session may cut this quantity in two or more fractions, so that the acquisition of large tracts of land in Texas is a thing of the past, excepting the transactions are with other parties than the State. The railroads have large tracts but are more disposed to lease than to sell; and all their lands being in alternate surveys of 640 acres each, the other alternates belonging to the schools, it becomes necessary, to acquire a solid body of land of any dimensions, to arrange with both owners. Had Texas lands been disposed of in larger tracts, they would now be all under fence and the home-seeker compelled to look elsewhere until such time as the cattle companies found it to their interest to divide and sell their lands.

I regard the homestead and pre-emption laws of the United States as far more beneficial than the continual changes which have taken place in this State; and while I would approve leases permitting the owner of alternate or railroad sections to lease the school sections, to give him control of his range, I would not approve the leasing of large solid bodies, even if, as in this State, the leased lands remained available for actual settlement. It would be unjust to the lessee to have his lease made null and void at any time, and the settler would be slow to enter a country skirted by another man's wire fences.

The probable tendency of the cattle business in Western Texas is toward the establishment of large ranches, divided up into moderate-sized pastures, whereby the owner can institute a system to better govern his herds. Horse pastures, bull pastures, calf pastures, breeding pastures, weaning pastures, and hay lands all require to be, and will be, separated; and pastures for wintering stock can be, and will be, preserved; but as every change of this kind requires absolute ownership of lands, and large sums of money in addition to the outlay for stock, it must necessarily follow that considerable time shall elapse before Texas becomes a perfect and magnificent stock farm, where every animal will be insured against severe weather and every range so conducted as to carry its full capacity of cattle and no more.

The ranges owned by individuals and companies, fenced and unfenced, run up from the 160-acre homestead to the 350,000-acre tracts of the wealthy individual and corporation; but, as before stated, it is not that the lands owned are immediately fenced. There are counties in which the State has not a foot of ground, and still by riding through and over the county, all is found open except here and there a farm is inclosed, while the stock owned by the farmer is ranging on the otherwise unoccupied lands, which he or some neighbor or non-resident may own. Nothing short of a survey would be sufficient to designate State lands from individual and railroad lands, even in the west, where the bulk of the State school lands are located. The State lands, even on the plains, are intersected with large bodies which individuals have acquired.

The Indian Territory is only second to Texas as a grazing country, if numbers be considered. A great many cattle have been passed over the line from Texas; some of the civilized Indians are large ranch-owners, and by arrangement with the Indian authorities there are always more or less cattle of non-residents there. Like in Texas, the eastern cattle are inferior in size, which is due to the rough and timbered ranges. The western prairie country produces better cattle. Here the tribes of Indians are now receiving rental, whereas it used to be paid to the individual who had some sort of a claim or right to be in the nation. In this case a lease brings into full use a large amount of valuable land.

In submitting this report I have to apologize for not going deeper into statistical details. Had time permitted I might have compiled the facts closer in connection with this great industry, but hope the outline presented may be sufficient for the purpose in view. All of which is respectfully submitted. I have the honor to remain,

Very respectfully, your obedient servant,

GEO. B. LOVING.

Hon. JOSEPH NIMMO, Jr.,
    Chief of Bureau of Statistics, Washington, D. C.

FORT WORTH, TEX., *February* 3, 1885.

DEAR SIR: I send you by this mail a map of Texas, divided into five different sections intended to divide the country, with reference to the class of cattle raised in each part of the State and its adaptability to stock-raising on the range.

That part of the State designated as East Texas is almost entirely a timbered country, being principally covered by a thick growth of pine; the bottom lands, however, on the different streams furnish reasonably fair grazing for stock. The country is principally settled by small farmers; that is to say, there are but few (if any) who make an exclusive business of raising stock in this portion of the State. However, most every farmer has more or less stock, numbering, generally, from fifteen to twenty one hundred head. These cattle manage to find sufficient feed during the spring and summer to keep them in reasonably fair condition, but are generally required to be fed, more or less, through the winter season. The feed usually consists of cotton seed or straw and is furnished without much cost to the owner. The cattle raised in this part of the State are a very inferior lot as compared with those raised further west, and consequently bring much less in the market. The average two-year-old raised in Eastern Texas is not as large as the one-year-old raised in the northwestern or western part of the State. Each farmer or stock owner in this part of the State usually sell off all their surplus or at least all their steer cattle every spring, which are usually bought up either for stocking the ranges of the western and northwestern portions of the State or for the Kansas or northern drive. They are generally shipped to some point further west in the State, or at least sufficiently far to put them beyond the timbered region, when they are placed on the trail, and in this way driven to market. Although this part of the State is really not adapted to stock-raising, and but few are owned by any one individual, yet taking in the entire eastern part of Texas there are altogether quite a number of cattle, probably one-half to three-quarters of a million head.

That part of the State designated as Central Texas was at one time (and up to within the last ten or fifteen years) a fine grazing country. It being also well adapted to agricultural purposes, it has during the last ten years been settled up by farmers, until there is no longer room for any large herds in this part of the State; not that it lacks the essentials of a good grazing country, but, on account of the fertility of the soil, it has been found more profitable for agricultural purposes. Still there are at this date a great many cattle raised in this part of the State, but on comparatively rather a small scale; that is, there are no large ranches and but very few in this part of the State that own over one thousand head; the average for Central Texas would probably be about one hundred. The cattle raised in this section were at one time as fine as could be found in any part of the State, but at the present time, on account of the country being to some extent overstocked, they are greatly inferior to those raised in the northwestern or western part of the State, but are considerable better than those raised in the eastern port. There are in this part of the State probably one and one-half million of cattle. The increase (in fact, almost all the steer cattle one year old and over) are annually driven to the northern States and Territories, there being in this locality but very few beeves kept until they arrive at maturity.

That part of the State designated as South Texas probably contains more cattle than any other division of the State, it being estimated that there are fully two and one-half million of cattle in this locality. The cattle raised in this section are of larger frames than those raised in the eastern or central portions of the State, but are inclined to be rough and bony, and are noted for the length of their horns and legs. There are a great many beeves matured in that part of the State lying next to the coast that find a market in New Orleans, in fact but few matured cattle are ever shipped from Southern Texas to any other market; but the majority of the surplus or steer cattle raised in this part of the State are driven to be matured in the northern ranges, being removed from Southern Texas at the ages of one and two years. They are now principally driven over what is known as the Fort Dodge and Griffin trail, which is outlined on the map referred to, from the crossing of the Colorado River to the crossing of the Red River, in Wilbarger County. I have not attempted to locate this trail further south than the Colorado River, from the fact that there is no designated route further south than that point. There is but little difference in the market value of cattle raised in Southern or Central Texas, though there is quite a difference in the quality. Southern Texas cattle, as a rule, are larger, while the Central Texas are more compact, "pony" built, and in this way make up in quality for the deficiency in size. The greater part of Southern Texas is alone adapted to grazing purposes, the land being regarded as unfit for agricultural purposes.

That part of the State designated as Western Texas is pre-eminently a stock-raising country, being entirely unsuited and almost totally worthless as an agricultural country. As is shown by the map, a great deal of this part of the State is rendered useless on account of the scarcity of water. All that part of it which is supplied by water is now stocked to almost within its full capacity. I estimate that there are in this part of the State, at this time, fully one and one-half million of cattle. They are, generally, a much better class than those raised in Southern Texas, and are second only to the cattle raised in the northwestern part of the State. A great deal of this is, comparatively, a new country, all that part of it lying tributary to the Pecos River and west having been only stocked within the last four or five years. This part of the State matures a very good class of beef, that will usually weigh in the Saint Louis and Chicago market about 900 pounds, gross, at three years old, and from 1,000 to 1,100 pounds, gross, at four years old. They generally become sufficiently fleshy at some time during the season to make good beef, without being driven to the northern ranges, as is required of the cattle from the southern part of the State. Western and Southern Texas are doubtless the best breeding portions of the State; that is to say, the ranchmen receive a larger percentage of calves from these two localities than are produced in any other part of the State.

That part of the State designated as Northwest Texas includes what is known as the Panhandle and is, without exception, the best stock country in Texas, as is evidenced by the fine herds which now occupy this portion of the State. The entire part of Northwest Texas is, comparatively, a new country, having been stocked within the past six or eight years. The western part is only partially used, at this time, on account of the scarcity of water, it being almost entirely on what is known as the "Staked Plains," which is, perhaps, as fine a grazing region as can be found in the United States, but is almost destitute of water and shelter. The former could, doubtless, be supplied with artesian wells or tanks made in the drains or basins; but will, probably, never be used to good advantage, on account of the scarcity of shelter, which could not be supplied with artificial means. All that part, however, east of these Staked Plains is reasonably well supplied with both water and shelter. Much of the range, however (as stated in my former report), is destroyed by prairie dogs, but still continues to furnish abundance of grass for all the stock that has, so far, been placed upon it. I regard this as the most valuable grazing section of the State, from the fact that it is not only a good breeding country; but, on account of the climate and the quality of the grass, is, perhaps, second only to the Northern Territories as a beef-producing range. This part of the State turns off, annually, a great number of beef cattle, a part of which are driven south to the Texas and Pacific Railway and shipped to Saint Louis and Chicago, while those in the more northern part are driven to Dodge and other shipping points in Kansas, and from thence shipped to the markets above mentioned. There is no difficulty found in this part of the State in introducing improved bulls and breeding up the herds; consequently, the cattle in the northwestern part of the State are much better improved than those further south, where, on account of the warm climate, it has been found exceedingly difficult to introduce improved bulls. The number of cattle in this part of the State will, probably, not fall short of two and one-half million. There is but little farming done in either Northwestern or Western Texas, the small amount of land cultivated being usually done by small stockmen and run in connection with their stock business in a small way, merely to furnish feed for their horses during the winter. In this part of the State, as well as in Western and Southern Texas, the cattle manage to live the entire season on such food only as nature provides for them, which was also the case, until the last few years, in Central Texas; but during the last winter (and to some extent for one or two winters previous) it has been found necessary to feed, in some localities, for a few months during the winter in the central part of the State.

You will notice from the map that I have marked a dotted line, designated as the quarantine line, which is intended to separate the southern and eastern portions of the State from the northern part, as near as possible on a line, so as to divide the cattle on the southern and eastern part, that may impart Texas fever, from those on the northern part, who will not impart it, but will contract the disease from those driven from the southern or eastern part. You will understand it is difficult to draw this line exact; that is, to locate or say just at what point the cattle will impart or contract the disease. I am of the opinion, however, that this line is as near correct as it can probably be made.

If I have not been sufficiently clear, or you should wish any further information on any point touching this interest, I shall take pleasure in answering any inquiries that you may wish to make.

I have the honor to be, very respectfully, your obedient servant,

GEO. B. LOVING.

Hon. JOSEPH NIMMO, Jr.,
Chief of Bureau of Statistics, Treasury Department, Washington, D. C.

APPENDIX No. 5.

STATEMENT PREPARED BY MR. D. W. HINKLE, OF SAN ANTONIO, TEX., IN REGARD TO THE RANGE AND RANCH CATTLE BUSINESS OF THE UNITED STATES.

1. There are in Texas 175,587,840 acres of land, about one-half of which is devoted to stock raising; the greater portion of these lands lie west of the Texas Central Railroad, and the principal part of them devoted strictly to *range* cattle west of the International and Great Northern Railroad, extending north to the upper Panhandle. All of the Indian Territory is used for range cattle, except lands occupied by towns and railroads, say about 40,000,000 acres, out of a total area of 44,154,240 acres.

2. As to the number of cattle raised in Texas annually, you will see by the comptroller's report of *tax-paying cattle*, 6,517,524 head reported on hand November 15, 1884. The product from that number of cattle would be a fraction less than 2,000,000 head of calves, one-half of which would be female cattle, leaving in round numbers about 900,000 head of male cattle for sale to beef growers and for driving purposes. In 1883 we had, as per comptroller's report same date, 6,054,488 head, showing that stocks had increased 463,036 head, though many female, as well as nearly all the young male cattle had been sold. It is safe to say that the State produces annually 1,000,000 head of cattle for sale, divided as per last year, 1884. (See comptroller's report.) Seven hundred and fifty thousand cattle shipped and driven to northern ranges, worth at points of delivery, at $16 per head, $12,000,000. Two hundred and fifty thousand head of beef cattle were shipped to the various markets North and South, (say Saint Louis, Chicago, New Orleans, Kansas City, Memphis, and others), worth, at $22 per head, $5,500,000. We have in the State a population of about 2,250,000 people, who all eat and largely of *beef*, and while the bulk of the beef eaten consists of female cattle, they are worth, at a low estimate to the raisers, say 300,000 head of cattle worth in Texas markets, $5,600,000, showing that Texas raises and *feeds* to a hungry world $24,100,000 worth of beef yearly.

The third question is answered in No. 2.

4. It is absolutely necessary to get a trail from Texas to the Northern States and Territories, owing to the fact that too few railroads lead from this State northward, and the roads now in operation could not, however willing, handle all of the cattle for export, and then it would give railroad companies a chance to pool on routes and make the expense of sending cattle to northern ranges too great.

Individually, I prefer to ship (have been a shipper for two years) rather than drive, and think the rail transportation *absolutely* necessary to this the greatest breeding country in the world.

Texas cattlemen *generally* own the land on which cattle are grown, and pastures ranging from 20,000 to 200,000 acres, securely fenced, are to be counted by scores; in fact, South and West and North Texas is nearly all owned by cattlemen, and a large per cent. of them have good fences. These are not farms, they are pastures. I name two men who own in this country pastures embracing more than 250,000 acres each. T. C. O'Conner, the richest cattleman in the United States, lives in Refugio County; R. King, in Nueces County. Many, very many, others own pastures of 100,000 acres and over.

You will see by the fact that as Texas is being fenced by large pasture owners, that in a few years railroads must furnish the necessary transportation to carry the cattle to market; in fact, the country south of the Galveston, Harrisburg and San Antonio Railroad is now so fenced as to depend on rail shipments, and a large per cent. of all the young cattle sent north for maturing comes from that region (would say at least 300,000 head). The letter to you from George Olds, esq., general traffic manager, is well conceived and deserves your consideration. He expresses my views about quarantine grounds. I think there should be quarantine grounds allotted to the railroads, and the points designated by him will suit us.

To sum up a very cursory report of so great a trade, we want to get our cattle to market; drive or ship by rail, prefer both, but if both can't be had, give us all you can. You can add *facts:* I know that Texas is *per se* the breeding country of the United States, and has and will produce more beef, or rather young cattle, than any

111

two States or Territories in the Union. We raise twelve calves for every cow owned (in her lifetime), Kansas raises about ten calves to the cow, Nebraska eight calves, Wyoming and Montana and Dakota about six calves to the cow, Oregon four calves to the cow (strictly range cattle).

You will see that with the above facts, that if Texas was cut off from the markets of the world, that the States and Territories quarantining against her cattle would enhance the value of *beef* and make the poor man pay more for it than he does now, and that it is due very largely to this State that the laboring classes in the East have been able to eat beef. Texas has more female cattle than all of the balance of the States west of the Mississippi River, and has been "*The Mother of the West*" in the cattle business. Her cowboys opened up to the world the markets of Kansas and other Northwestern States. They drove the Indians from the great northern plain and opened them up to civilization.

As to the subject of artesian wells and the practicability of furnishing water where none now exists, I am too little posted to give you the data requested, but I think in the near future large tracts of dry lands in Texas and other Territories will be furnished by that means and thus add to the beef production of the country. I estimate that there are about 23,500,000 acres in this State now unavailable on account of the scarcity of water, which can and will be brought into use through the means of artesian wells. Fully 10,000,000 acres are in the same condition in the Indian Territory and 28,000,000 acres in New Mexico.

There is no doubt in my mind that it will always pay stockmen and beef eaters better if they will allow Texas to breed cattle and then sell the young stock to northern ranchmen to be matured. Texas raises a greater number of calves to a given number of cows than any other State north of it, and our young cattle make larger and better beef by being grown on northern ranges. Our climate, warm at nearly all seasons of the year, is especially adapted to breeding purposes, and after a calf is twelve months old or over, it is then able to stand the colder climate of the North, and in a year or two mature into a beef steer. weighing more than the same animal grown here.

To describe the drive, and how Texas cattle are handled, would be almost impossible, unless you knew something of range work. We commence in the early spring with mounted men to drive the cattle on a certain range to a pen, where we turn out all not needed for driving purposes (most ranges have several pens). Those to be driven are kept under herd until, after repeating the same operation over all parts of the range and putting all the bunches together, a herd is formed ; it sometimes takes many ranches or ranges to furnish a herd large enough to drive north, though there are a large number of ranches able to furnish several herds each. A herd generally consists of twenty-five hundred to three thousand head of cattle. After enough cattle are bunched together to form a herd, a boss man, with eight hands, a wagon for hauling provisions, and a cook, who is also the driver of the wagon, with not less than four horses to each man, starts to go to the trail, taking the nearest route on which there is grass and water, from the point at which the cattle are started to the nearest point on the trail ; the cattle are driven slowly, allowing time for grazing and watering, and at night are stopped, and will generally lie down about dark in a space of about 2 acres ; the drivers ride around them all night, taking watches just like sentinels around a camp. Our main trail commences at Bandera, the county seat of the county of the same name, runs in a northerly direction to Fort Griffin, thence to Doan's store, on Red River, where it is proposed the national trail shall commence, thence to Dodge City, Kans., thence to Ogalalla, Nebr., where the trails divide, going in all directions northward, west, or east, to points where the cattle are to be delivered to northern buyers. Cattle are driven about 15 miles per day, and some herds, for delivery in Montana, are on the trail ninety days, and even more.

The comptroller of the State certifies that taxes have been paid to the 15th November, 1884, on 6,517,524 head. Value, $81,052,616.

I would say there are in the State not less than 7,000,000 cattle, value $105,000,000. I send comptroller's report. There are many ranges in the extreme western part of the State, reaching from the mouth of Devil's River west to El Paso, on the Rio Grande, and north to the extreme northern part of the Panhandle, so large that it would be impossible to make a close estimate of the number of cattle on them.

The following certificates of the comptroller of Texas show the number and valuation of cattle, horses, sheep, and hogs assessed for taxation in that State for the years 1883 and 1884:

(Executive department, office of comptroller, Austin, Tex.)

I, William J. Swain, comptroller of public accounts of the State of Texas, do hereby certify that the assessment rolls for the year 1884 on file in this office show the numbers of cattle, horses, sheep, and hogs assessed for taxation for said year to be as follows:

Animals.	Number.	Value.
Cattle	6, 517, 524	$81, 052, 616
Horses	1, 154, 090	32, 109, 577
Sheep	4, 691, 008	9, 291, 890
Hogs	1, 403, 870	2, 137, 978

In testimony whereof I hereunto sign my name and cause the seal of this office to be affixed this the 15th day of November, A. D. 1884.

WM. J. SWAIN, *Comptroller.*

(Executive department, office of comptroller, Austin, Tex.)

I, Wiliam J. Swain, comptroller of public accounts of the State of Texas, do hereby certify that the assessment rolls for the year 1883 on file in this office show the numbers of cattle, horses, sheep, and hogs assessed for taxation for said year to be as follows:

Animals.	Number.	Value.
Cattle	6, 054, 488	$71, 393, 319
Horses	1, 054, 452	27, 678, 508
Sheep	4, 491, 600	9, 228, 234
Hogs	1, 044, 762	1, 673, 298

In testimony whereof I hereunto sign my name and cause the seal of this office to be affixed this the 29th day of September, A. D. 1884.

WM. J. SWAIN, *Comptroller.*

APPENDIX No. 6.

LETTER ADDRESSED TO THE CHIEF OF THE BUREAU OF STATISTICS BY PROF. ELIAS LOOMIS, LL. D. OF YALE COLLEGE, IN REGARD TO THE PRINCIPAL SOURCES OF THE RAINFALL OF DIFFERENT SECTIONS OF THE UNITED STATES.

YALE COLLEGE, *February* 23, 1885.

DEAR SIR: In reply to your letter of the 14th ultimo I have to state that there is no doubt that the westerly winds which blow over the Rocky Mountains are very dry winds when they reach the eastern slope of those mountains; and they appear to have lost a very considerable part of their moisture by the precipitation which took place on the western slope of the Sierra Nevadas. I have examined this subject in a paper published in the American Journal of Science for July, 1881, and I herewith send you a copy of this paper. As the result of this dryness, the mean annual rainfall between the Sierra Nevadas and the meridian of 100 degrees is, with slight exceptions, less than 15 inches. This is shown by the latest rain-charts published by the Smithsonian Institution.

Throughout all the southern part of the United States east of the Rocky Mountains, with the exception of the Atlantic coast, is evidently due to vapor which comes from the Gulf of Mexico. This influence is very decided up to the parallel of 36 degrees, and is probably felt in a diminished degree still further north.

Near the Atlantic coast the amount of rainfall is evidently increased by vapor which comes from the Atlantic Ocean. For the remaining portion of the United States east of the Rocky Mountains, the vapor which furnishes the rain may come to some extent from these two sources, but it is chiefly derived from the chain of the great lakes from the rivers, small lakes, and collections of water, and from the moist earth.

The rainfall in the western portion of the United States within 150 miles of the Pacific Ocean is evidently derived mainly from vapor which rises from the Pacific Ocean. This is indicated by the fact that the precipitation occurs almost wholly on the west side of the ridge of the Sierra Nevadas, and there is but little rainfall on the east side.

I am, with much respect, yours truly,

ELIAS LOOMIS.

114

APPENDIX No. 7.

LETTER ADDRESSED TO THE CHIEF OF THE BUREAU OF STATISTICS BY MR. SILAS BENT, OF SAINT LOUIS, IN REGARD TO THE METEOROLOGY OF THE GREAT INTERIOR DRY AREA OF THE UNITED STATES.

GRANITE BLOCK, CORNER FOURTH AND MARKET STREETS,
Saint Louis, February 19, 1885.

DEAR SIR: Your favor of 13th instant, together with map showing annual rainfall in the United States, is received, for which I thank you, as well as for your criticism of my address upon the "Meteorology of the Mountains and Plains of North America," &c., in reply to which I have to say that my treatment of the subject, necessarily very brief, did not aim to go farther than to announce the operations of general laws, and to only touch upon such modifications of those laws occasioned by local influences as were absolutely necessary for a fair presentation of the hypothesis.

If the maps you send were made from observations taken equally often all over the United States territory and included the snowfall as well as the rainfall, then it would be almost conclusive against the general theory; but this, I take it, is not the case, and the precipitation of moisture in the form of snow on the tops of the mountains (which from their reservoirs keep in perennial flow all the great rivers of the continent), as well as along what might be termed the water-belts, extending from the mouth of the Columbia River to the mouth of the Saint Lawrence and Kennebec Rivers, is not shown on the map, yet this is a potential factor in the consideration of the subject as a whole.

The rainfall alone, as shown by the map, would not keep the Great Lakes in supply without the addition of the snow that falls into them, and by the map there is no rainfall shown capable of sustaining all the great rivers that radiate from the region of the Yellowstone Park or the "water dome" of the continent. But my main object in discussing these points in the address was to show that if it were not for the mountain ranges running north and south, and therefore, according to my theory, at right angles to the *moisture-laden* winds from the west, the arid plateau and plains of Arizona, Utah, and Nevada and of New Mexico, Colorado, and Wyoming, would be as prolific and luxuriant as the valley of the Columbia River and Manitoba, for if this moisture were brought to these high latitudes of the water belt by a wind from the south, its precipitation would be distributed all along the way over the arid plains of Arizona and Utah and of New Mexico and Colorado, and the sterility of those plains would not exist. Their very sterility, therefore, shows that south winds do not prevail there, and that the west winds that do prevail are robbed of their moisture by the condensing power of the mountain ranges which stand across their path before they can reach these plains.

The map, no doubt, shows correctly the rainfall over the eastern half of our country; but how much of that, so represented, comes from the Gulf of Mexico and Atlantic, and how much from the snows of the northwest converted into rain before it falls cannot be yet determined, though I by no means pretend that by far the greater portion of that rainfall does not come from the Gulf and the Atlantic. But still, if the snowfall upon the western mountains and northern plains could be also as fully and fairly shown as the rainfall is in the eastern half of the country, I think the face of the map would be very materially changed and its relative exhibits correspondingly modified.

I write under a press of disturbing business thoughts, but hope you can understand me, and believe me, very respectfully, yours,

SILAS BENT.

Hon. JOSEPH NIMMO, Jr.,
    Chief of Bureau of Statistics, Washington, D. C.

APPENDIX No. 8.

*LETTER IN REGARD TO THE PRECIPITATION OF MOISTURE THROUGH-
OUT THE GREAT DRY AREA OF THE INTERIOR, BY SILAS BENT, ESQ.,
SAINT LOUIS.*

GRANITE BLOCK,
CORNER FOURTH AND MARKET STREETS, *Saint Louis, April 9,* 1885.

DEAR SIR: Your favor of the 17th ultimo, with papers from the Signal Bureau, I found awaiting me on my return home a few days ago. I have not had time to examine the tables, but assuming that your analysis of them is correct, and that they "show that the average precipitation during the summer months throughout the dry area east of the Rocky Mountain range is considerably greater than during the winter months," and that "in Idaho and Washington Territories the reverse, however, appears to be the case," it would, of course, be desirable with me to harmonize these facts with the theory advanced in my recent paper upon the meteorology of the mountains and plains of North America. This, however, I am not sure I can fully do, for I have great doubts as to the *whole* truth being told by these tables. The *rain-gauges* used by the weather bureau are accurate enough for all practical purposes, and no doubt show correctly the precipitation that takes place in that form at the localities where they are used, but the *snow-gauges* are quite inadequate to show the amount of precipitation of moisture that reaches the earth's surface in the form of snow, or the point at which the congealation of vapor into snow has occurred. Tables or maps, therefore, made from such records give but a one-sided view of the subject, and this is the difficulty that stands in the way of any examination of the meteorological problem where the annual precipitation is divided into rainfall and snowfall, as is the case throughout the dry area east of the Rocky Mountain range. But, on the Pacific coast and western slope of the Sierra Nevada range, below the snow limit, where the precipitation is almost altogether as rain, it is not difficult to show why that precipitation should be much greater in winter than in summer, as I shall now proceed to do.

The ocean temperature of the North Pacific remains pretty much the same throughout the year, and is, as I have before said, about 70° or 75° F. The temperature of the land, however, along the coast of Oregon and Washington Territory and the lower regions of Idaho is much higher than that of the ocean in the summer time, and much lower in the winter season. The vapor-laden west winds, which come to those coasts from across the Pacific, partake of the temperature of the ocean, and being cooler than the land in summer, are expanded by the contact rather than contracted, and, of course, yield no precipitation, but in the winter, being warmer than the land, they are contracted by the contact, and give forth the mists and rain which envelop that region throughout that season, and which mists and rain are congealed into snow only when those winds reach the mountains where the temperature is below the freezing point.

The equable character of the climate on that coast, caused by these west winds, is shown by the fact that thunder-storms and tornadoes are almost unknown there, these phenomena being caused by the meeting of currents in the atmosphere of different temperatures, as described in extreme cases in the article upon the "Birth of the Tornado," which I sent you a short time since.

From information derived from residents along the foot-hills of the eastern slope of the Rocky Mountains, who are familar with the weather of the plains or dry area of that region, I am of the opinion that by far the greater amount of precipitation upon those plains is in the form of snow, which falls in the winter, and which, if it could be measured, would reverse the showing of these tables from the weather bureau. This, however, can be only definitely settled when the appliances for snowfall measurement can be made more accurate than any yet devised.

With many thanks for the interest and trouble you bestow upon this matter, and with the hope that it may lead to profitable investigation in the interest of science, I am, very sincerely yours,

SILAS BENT.

Hon. JOSEPH NIMMO, Jr.,
Chief of Bureau of Statistics, Treasury Department, Washington, D. C.

APPENDIX No. 9.

LETTER ADDRESSED TO THE CHIEF OF THE BUREAU OF STATISTICS, IN REGARD TO THE SOURCES OF PRECIPITATION THROUGHOUT THE DRY AREA, BY CAPT. SAMUEL M. MILLS, ACTING CHIEF SIGNAL OFFICER UNITED STATES ARMY.

SIGNAL OFFICE, WAR DEPARTMENT,
Washington City, March 6, 1885.

SIR: Referring to your letter of the 13th ultimo, in which you state that in the preparation of a report in regard to the range and ranch cattle area of the United States, you desire to describe the dry area of this country, and for that purpose submit certain inquiries to obtain information on the subject, I have the honor to say that your questions relate to general theories which are not easily discussed in a few words.

It seems probable that evaporation from the Kuro-Siwo is no more important than that from the remainder of the Pacific Ocean.

The southwest wind that, north of California, passes over the Rocky Mountains, and deposits rain on our Pacific coast, undoubtedly draws most of its moisture from the Pacific Ocean; it loses more of its moisture on the immediate coast than in the neighborhood of the crest of the Rocky Mountains, but is by no means depleted; on the average its dew-point falls about 15 degrees Fahrenheit before reaching the crest. This corresponds to a loss of about 40 per cent. of its moisture. Having passed the crest it does not furnish any more rain until its 60 per cent. residuum has been increased either by local evaporation or by mixing with moist air from some distant source, such as the Atlantic, Gulf of Mexico, Great Lakes, &c.

As any rainfall immediately begins to evaporate, and mixes with what is already in the air, it is impracticable to state what proportion of the rainfall over the Great Lakes or over any other section comes directly from the Gulf of Mexico and Caribbean Sea.

I am, very respectfully, your obedient servant,

S. M. MILLS,
Captain Fifth Artillery, Acting Chief Signal Officer U. S. Army.

Mr. JOSEPH NIMMO, Jr.,
Chief Bureau of Statistics, Treasury Department.

117

APPENDIX No. 10.

TABLES SHOWING THE MONTHLY PRECIPITATION AT VARIOUS POINTS THROUGHOUT THE DRY AREA, FURNISHED BY CAPT. SAMUEL M. MILLS, U. S. ARMY, ACTING CHIEF SIGNAL OFFICER.

SIGNAL OFFICE, WAR DEPARTMENT,
Washington City, March 13, 1885.

SIR: In reply to your letter of the 7th instant, requesting a statement of the precipitation at the points indicated therein, I have the honor to inclose herewith an extract from the records of this office.

I am, very respectfully, your obedient servant,

S. M. MILLS,
Captain Fifth Artillery, Acting Chief Signal Officer U. S. Army.

Mr. JOSEPH NIMMO, Jr.,
Chief Bureau of Statistics, Treasury Department.

Precipitation (in inches and hundreÎths) at various points, from the records of the Signal Office.

BOISE CITY, IDAHO.

Year.	January.	February.	March.	April.	May.	June.	July.	August.	September.	October.	November.	December.	Annual amount.
1877							0.35	0.09	0.27	0.85	2.05	0.01	
1878	1.73	2.18	1.63	0.37	1.18	0.86	0.31	0.50	0.27	0.30	0.53	0.35	10.21
1879	3.62	1.42	3.04	1.42	0.92	1.43	(*)	0.03	0.14	0.76	1.20	3.65	17.63
1880	0.90	0.94	0.50	1.50	1.57	0.11	0.02	0.02	0.11	0.50	0.48	4.01	10.66
1881	3.62	3.51	0.64	1.34	0.07	0.29	0.13	0.00	0.25	2.12	0.94	0.65	13.56
1882	1.62	1.73	1.54	2.33	0.34	0.29	(*)	0.00	1.36	2.94	0.08	2.20	14.43
1883	3.77	1.20	0.28	0.61	2.12	0.20	(†)	(*)	0.20	4.06	0.46	2.27	
1884	1.75	1.32	2.78	0.78	0.92	3.41	0.60	0.07	2.11	1.52	0.12	5.67	21.05
Mean	2.43	1.76	1.49	1.19	1.02	0.94	0.20	0.09	0.59	1.63	0.73	2.35	14.59

* Inappreciable.   † No record.

CHEYENNE, WYO.

Year.	January.	February.	March.	April.	May.	June.	July.	August.	September.	October.	November.	December.	Annual amount.
1870											0.41	0.18	
1871	0.28	0.07	0.11	0.95	2.14	2.25	1.27	0.36	0.74	0.24	0.66	0.16	9.23
1872	0.02	0.27	0.38	1.61	1.99	1.84	3.90	2.05	1.03	0.33	0.03	0.03	13.48
1873	0.03	0.02	0.38	0.92	2.41	1.77	1.10	2.07	0.36	0.70	0.17	0.08	10.01
1874	0.11	0.11	0.74	0.61	1.50	1.34	1.87	0.44	0.93	1.86	0.04	0.16	9.71
1875	0.42	0.06	0.23	0.50	1.20	0.29	4.47	2.12	1.34	0.60	0.84	0.03	12.10
1876	0.02	0.06	0.54	0.23	2.50	0.10	0.79	0.26	0.00	0.00	0.32	0.21	5.03
1877	0.20	0.14	0.98	1.11	2.24	1.27	0.43	0.83	2.02	1.99	0.17	0.33	11.71
1878	0.08	0.13	1.16	0.19	4.46	1.71	1.43	2.50	0.75	0.04	0.00	0.19	12.64
1879	0.32	0.20	0.44	1.66	1.30	0.07	1.04	1.26	0.00	0.65	0.23	0.17	7.34
1880	0.20	0.09	0.06	0.17	0.44	1.06	1.88	2.23	1.05	0.76	0.36	0.08	8.38
1881	0.36	0.22	0.32	2.32	1.14	1.22	1.40	1.97	1.75	0.88	0.29	0.01	11.88
1882	0.14	0.05	0.06	0.46	2.73	1.85	2 30	0.23	0.35	0.31	0.06	0.10	8.64
1883	0.88	0.25	0.85	2.76	3.68	3.67	1.45	2.18	0.90	1.66	0.16	0.80	19.24
1884	0.76	0.26	1.59	1.33	4.83	1.50	0.60	2.07	1.25	0.50	0.18	0.67	15.54
Mean	6.27	0.14	0.56	1.06	2.33	1.42	1.71	1.47	0.89	0.75	0.26	0.21	11.07

Precipitation (in inches and hundredths) at various places, &c.—Continued.

DAYTON, WASH.

Year.	January.	February.	March.	April.	May.	June.	July.	August.	September.	October.	November.	December.	Annual amount.
1879												4.55	
1880	3.37	2.19	1.89	3.81	2.78	1.00	1.68	1.29	0.19	1.65	2.00	7.93	29.78
1881	5.03	5.04	1.84	3.51	0.45	1.61	0.65	0.22	1.47	3.04	2.47	2.37	27.70
1882	2.56	6.16	1.97	4.08	1.93	0.77	0.83	0.14	0.94	4.41	2.61	7.12	33.52
1883	5.48	1.17	2.44	1.64	2.90	0.08	0.00	0.30	0.09	1.44	3.11	2.79	21.44
1884	3.14	5.66	1.79	2.40	0.81	2.02	0.32	0.09	1.40	3.45	0.25	5.10	26.43
Mean	3.92	4.04	1.99	3.09	1.77	1.10	0.70	0.41	0.82	2.80	2.09	4.98	27.75

DEADWOOD, DAK.

Year.	January.	February.	March.	April.	May.	June.	July.	August.	September.	October.	November.	December.	Annual amount.
1878	0.30	1.01	3.85	8.77	7 80						0.75	3.63	
1879	0.58	0.72	0.51	7.69	5.03	4.67	1.82	1.49	0.32	4.26	0.27	1.14	28.50
1880	0.56	1.14	0.75	1.57	2.43	3.33	1.51	3.33	0.30	1.27	2.37	0.64	19.20
1881	3.10	1.26	2.59	2.05	3.70	3.04	1.56	0.56	1.80	0.58	0.84	0.05	21.13
1882	0.33	0.21	1.29	7.31	7.05	5.78	4.81	1.97	0.28	0.88	1.35	2.57	33.83
1883	0.74	1.32	0.84	5.69	10.33	5.26	1.82	1.32	0.11	0.80	0.45	1.01	29.69
1884	0.85	1.01	2.61	2.29	1.72	2.51	3.51	3.07	1.99	1.48	1.46	1.79	24.29
Mean	0.92	0.95	1.78	5.05	5.44	4.10	2.50	1.96	0.80	1.54	1.07	1.55	26.11

DENVER, COLO.

Year.	January.	February.	March.	April.	May.	June.	July.	August.	September.	October.	November.	December.	Annual amount.
1871												0.51	
1872	0.55	0.22	1.71	2.09	3.74	2.07	2.69	1.75	1.57	0.68	0.69	0.29	18.05
1873	0.13	0.24	0.22	2.43	0.75	2.24	2.00	1.41	0.89	0.73	0.16	0.61	11.81
1874	0.84	0.53	0.49	1.70	2.43	1.21	3.35	0.68	1.34	0.64	0.08	0.17	13.46
1875	0.38	0.60	0.39	2.24	1.94	0.43	4.32	1.97	2.89	0.22	1.28	0.59	17.25
1876	0.21	0.11	1.80	1.22	8.57	1.10	1.16	2.03	0.60	0.12	1.50	1.70	20.12
1877	1.90	0.40	1.40	2.77	2.30	1.93	0.33	1.30	0.38	2.15	0.73	0.79	16.38
1878	0.10	0.48	1.82	0.05	2.90	2.78	1.38	2.25	1.23	0.80	0.67	1.05	15.51
1879	0.40	0.39	1.00	2.62	3.36	0.32	0.64	1.38	0.02	0.19	0.21	0.33	10.86
1880	0.38	0.32	0.21	0.31	1.11	1.22	1.38	1.46	0.89	1.37	0.83	0.10	9.58
1881	0.49	1.22	0.87	0.50	2.21	0.09	2.50	2.33	0.57	0.32	1.68	0.00	12.78
1882	0.57	0.20	0.20	1.47	2.98	4.96	0.66	1.20	0.06	0.75	0.71	0.73	14.49
1883	2.35	0.45	0.21	3.10	4.30	0.85	2.27	0.75	1.08	1.49	0.32	2.32	19.49
1884	0.22	0.86	0.93	3.33	4.61	1.47	0.65	1.71	0.13	0.21	0.19	0.76	14.98
Mean	0.66	0.46	0.87	1.83	3.17	1.59	1.79	1.56	0.90	0.74	0.70	0.71	14.98

DODGE CITY, KANS.

Year.	January.	February.	March.	April.	May.	June.	July.	August.	September.	October.	November.	December.	Annual amount.
1874										0.22	0.23	0.05	
1875	0.12	0.10	0.04	0.72	2.26	0.73	3.28	2.06	1.32	0.06	0.00	0.09	10.78
1876	0.00	0.05	3.59	0.16	1.15	2.53	2.26	1.03	2.13	1.00	1.35	0.15	15.40
1877	0.18	0.56	0.25	3.38	4.96	3.92	1.79	4.09	0.50	3.34	0.56	4.36	27.89
1878	0.21	1.13	1.01	1.06	4.63	2.19	1.61	4.48	0.76	0.09	0.60	0.19	17.96
1879	0.87	0.08	0.17	0.40	0.90	4.40	3.90	3.75	0.80	(*)	0.04	0.12	15.43
1880	(*)	(*)	0.04	0.11	3.01	1.59	4.00	5.17	0.32	1.42	2.43	0.03	18.12
1881	0.15	1.63	0.50	2.38	12.82	1.77	5.06	2.36	3.13	2.19	0.95	0.61	33.55
1882	0.52	0.22	0.24	0.68	3.87	1.51	3.04	1.07	0.15	1.62	0.11	0.11	13.14
1883	0.44	1.42	0.42	2.40	5.41	4.31	2.61	5.66	1.32	3.32	0.12	1.07	28.50
1884	0.08	0.28	1.91	1.07	4.47	7.67	6.40	4.82	0.23	1.50	0.83	1.10	30.36
Mean	0.26	0.55	0.82	1.24	4.35	3.06	3.40	3.45	1.07	1.34	0.66	0.72	21.11

* Inappreciable.

EAGLE ROCK, IDAHO.

Year.	January.	February.	March.	April.	May.	June.	July.	August.	September.	October.	November.	December.	Annual amount.
1880												4.50	
1881	3.66	5.14	0.97	3.13	0.74	1.09	1.21	0.95	0.00	1.71	1.91	0.80	21.31
1882	4.41	1.25	3.45	3.35	0.30	0.52	0.30	0.07	1.17	1.50	0.49	1.24	18.05
1883	2.08	2.38	0.41	0.76	1.12	(*)							
Mean	3.38	2.92	1.61	2.41	0.72	0.80	0.76	0.51	0.58	1.60	1.20	2.18	19.68

* Station closed June 15, 1883.

Precipitation (in inches and hundredths) at various points, &c.—Continued.

EL PASO, TEX.

Year.	January.	February.	March.	April.	May.	June.	July.	August.	September.	October.	November.	December.	Annual amount.
1878							1.25	2.55	0.66	1.02	0.66	0.11	
1879	1.57	0.83	0.18	0.07	0.00	0.08	2.47	0.35	0.04	0.95	0.01	0.26	6.81
1880	1.01	(*)	0.30	0.10	0.00	0.00	6.54	3.60	0.80	0.47	0.02	1.53	14.37
1881	0.35	0.24	0.01	0.22	1.83	0.02	8.18	3.15	1.44	1.45	0.50	0.78	18.17
1882	0.64	0.78	0.38	0.00	0.10	0.43	1.26	2.82	0.40	0.00	1.46	0.00	8.27
1883	0.10	0.40	2.09	0.10	0.02	0.04	2.84	1.34	2.51	2.03	0.61	0.84	12.92
1884	0.55	0.84	0.33	0.91	(*)	0.11	0.46	3.98	3.68	5.15	0.22	2.07	18.30
Mean	0.70	0.52	0.55	0.23	0.32	0.11	3.29	2.54	1.36	1.58	0.50	0.80	13.14

* Inappreciable.

FORT BENTON, MONT.

Year.	January.	February.	March.	April.	May.	June.	July.	August.	September.	October.	November.	December.	Annual amount.
1871												1.30	
1872	0.27	0.34	0.82	0.67	0.64	1.14	4.62	0.61	1.82	0.19	0.61	0.59	12.32
1873	0.60	0.65	0.23	1.14	3.03	1.67	1.29	1.59	0.58	0.19	0.86	0.12	11.95
1874	0.67	0.10	0.64	0.43	2.98	2.13	0.10	1.17	0.49	0.56	0.58	0.60	10.45
1875	0.66	1.11	0.22	1.04	1.60		2.24	1.19	0.13	0.71	0.85	0.43	12.75
1876	0.71	0.28	1.53	1.25	11.06	1.45	2.31						
1880							1.12	1.56	0.32	1.09	1.44	1.39	
1881	2.27	0.66	0.29	0.18	1.43	3.46	2.28	1.18	1.32	1.94	1.73		16.81
1882	0.75	0.38	1.09	1.22	0.35	0.13	0.85	0.27	2.89	0.86	0.39	1.00	10.18
1883	0.75	0.45	1.34	1.02	3.31	1.93	0.16	1.01	0.93	1.64	0.36	0.11	13.01
1884	0.56	(*)	(*)	(*)	1.09	2.18	3.09	0.79	1.44	0.36	0.29	1.01	
Mean	0.80	0.50	0.77	0.87	2.83	1.85	1.81	1.04	1.10	0.84	0.79	0.66	12.50

*Incomplete.

FORT BUFORD, DAK.

Year.	January.	February.	March.	April.	May.	June.	July.	August.	September.	October.	November.	December.	Annual amount.
1879	0.02	0.59	0.03	2.75	5.56	3.35	3.63	0.18	0.00	1.55	0.37	1.68	19.71
1880	0.10	0.51	0.21	0.74	4.02	5.46	4.17	2.36	1.04	0.90	0.66	3.08	23.25
1881	1.98	1.10	1.17	1.34	1.00	3.44	1.32	1.10	0.58	0.39	0.39	0.09	13.90
1882	0.26	0.29	0.69	0.94	1.61	1.87	2.25	0.16	2.86	1.00	0.29	0.51	12.73
1883	1.98	0.36	0.91	0.48	0.59	0.97	1.69	1.96	0.22	1.41	0.14	0.11	10.82
1884	0.11	0.12	0.10	1.30	0.14	0.99	1.87	1.06	0.53	0.44	0.31	0.40	7.37
Mean	0.74	0.50	0.52	1.26	2.15	2.68	2.49	1.14	0.87	0.95	0.36	0.98	14.63

FORT CUSTER, MONT.

Year.	January.	February.	March.	April.	May.	June.	July.	August.	September.	October.	November.	December.	Annual amount.
1879									0.03	2.04	0.18	1.53	
1880	0.32	0.60	0.36	1.31	5.63	3.17	2.51	2.55	0.20	1.19	0.54	1.27	19.65
1881	2.84	0.51	0.17	0.78	1.80	1.57	1.41	0.03	1.09	0.80	0.66	0.22	11.88
1882	0.40	0.02	0.07	1.12	4.45	2.43	0.54	0.11	1.28	0.29	0.15	1.19	12.05
1883	0.22	0.09	1.03	1.86	2.96	1.50	0.77	1.01	0.46	0.97	1.10	1.87	13.84
1884	2.85	1.29	1.02	0.77	1.19	3.87	0.80	2.09	1.42	0.66	0.37	0.27	16.60
Mean	1.33	0.50	0.53	1.17	3.21	2.51	1.21	1.16	0.75	0.99	0.50	1.06	14.80

FORT ELLIOTT, TEX.

Year.	January.	February.	March.	April.	May.	June.	July.	August.	September.	October.	November.	December.	Annual amount.
1879												0.10	
1880	(*)	0.05	0.40	0.16	4.48	4.50	2.11	1.70	0.54	2.40	0.10	0.35	16.79
1881	0.47	0.74	(*)	1.26	5.27	0.10	3.28	0.49	3.18	0.69	0.42	0.26	16.16
1882	0.33	0.16	0.53	0.66	7.48	1.54	5.65	1.55	3.18	2.32	0.96	0.40	24.76
1883	(*)	0.53	0.04	0.82	4.56	1.66	2.87	6.56	4.97	5.32	0.04	0.84	28.21
1884	0.61	0.27	0.34	1.08	6.29	6.86	1.29	5.60	0.84	5.54	2.14	3.05	33.91
Mean	0.28	0.35	0.26	0.80	5.62	2.93	3.04	3.18	2.54	3.25	0.73	0.83	23.97

* Inappreciable.

Precipitation (in inches and hundredths) at various points, &c.—Continued.

FORT KEOGH, MONT.

Year.	January.	February.	March.	April.	May.	June.	July.	August.	September.	October.	November.	December.	Annual amount.
1879	0.26	0.69	0.28	2.20	2.75	5.23	5.90	1.84	0.44	2.47	0.11	0.58	22.75
1880	0.32	0.17	0.51	0.48	3.51	3.05	2.66	2.10	0.07	0.29	0.56	1.12	14.84
1881	2.35	0.36	0.31	0.35	0.76	4.44	0.39	0.93	0.55	0.46	0.44	0.10	11.44
1882	0.18	0.18	0.41	2.06	2.57	1.76	0.58	(*)	1.21	0.62	0.19	0.37	10.13
1883	0.18	0.11	0.39	1.37	2.80	(†)	......	......	......	......	......	......	......
Mean	0.66	0.30	0.38	1.29	2.48	3.62	2.38	1.22	0.57	0.96	0.32	0.54	14.79

*Inappreciable.   †Station closed June 30, 1883.

FORT SILL, IND. T.

Year.	January.	February.	March.	April.	May.	June.	July.	August.	September.	October.	November.	December.	Annual amount.
1876												1.08	......
1877	0.12	3.06	0.11	0.90	7.24	5.57	4.49	2.50	5.98	6.86	4.65	6.97	48.45
1878	1.91	1.83	0.35	1.85	4.06	8.86	5.13	2.03	1.26	0.71	2.69	3.01	33.69
1879	2.73	0.21	1.47	6.93	2.30	5.97	1.53	2.36	0.47	0.28	0.27	0.55	25.07
1880	0.58	0.59	3.03	1.58	9.74	5.76	5.57	3.96	1.17	0.54	0.60	0.63	33.75
1881	1.92	3.45	1.28	2.63	6.04	0.21	1.97	0.84	4.46	1.74	1.38	2.30	28.22
1882	0.80	1.66	1.53	1.61	4.40	3.25	4.66	3.30	4.71	2.87	2.01	0.33	31.13
1883	0.20	2.27	1.68	1.55	1.46	5.55	2.30	......	1.44	......	......	......	......
1884	......	......	......	......	......	......	0.23	1.21	2.24	......	......	......	......
Mean	1.18	1.87	1.35	2.44	5.03	5.02	3.24	2.31	2.72	2.17	1.93	2.12	33.38

FORT WASHAKIE, WYO.

Year.	January.	February.	March.	April.	May.	June.	July.	August.	September.	October.	November.	December.	Annual amount.
1882	......	......	0.15	1.80	5.77	1.51	0.57	0.25	0.46	0.85	0.69	0.52	......
1883	0.83	0.65	0.35	3.32	3.57	(*)	......	......	......	......	......	......	......
Mean	0.83	0.65	0.25	2.56	4.67	1.51	0.57	0.25	0.46	0.85	0.69	0.52	......

*Station closed June 15, 1883.

LEWISTON, IDAHO.

Year.	January.	February.	March.	April.	May.	June.	July.	August.	September.	October.	November.	December.	Annual amount.
1880	0.33	0.20	0.29	0.59	1.59	1.07	1.87	1.09	0.20	1.54	2.33	6.31	17.41
1881	4.46	4.33	0.49	2.60	0.23	2.30	0.89	0.31	1.17	1.52	1.19	1.07	20.56
1882	1.46	0.78	0.67	0.80	0.65	0.36	0.29	0.06	0.69	2.83	1.27	4.88	14.74
1883	3.56	0.82	3.21	1.12	2.01	0.01	(*)	(*)	0.04	1.84	1.86	1.36	15.83
1884	2.15	3.10	1.25	1.45	0.50	5.66	1.30	0.06	1.01	2.08	0.36	2.79	21.71
Mean	2.39	1.85	1.18	1.31	1.00	1.88	0.87	0.30	0.62	1.96	1.40	3.28	17.85

*Inappreciable.

NORTH PLATTE, NEBR.

Year.	January.	February.	March.	April.	May.	June.	July.	August.	September.	October.	November.	December.	Annual amount.
1874	......	......	......	......	......	......	......	......	......	1.46	0.57	0.34	......
1875	0.24	0.26	0.40	6.21	1.69	1.62	2.12	0.66	1.40	0.14	0.52	0.09	15.35
1876	0.09	0.49	0.13	0.80	2.97	0.49	1.16	2.46	1.47	1.07	0.49	0.51	11.84
1877	1.38	0.37	0.19	0.37	3.22	2.99	2.04	5.03	4.49	1.23	0.30	3.86	25.47
1878	0.00	0.18	1.40	1.15	3.24	5.85	3.58	1.52	0.91	0.13	0.46	0.20	18.62
1879	2.33	0.43	0.11	1.92	2.25	3.31	8.47	0.16	0.40	0.21	0.10	0.37	20.06
1880	0.03	0.03	0.18	0.16	2.28	3.12	2.87	3.96	1.53	2.72	0.23	0.37	17.48
1881	0.16	0.76	1.26	0.87	4.84	6.12	3.09	0.75	2.36	2.22	0.37	0.13	22.93
1882	0.46	0.13	0.04	1.94	3.98	4.84	2.65	1.68	0.28	1.23	0.01	0.71	17.95
1883	1.20	1.38	0.47	3.11	4.77	7.49	1.39	4.51	1.08	3.47	0.42	1.43	30.01
1884	0.10	0.23	1.82	2.14	2.40	1.39	2.19	2.13	0.08	0.74	0.04	0.27	13.53
Mean	0.60	0.39	0.64	1.84	3.09	3.72	2.96	2.29	1.40	1.33	0.32	0.75	19.32

Precipitation (in inches and hundredths) at various points, &c.—Continued.

SANTA FÉ, N. MEX.

Year.	January.	February.	March.	April.	May.	June.	July.	August.	September.	October.	November.	December.	Annual amount.
1871											0.00	0.00	
1872	0.34	0.20	0.13	0.14	0.45	2.44	2.63	2.98	0.27	0.25	0.01	0.04	9.87
1873	0.55	0.40	0.15	0.26	0.33	1.72	1.02	2.79	1.23	0.07	0.38	0.83	9.73
1874	1.39	1.60	1.51	1.71	0.70	0.54	3.92	1.73	1.52	2.47	0.58	2.26	19.93
1875	0.67	0.72	1.37	0.33	0.88	0.33	6.91	1.57	4.14	0.06	1.50	0.47	18.97
1876	0.61	0.40	0.64	0.46	0.83	1.62	5.43	2.13	0.85	0.75	0.97	0.38	15.07
1877	0.18	1.08	0.14	1.83	0.92	0.13	3.54	1.72	0 96	1.32	0.70	0.63	13.15
1878	0.21	0.89	0.73	0.22	1.01	3.18	3.20	5.12	1.03	0.00	3.15	0.78	19.52
1879	0.77	2.23	0.15	0.48	0.37	0.51	2.34	2.30	1.07	1.38	1.34	0.50	11 44
1880	0.28	0.94	0.15	0.05	0.52	0.65	2.69	1.79	1.13	0.75	0.28	0.66	9.89
1881	0.38	0.22	0.57	0.98	2.31	0.08	4.72	6.28	0.91	4.19	1.11	(*)	
1882	0.47	0.06	0.23	0.26	1.06	1.36	1.17	4.69	0.62		0.90	0.55	11.37
1883	0.42	0.96	0.40	0.11	0.87	(†)							
1884												‡1.77	
Mean	0.52	0.64	0.51	0.57	0.85	1.14	3.41	3.01	1.25	1.02	0.91	0.74	13.89

* No record.   † Station closed June 15, 1883.   ‡ Station reopened December 1, 1884.

SILVER CITY, N. MEX.

Year.	January.	February.	March.	April.	May.	June.	July.	August.	September.	October.	November.	December.	Annual amount.
1878					0.00	0.05	3.92	7.70	0.27	(*)	3.81	0.77	
1879	2.78	1.12	0.32	0.01	0.00	0.08	1.37	3.85	2 41	1.06	0.28	0.49	13.77
1880	0.79	0.85	0.53	0.30	0.00	0.99	3.05	3.51	3.57	1.66	0.00	1.65	16.90
1881	0.02	0.73	0.91	0.48	1.01	0.43	9.62	8 69	3.89	3.21	1.55	0 28	30.82
1882	1.83	2.06	1.17	0.08	1.37	1.92	1.84	6.00	1.05	0.00	1.37	0.58	19.27
1883	1.68	0.63	1.57	(†)									
Mean	1.42	1.08	0.90	0.22	0.48	0.69	3.96	5.95	2.24	1.19	1.40	0.75	20.19

* Inappreciable.   † Station closed March 31, 1883.

SPOKANE FALLS, WASH.

Year.	January.	February.	March.	April.	May.	June.	July.	August.	September.	October.	November.	December.	Annual amount.
1881		3.85	1.07	1.20	0.50	1.23	2.25	0.45	2.55	2.41	2.23	2.44	
1882	4.54	2.25	1.04	2.84	1.54	1.17	0.88	0.14	0.80	4.81	2.44	3.54	25.99
1883	2.13	2.95	0.75	1.93	2.11	0.60	0.00	0.15	0.08	1.48	1.98	0.21	14.37
1884	1.79	3.04	1.54	1.33	0.56	2.58	1.06	0.54	2.43	1.82	0.59	3.28	20.56
Mean	2.82	3.02	1.10	1.82	1.18	1.40	1.05	0.32	1.46	2.63	1.81	2.37	20.31

UMATILLA, OREG.

Year.	January.	February.	March.	April.	May.	June.	July.	August.	September.	October.	November.	December.	Annual amount.
1877								0.02	0.59	0.68	1.92	0.64	
1878	1.14	1.26	1.72	0.01	0.36	0.02	0.32	0.15	1,14	0.56	0.72	0.36	7.76
1879	0.95	1.81	1.30	1.49	1.96	0.28	0.21	0.03	0.83	0.33	0.61	0.78	10.58
1880	0.56	0.54	0.35	0.97	0.57	0.38	0.48	1.14	0.18	0.35	0.54	3.65	9.71
1881	2.45	1.92	0.44	0.89	0.06	0.96	0.53	0.73	0.74	1.54	0.98	0.45	11.69
1882	0.71	0.73	0.32	0.76	0.26	0.17	0.04	0.00	1.20	1.79	0.81	1.96	8.75
1883	2.56	0.57	1.20	(*)									
Mean	1.40	1.14	0.89	0.82	0.64	0.36	0.32	0.34	0.78	0.88	0.93	1.31	9.70

* Station closed March 31, 1883.

WEST LAS ANIMAS, COLO.

Year.	January.	February.	March.	April.	May.	June.	July.	August.	September.	October.	November.	December.	Annual amount.
1882	(*)	0.02	0.10	0.98	5.06	2.49	1.69	1.89	(†)	0.25	0.01	0.08	
1883	0.14	0.52	0.15	0.93	1.50	2.63	0.67	0.65	1.35	0.69	0.21	1.68	11.12
1884	0.26	0.50	1.19	1.05	4.46	2.79	1.75	2.17	0.06	0.43	0.32	0.72	15.70
Mean	0.20	0.35	0.48	0.99	3.67	2.64	1.37	1.57	0.47	0.46	0.18	0.83	13.41

* Incomplete.   † Inappreciable.

SIGNAL OFFICE, WAR DEPARTMENT,
Washington, March 11, 1885.

APPENDIX No. 11.

STATEMENTS IN REGARD TO THE AVERAGE ANNUAL RAINFALL OF DIFFERENT SECTIONS OF THE UNITED STATES.

(Prepared by the Chief Signal Officer of the United States Army.)

SIGNAL OFFICE, WAR DEPARTMENT,
Washington City, February 16, 1885.

SIR: Referring to your letter of the 9th instant, requesting certain meteorological data, I have the honor to inclose herewith an extract from the records of this office.

I am, very respectfully, your obedient servant,

W. B. HAZEN,
Brig. and Bvt. Maj. Genl., Chief Signal Officer U. S. A.

Mr. JOSEPH NIMMO, Jr.,
Chief Bureau of Statistics, Treasury Department, Washington, D. C.

Average annual rainfall of different sections of the United States.

Location.	Rainfall.	Location.	Rainfall.
	Inches.		*Inches.*
NEW ENGLAND.		**FLORIDA PENINSULA.**	
Eastport, Me	49. 02		
Portland, Me	38. 67	Cedar Keys, Fla	58. 95
Mount Washington, N. H.	83. 86	Key West, Fla	40. 66
Boston, Mass	48. 21	Sanford, Fla	44. 61
Block Island, R. I	52. 26	Punta Rasa, Fla	42. 61
New Haven, Conn	50. 99		
New London, Conn	47. 75	**EASTERN GULF STATES.**	
		Atlanta, Ga	56. 91
MIDDLE ATLANTIC STATES.		Pensacola, Fla	70. 22
		Mobile, Ala	65. 84
Albany, N. Y	38. 05	Montgomery, Ala	53. 68
New York City, N. Y.	42. 68	Vicksburg, Miss	60. 44
Philadelphia, Pa	41. 22	New Orleans, La	64. 69
Atlantic City, N. J	42. 18		
Barnegat City, N. J	51. 74	**WESTERN GULF STATES.**	
Cape May, N. J	47. 63		
Sandy Hook, N. J.	51. 26	Shreveport, La	54. 11
Delaware, Breakwater, Del	31. 76	Fort Smith, Ark	46. 65
Baltimore, Md	41. 98	Little Rock, Ark	57. 64
Washington, D. C	43. 30	Galveston, Tex	51. 43
Cape Henry, Va	57. 82	Indianola, Tex	38. 22
Chincoteague, Va	37. 60	Palestine, Tex	43. 49
Lynchburg, Va	41. 34		
Norfolk, Va	52. 13	**RIO GRANDE VALLEY.**	
		Brownsville, Tex	32. 02
SOUTH ATLANTIC STATES.		Rio Grande City, Tex	25. 12
Charlotte, N. C	51. 24		
Hatteras, N. C	75. 44	**OHIO VALLEY AND TENNESSEE.**	
Kitty Hawk, N. C	64. 90		
Macon, Fort, N. C	63. 81	Chattanooga, Tenn	59. 42
Smithville, N. C	52. 86	Knoxville, Tenn	53. 20
Wilmington, N. C	57. 42	Memphis, Tenn	55. 38
Charleston, S. C	59. 89	Nashville, Tenn	53. 63
Augusta, Ga	49. 91	Louisville, Ky	48. 83
Savannah, Ga.	52. 86	Greencastle, Ind	
Jacksonville, Fla	55. 33		

Average annual rainfall of different sections of the United States—Continued.

Location.	Rainfall.	Location.	Rainfall.
	Inches.	NORTHERN SLOPE—Continued.	*Inches.*
OHIO VALLEY AND TENNESSEE—Cont'd.		Maginnis, Fort, Mont	13.29
Indianapolis, Ind	47.59	Poplar River, Mont	8.24
Cincinnati, Ohio	44.09	Shaw, Fort, Mont	13.87
Columbus, Ohio	44.62	Deadwood, Dak	26.47
Pittsburgh, Pa	37.04	Cheyenne, Wyo	10.72
		North Platte, Nebr	19.97
LOWER LAKES.			
		MIDDLE SLOPE.	
Buffalo, N. Y	37.0g		
Oswego, N. Y	36.05	Denver, Colo	14.98
Rochester, N. Y	37.23	Pike's Peak, Colo	31.60
Erie, Pa	42.39	West Las Animas, Colo	13.41
Cleveland, Ohio	38.40	Dodge City, Kans	20.09
Sandusky, Ohio	41.78	Elliott, Fort, Tex	21.48
Toledo, Ohio	33.07		
Detroit, Mich	35.27	SOUTHERN SLOPE.	
		Sill, Fort, Ind. T	33.38
UPPER LAKES.		Concho, Fort, Tex	29.18
		Davis, Fort, Tex	19.83
Alpena, Mich	38.21	Stockton, Fort, Tex	19.43
Escanaba, Mich	35.30		
Grand Haven, Mich	39.17	SOUTHERN PLATEAU.	
Mackinaw City, Mich	38.97		
Marquette, Mich	32.68	Santa Fé, N. Mex	13.89
Port Huron, Mich	35.26	El Paso, Tex	12.11
Chicago, Ill	37.57	Apache, Fort, Ariz	22.75
Milwaukee, Wis	33.87	Grant, Fort, Ariz	15.71
Duluth, Minn	33.87	Prescott, Ariz	14.51
		Thomas, Camp, Ariz	10.31
UPPER MISSISSIPPI VALLEY.		Yuma, Ariz	2.04
Saint Paul, Minn	29.83		
La Crosse, Wis	34.26	MIDDLE PLATEAU.	
Davenport, Iowa	35.96		
Des Moines, Iowa	42.72	Winnemucca, Nev	9.62
Dubuque, Iowa	39.41	Salt Lake City, Utah	16.91
Keokuk, Iowa	38.57	Thornburgh, Fort, Utah	
Cairo, Ill	46.33		
Springfield, Ill	48.61	NORTHERN PLATEAU.	
Saint Louis, Mo	37.88		
		Boise City, Idaho	13.30
MISSOURI VALLEY.		Lewiston, Idaho	17.85
		Dayton, Wash	28.11
Lamar, Mo		Spokane Falls, Wash	20.31
Leavenworth, Kans	38.37		
Omaha, Nebr	36.45	NORTH PACIFIC COAST.	
Bennett, Fort, Dak	18.17		
Huron, Dak	25.68	Canby, Fort, Wash	45.71
Yankton, Dak	28.21	Olympia, Wash	59.72
		Tatoosh Island, Wash	75.18
EXTREME NORTHWEST.		Portland, Oreg	54.64
		Roseburg, Oreg	35.72
Moorhead, Minn	29.48		
Saint Vincent, Minn	18.62	MIDDLE PACIFIC COAST.	
Bismarck, Dak	21.27		
Buford, Fort, Dak	16.08	Cape Mendocino, Cal	17.99
Totten, Fort, Dak	17.36	Red Bluff, Cal	28.27
		Sacramento, Cal	21.68
NORTHERN SLOPE.		San Francisco, Cal	22.80
Assinaboine, Fort, Mont	13.93	SOUTH PACIFIC COAST.	
Benton, Fort, Mont	12.50		
Custer, Fort, Mont	14.36	Los Angeles, Cal	14.56
Helena, Mont	15.13	San Diego, Cal	9.48

SIGNAL OFFICE, WAR DEPATMENT,
Washington City, February 14, 1885.

The mean annual and mean monthly rainfall, in inches and hundredths of an inch, as registered at twenty-seven stations in Texas and one in Louisiana, of the United States Army Signal Service, for the periods set opposite the names of the several stations respectively.

[The mean monthly columns embrace each month of the whole time stated for which a record was kept. The mean annual column includes only those years in which registration was made for every month of the year. The small figures placed above each monthly mean indicate the number of years on which computation is made, and those in the annual column the number of full years embraced. It will be observed that all the stations in Texas, except Galveston and Palestine, are situated west of the meridian of longitude 96° 30' west of Greenwich, and that the record for Palestine is only for eight months of 1882. The record for Shreveport, La., is given as being the station nearest to and as approximately indicating the rainfall throughout the northeastern section of Texas.]

Stations.	January.	February.	March.	April.	May.	June.	July.	August.	September.	October.	November.	December.	Period of registration.	Mean annual rainfall.
Brackettville	5 1.44	5 0.81	5 1.49	5 2.70	6 5.39	6 2.16	6 2.20	6 2.61	6 2.71	6 0.56	5 0.76	5 1.30	May 1, 1877, to October 1, 1882	4 29.12
Brownsville	6 2.59	5 2.19	5 1.55	6 0.82	4 2.68	4 1.16	6 2.48	5 7.76	5 4.89	5 4.29	5 2.06	5 2.16	January 1, 1877, to August 1, 1882	5 33.35
Castroville	5 1.36	5 1.44	5 1.33	5 2.31	4 3.07	4 1.31	4 3.10	5 2.70	4 1.92	5 1.71	5 1.22	5 1.37	August 1, 1877, April 1, 1882	4 22.71
Coleman City	5 1.22	5 1.48	5 1.34	5 1.88	5 3.26	6 3.36	5 4.48	6 2.35	4 4.94	4 2.18	4 1.14	4 2.67	July 1, 1877, to September 1, 1882	3 27.71
Concho	5 1.27	5 0.60	5 0.79	5 1.67	6 2.87	6 2.65	6 2.92	6 4.30	5 4.65	5 1.53	5 1.09	5 1.29	April 1, 1877, to September 1, 1882	4 25.07
Corsicana														4 39.35
Decatur	5 1.64	5 2.78	6 1.14	6 2.21	6 4.11	6 3.40	6 5.32	6 1.60	5 4.86	4 1.75	5 2.48	5 1.48	March 1, 1877, to September 1, 1882	4 28.63
Denison	7 2.22	7 3.53	7 2.34	7 3.95	7 4.65	4 4.89	8 5.00	8 3.23	7 3.06	7 3.01	7 2.87	7 2.41	July 1, 1875, to September 1, 1882	6 47.92
Eagle Pass	5 1.34	5 1.10	4 1.04	4 1.21	5 4.14	5 2.11	5 3.34	5 3.54	6 4.16	5 2.14	5 0.57	5 1.41	July 1, 1873, to September 1, 1882	4 26.06
El Paso	4 0.89	4 0.46	4 0.22	4 0.10	4 0.48	4 0.13	5 3.94	4 2.49	3 0.73	4 0.97	4 0.30	4 0.67	July 1, 1875, to September 1, 1882	3 13.12
Fort Davis	3 0.81	3 0.25	4 0.20	3 0.33	3 1.73	3 2.46	4 4.43	3 4.98	3 1.82	4 2.88	3 0.40	4 0.40	April 1, 1878, to August 1, 1882	2 22.45
Fort Elliott	5 0.27	5 0.32	5 0.31	5 0.69	4 5.74	5 2.05	5 3.68	5 1.25	5 1.86	5 1.55	5 0.26	5 0.24	February 1, 1880, to September 1, 1882	2 16.47
Fort Griffin	5 1.25	5 1.10	5 0.53	5 2.08	5 3.18	4 4.38	5 3.03	5 1.25	5 2.73	5 2.85	5 2.26	5 1.82	June 1, 1877, to May 1, 1882	4 24.57
Fort McKavett	5 1.13	5 1.30	5 0.60	6 1.33	6 2.77	6 1.84	6 3.18	6 3.15	6 2.95	5 3.07	5 1.41	5 1.17	July 1, 1877, to September 1, 1882	4 22.71
Fredericksburg	5 1.12	5 1.81	5 1.46	6 3.14	6 4.21	6 1.96	6 2.95	6 2.28	5 3.46	5 2.40	5 2.15	5 1.50	April 1, 1877, to September 1, 1882	4 28.10

The mean annual and mean monthly rainfall, in inches and hundredths of an inch, as registered at twenty-seven stations in Texas, &c.—Continued.

Stations.	January.	February.	March.	April.	May.	June.	July.	August.	September.	October.	November.	December.	Period of registration.	Mean annual rainfall.
Galveston	3.55	3.27	2.82	3.22	3.99	4.31	3.99	6.00	6.59	5.41	5.59	4.85	April 1, 1871, to September 1, 1882	51.84
Graham	1.29	2.53	1.17	2.28	2.85	2.03	5.24	5.16	2.94	2.40	1.21	2.31	January 1, 1880, to October 1, 1882	25.11
Henrietta	1.63	1.14	1.81	2.86	2.63	3.26	2.24	3.98	1.51	1.38	1.22	0.87	April 1, 1879, to September 1, 1882	22.73
Indianola	2.18	2.12	2.40	1.51	2.92	2.40	2.76	4.74	6.22	3.91	3.22	3.56	May 1, 1872, to September 1, 1882	38.65
Jacksboro'	0.86	1.86	1.03	1.77	3.50	4.10	4.88	2.24	2.73	2.61	1.83	1.25	January 1, 1878, to September 1, 1882	26.20
Laredo	1.38	2.29	1.74	1.31	2.51	1.62	2.40	5.74	1.02	1.40	1.10	1.22	January 1, 1877, to October 1, 1882	24.16
Mason	1.37	1.48	1.02	2.28	0.70	1.63	2.45	2.08	1.05	2.06	1.51	1.84	June 1, 1877, to May 1, 1882	24.90
Palestine	1.65	3.68	3.37	3.42	7.56	0.83	6.52	5.32	3.96				January 1, 1882, to September 1, 1882	0
Rio Grande City	1.26	0.91	1.58	0.83	2.69	0.66	1.87	5.90	2.40	2.49	0.86	1.65	April 1, 1877, to September 1, 1882	25.27
San Antonio	1.73	2.16	1.66	3.09	3.74	2.14	3.28	3.67	4.27	2.79	2.10	2.31	March 1, 1877, to September 1, 1882	32.77
Stockton	0.36	0.51	0.55	0.30	1.20	2.10	2.23	3.08	3.72	1.07	0.55	0.66	May 1, 1877, to September 1, 1882	15.91
Uvalde	0.80	1.17	1.50	1.79	3.28	0.90	2.24	3.19	2.48	1.26	1.37	1.93	April 1, 1877, to September 1, 1882	24.00
Shreveport, La	4.88	4.99	4.97	6.09	4.74	2.90	4.63	2.13	4.67	3.93	4.19	5.05	October 1, 1871, to October 1, 1882	53.07

APPENDIX No. 12.

TABLES PREPARED BY THE CHIEF SIGNAL OFFICER OF THE UNITED STATES ARMY, SHOWING THE AVERAGE MONTHLY RAINFALL AT DIFFERENT POINTS IN CALIFORNIA, OREGON, WASHINGTON TERRITORY NEVADA, AND ARIZONA.

SIGNAL OFFICE, WAR DEPARTMENT.
Washington City, February 26, 1885.

SIR: Referring to your letters of the 14th and 19th instant, requesting certain rainfall data for California, Oregon, and Washington Territory, I have the honor to transmit herewith an extract from the records of this office.

I am, very respectfully, your obedient servant,

W. B. HAZEN,
Brig. and Bvt. Maj. Gen'l, Chief Signal Officer U. S. Army.

Mr. JOSEPH NIMMO, Jr.,
Chief, Bureau of Statistics, Treasury Department, Washington, D. C.

Statement showing the average annual precipitation, in inches and hundredths, at the below-named stations of the Signal Service, United States Army, computed from the commencement of observations at each, to and including December, 1884, from the records on file at the office of the Chief Signal Officer of the Army.

Stations.	January.	February.	March.	April.	May.	June.	July.	August.	September.	October.	November.	December.
Boise City, Idaho	2.43	1.76	1.49	1.19	1.02	0.94	0.20	0.09	0.59	1.63	0.73	2.35
Cape Mendocino, Cal	2.09	2.40	2.60	3.13	1.00	0.47	0 22	0.11	0.93	1.74	1.39	2.42
Fort Bidwell, Cal. *	3.41	2.52	1.82	1.62	1.35	0.58	0.26	0.17	0.36	1.19	1.86	3.13
Fort Canby, Wash.†	{8.40 {6.45	9.95 5.20	8.82 2.18	3.59 2.98	3.32 1.30	2.21 2.16	1.69 1.73	1.36 1.23	3.01 4.72	4.90 5.94	9.11 6.20	7.72 5.89
Los Angeles, Cal	2.21	4.30	3.44	2.00	0.57	0.22	‡)	(‡)	(‡)	0.59	0.96	3.92
Olympia, Wash	8.80	9.74	5.53	4.24	2.58	1.21	0.83	0.85	2.99	5.44	7.31	9.62
Portland, Oreg	7.06	7.86	6.88	3.49	2.35	1.79	0.79	0.77	1.82	4.88	7.08	8.22
Red Bluff, Cal	6,08	4.47	3.55	3.09	1.20	0.28	0.01	0.04	0.42	1.43	2.20	5.36
Roseburg, Oreg	6.47	4.75	3.95	3.00	1.77	1.01	0.47	0.39	0.95	2.91	3.40	6.31
Sacramento, Cal	3.97	3.83	3.81	3.78	0.78	0.31	(‡)	(‡)	0.33	1.04	1.17	4.05
San Diego, Cal	1.81	2.61	1.38	0 84	0.41	0.07	0.02	0.21	0.05	0.48	0.66	2.33
Spokane Falls, Wash	2.82	3.02	1.10	1.82	1.18	1.40	1.05	0.32	1.46	2.63	1.81	2.37
Tatoosh Island, Wash	13.32	6.04	2.41	3.31	4.45	3.98	1.73	5.49	6.15	6.66	11.32	11.46
Winnemucca, Nev	1.18	0.95	0.89	1.03	0.91	0.72	0.13	0.10	0.39	0.63	0.48	1.27
Yuma, Ariz	0.38	0.04	0.24	0.09	0.06	0.01	0.20	0.26	0.09	0.04	0.03	0.49

* From post surgeons' reports.
† The data in the upper line is from post surgeons' reports, covering the period 1871 to 1880, inclusive.
‡ Inappreciable—less than .01 of an inch.

SIGNAL SERVICE, WAR DEPARTMENT,
Washington City, February 25, 1885.

127

APPENDIX No. 13.

STATEMENT SHOWING THE NUMBER OF ACRES PATENTED AND UNPATENTED IN THE STATE OF TEXAS, FROM THE ANNUAL REPORT OF THE COMMISSIONER OF THE GENERAL LAND OFFICE OF THAT STATE.

County.	Patented.	Unpatented.	County.	Patented.	Unpatented.
	Acres.	*Acres.*		*Acres.*	*Acres.*
Anderson	615	10, 240	Ellis	1, 892	....
Andrews	26, 720	12, 320	El Paso	72, 640	1, 254, 400
Angelina	38, 985	12, 585	Encinal	374, 207⅔	87, 870
Aransas	640	640	Erath	111, 345⅔	3, 520
Archer	64, 307	7, 521	Falls	....	....
Armstrong	215, 380	2, 541½	Fannin	4, 013¾	320
Atascosa	75, 390	7, 479	Fayette	....	....
Austin	26, 240	640	Fisher	280, 802	3, 250
Bailey	....	....	Floyd	307, 256⅔	640
Bandera	91, 275	77, 126	Fort Bend	42, 222	41, 998
Bastrop	....	....	Franklin	1, 600	2, 560
Baylor	176, 213	48, 320	Freestone	640	1, 089
Bee	27, 080	1, 384½	Frio	114, 880	15, 486
Bell	9, 323	4, 139	Gaines	207, 720	....
Bexar	30, 257	9, 777	Galveston	1, 280	1, 280
Blanco	45, 898	11, 912	Garza	229, 935	59, 308
Borden	210, 643½	83, 524	Gillespie	104, 495	5, 606
Bosque	3, 940	1, 280	Goliad	10, 480	2, 409
Bowie	23, 356	1, 062	Gonzales	960	....
Brazos	....	1, 157½	Gray	174, 720	34, 560
Brazoria	74, 240	5, 760	Grayson	2, 565	....
Briscoe	230, 948	640	Grimes	....	....
Brown	86, 495½	14, 608	Greer	....	....
Burleson	....	....	Gregg	....	....
Burnet	26, 949	17, 670	Guadalupe	10, 880	640
Caldwell	8, 320	....	Hale	275, 559	51, 840
Calhoun	1, 871	....	Hall	239, 700	2, 816
Callahan	138, 557½	1, 681	Hamilton	15, 643	24, 404
Cameron	6, 448	68, 160	Hansford	105, 060	166, 720
Camp	....	....	Hardeman	388, 443	208, 971
Carson	157, 960	3, 200	Hardin	33, 672	31, 294
Cass	1, 495½	640	Harris	70, 675	8, 139
Castro	194, 780	....	Harrison	1, 920	57, 360
Chambers	46, 080	23, 680	Hartley	94, 080	....
Cherokee	4, 160	....	Haskell	67, 184	31, 828
Childress	204, 160	16, 000	Harp	7, 736	4, 178
Clay	67, 500½	1, 920	Henderson	....	6, 572
Coleman	155, 630½	4, 480	Hemphill	123, 520	87, 280
Cottle	84. 538⅔	12, 613½	Hidalgo	58, 109	200, 650
Collingsworth	291, 200	640	Hill	2, 978	2, 560
Cochran	....	....	Hockley	426⅔	....
Collin	....	....	Howard	227, 766⅓	77, 615
Colorado	38, 501½	4, 480	Hood	1, 600	....
Comal	25, 211	2, 539½	Hopkins	640	....
Comanche	77, 964	640	Houston	320	1, 280
Concho	140, 393	26, 463	Hunt	....	....
Cooke	21, 070¾	640	Hutchinson	185, 615	55, 640
Coryell	9, 819	4, 141	Jack	37, 366⅔	7, 718½
Crockett	1, 620, 060	732, 939	Jackson	13, 120	746⅔
Crosby	213, 895	....	Jasper	44, 640	63, 682
Dallas	3, 200	....	Jefferson	127, 676	1, 280
Dallam	152, 000	5, 440	Johnson	27, 960	5, 120
Dawson	186, 197	....	Jones	104, 734½	2, 960
Deaf Smith	231, 640	640	Karnes	4, 531	2, 560
Denton	5, 825	2, 578	Kaufman	....	640
De Witt	24, 484	....	Kendall	79, 865	3, 178
Delta	640	....	Kerr	177, 221⅔	27, 581
Dickens	165, 448	1, 280	Kent	164, 266	142, 520
Dimmit	125, 011½	11, 807	King	82, 314⅔	68, 504
Donley	206, 516	5, 760	Kimble	254, 133	60, 426
Duval	276, 128	29, 660	Kinney	176, 010	99, 433
Eastland	34, 560	2, 560	Knox	110, 547	162, 221
Edwards	261, 986	56, 219	Lamar	4, 086½	....

Statement showing the number of acres patented and unpatented, &c.—Continued.

County.	Patented.	Unpatented.	County.	Patented.	Unpatented.
	Acres.	*Acres.*		*Acres.*	*Acres.*
Lamb	20,000	2,560	Robertson	1,280	2,580
Lampasas	61,437½	15,554	Rockwell		
La Salle	268,243	6,720	Runnels	126,256	25,419
Lavaca	13,868	320	Rusk		
Leon	3,840		Sabine	20,444	9,320
Liberty	35,760	34,709	San Augustine	22,120	640
Lipscomb	47,760	237,080	San Jacinto	213½	9,600
Limestone	4,160	1,920	San Patricio	7,674	
Live Oak	121,041	2,560	San Saba	92,571	5,422
Lee			Scurry	81,159	39,680
Llano	44,100	3,840	Shackelford	175,765	
Lubbock	257,262	640	Shelby	640	2,346
Lynn	254,320	640	Sherman	290,840	
Madison			Smith	640	640
Marion	1,280	640	Somervell		
Martin	210,563		Starr	168,080	57,808
Mason	80,571	3,921	Stephens	130,610	2,560
Matagorda	4,800		Stonewall	111,220	147,086
Maverick	53,843	4,997½	Swisher	280,287	12,800
McCulloch	22,067	2,240	Tarrant	11,039	560
McLennan			Taylor	86,123	26,158
McMullen	113,577	16,200	Terry	263,360	
Medina	130,230	19,358	Throckmorton	23,147	3,419
Menard	163,395	12,760	Titus	1,920	2,880
Milam			Tom Green	1,379,341	1,209,074
Mitchell	224,473	82,288	Travis	21,229	6,080
Montague	24,720	4,597	Trinity	11,925	640
Montgomery	8,426	640	Tyler	60,160	1,280
Moore	261,698		Upshur	1,600	640
Morris	1,920	2,560	Uvalde	187,831	12,935
Motley	201,144	16,685	Van Zandt	480	742
Nacogdoches	3,247	5,760	Victoria	41,892	5,917
Navarro	2,415	493	Walker	640	1,280
Newton	64,481	49,449	Waller	40,873	39,040
Nolan	177,746	67,200	Washington		
Nueces	100,355	5,848	Webb	95,786	22,203
Ochiltree	150,820	127,360	Wharton	118,650	30,967
Oldham	146,680	2,133	Wheeler	293,208	1,920
Orange	14,720	1,299	Wichita	74,808	14,328
Palo Pinto	148,680	4,673	Wilbarger	56,787	19,715
Panola	3,894	1,070	Williamson	5,760	553
Parker	110,535		Wilson	2,880	1,280
Parmer			Wise	17,660	1,267
Pecos	1,240,177	1,357,922	Wood	438½	533
Polk	16,688	11,435	Yoakum	257,920	
Potter	199,023	40,640	Young	28,125	1,280
Presidio	1,746,250	1,807,515	Zapata	62,051	48,580
Rains	3,872		Zavala	75,345	33,132
Randall	209,380	640			
Red River	15,060	4,667	Total	21,584,828	10,131,273
Refugio	640				
Roberts	84,800	60,840			

	Acres.
Total patented	21,548,828
Total unpatented	10,131,273
Grand total	31,716,101
Add under act of 1883	1,000,000
Total	32,716,101
Sales under acts of 1874, 1879, and 1881	6,072,603
Sales under act of 1883 (Land Board)	1,965,201
Total of sales	8,037,804

RECAPITULATION.

	Acres.
Total school land	32,716,101
Total sales	8,037,804
Balance to credit of fund	24,678,297

APPENDIX No. 14.

*LETTER FROM DR. FRANKLIN B. HOUGH, IN REGARD TO THE EFFECT
OF FORESTS IN INCREASING THE AMOUNT OF RAINFALL.*

ALBANY, N. Y., *April 20*, 1885.

DEAR SIR: Your letter of the 10th instant has been forwarded to me from Lowville, and I have delayed reply on account of sickness. I find myself slowly recovering, and hope to be well again soon.

Of course, trees in a forest do not "attract" rain in the ordinary sense of that word, but they do this: They shade the ground from the sun, and shelter it from drying winds. They prevent snows from drifting, and delay the thawing of winter frosts. All of these tend to maintain humidity in the soil, to encourage the percolation of rains, and to diminish or wholly prevent the flowing off of water from the surface. They equalize the flow of streams, and prevent erosions.

But in the season of active vegetation there is an active evaporation going on from the leaves, the water being drawn from the soil, and sometimes from a considerable depth. This evaporation is doubtless less than would have happened with full exposure to sun and winds. It tends to render the air within the woods more humid. It is also a *cooling* process. By increasing the humidity and reducing the temperature, we evidently tend to approach the dew-point. In some climates it actually does reach this point and cause rain, where it would not have rained on a cleared area.

I have often seen in a "dry spell" a passing cloud send down filaments of rain which vanished and dried up before they reached the ground. I have also seen, where this cloud passed over a forest of considerable area, that these filaments of rain became a copious shower, which dried up when they came over the heated and naked fields beyond, something like the following sketch:

In some districts, where rocks and bowlders, once thickly covered with shrubbery, vines, and vegetation, have been cleared off and the stones exposed to the sun, they are now troubled with protracted drought, unknown in early days. The cause is evidently due to the stones becoming heated and remaining warm till into the night, preventing showers of rain and the deposit of dew.

I consider fires—annually set by the Indians from time immemorial and until white settlement—as sufficient to account for "oak openings," "barrens," and very many of the prairies. They all will bear trees under protection, and the climate improves. An obvious cause of failure of wells, &c., in the Western States, east of the Mississippi, can be found in the deepening of channels by the clearing of woods that once bordered the streams.

I have more confidence in the possibility of improving the plains, say out to 100° west longitude, than some have, but would not advise attempting too much at once. I would begin along the streams and gradually encroach upon the arid lands, where possibly I would divide up the country into compartments by planting belts of cotton-

130

wood, gray willow, carrageen, and other hardy trees and shrubs, and under their shelter others of less hardy but more valuable kinds.

There appears to be evidence that there is now a great deal more water in the land-locked basin of the Great Salt Lake in Utah than formerly. It has probably been brought in by the winds and condensed from the already half depleted moisture of the air by the cultivation introduced by man.

I do not know that I have answered your inquiries fully; there are some facts about the effect of woodlands upon climate that cannot be answered until further researches have determined facts now unknown.

Very truly yours,

FRANKLIN B. HOUGH.

Mr. J. NIMMO,
Chief of Bureau of Statistics.

11991 R C——10

APPENDIX No. 15.

LETTER FROM GEORGE B. LOVING, ESQ., OF FORT WORTH, TEX., IN REGARD TO THE LOSSES OF CATTLE DURING THE WINTER OF 1884-'85, THE DECLINE IN THE VALUE OF STOCK, AND THE FUTURE OF THE STOCK-GROWING INTERESTS OF TEXAS.

[Daily and Weekly Gazette, George B. Loving, proprietor.]

FORT WORTH, TEX., *April* 15, 1885.

DEAR SIR: Absence from the city and pressure of business has prevented me from answering your several letters sooner. The loss of cattle during the past winter has been very heavy in some localities, while in others it has been much less. The loss in that part of the State known as the Panhandle will probably not exceed 5 per cent., and the same may be said of the extreme western part of the State in what is known as the Pecos River country. In some localities in the central part of the State the loss is estimated as high as 30 to 40 per cent. Taking the entire State, it will probably average between 15 and 20 per cent. The loss during the past winter has been the heaviest ever known in Texas for some length of time and will probably not occur again for many years; although, from present appearances, there is a strong probability that the entire grazing country in Texas will be largely overstocked within the next few years, caused by the outlets for surplus cattle being cut off by the recent enactment of quarantine laws in Kansas and other States and Territories. These laws, if enforced, will very materially injure the stock business in this State, from the fact that in order to carry it on successfully, an outlet must be found for our surplus stock cattle each year. Stock cattle in Texas have declined in value fully one-third in the last six or eight months. This decline was first caused by the stringency in money matters, but has been greatly increased within the last few months by the quarantine laws referred to above.

Nearly the entire drive from Texas, heretofore by trail, has been made between the 1st of March and the 1st of July. It will be impossible to drive Texas cattle to Kansas, if they must enter that State between the 1st of December and 1st of March, as the latter date is too early to handle cattle from this State, while December is too late, the cold weather making it impossible to handle them at that time. Heretofore thousands of cattle have been contracted for earlier than this for the spring drive, while this spring comparatively nothing has been done in that respect. The depression in the cattle business here, now that winter is over, is almost entirely due to the rigid quarantine laws enacted by Kansas and other Northern and Western Territories. In reference to Mr. Atwater's suggestion as to the days of free grazing in Texas being over, will say that there will doubtless be for many years to come still much free grazing in this State, although there is a very considerable disposition among the cattlemen to buy or lease their ranges where it can be done. The grazing section of Texas being unsuited for agricultural purposes, it will be impossible for ranchmen to ever grow feed to fatten their cattle on during the winter. They may, however, by buying or leasing and inclosing their ranges be able to protect the grass to a considerable extent; as by this arrangement their range would not be subjected to the drifts of neighboring herds, and would enable them to regulate the number of cattle grazed on any given quantity of land in such a way as not to permanently injure the range.

Instead of cattlemen being hopeful of better times my observation has led me to believe quite the reverse. The majority of cattle ranches now in Texas are now for sale at fully 25 per cent. less than they could have been bought for twelve months ago, and, generally speaking, it may safely be said that a large majority of the ranchmen of Texas would willingly retire from the business if they could dispose of their holdings at anything like a reasonable price. There is considerable talk of trying to establish a trail through the neutral strip and the eastern part of Colorado, thus avoiding Kansas, but I am of the opinion that this route is not feasible, first on account of the scarcity of water in Eastern Colorado, and, secondly, for the reason that in all probability the ranchmen and citizens of eastern Colorado would soon raise the same objection to the establishment of a trail through the eastern part of their State that has been made by the Kansas people. I see no solution of this vexed question, which threatens to disastrously end a business that has heretofore been extensively and lucratively carried on in this State, except by the establishment of a permanent cattle trail, thus making an outlet for the surplus of the cattle raised in this State.

Referring to your inquiry as to the number of cowboys employed in this State, will say that I cannot even approximate the number, and know of no data by which I could be able to arrive at the desired information.

The enactment of the quarantine laws referred to does not interfere with the shipment of fat cattle ready for the butchers direct from Texas to Saint Louis or Chicago; but this outlet is not sufficient, from the fact that Texas has for several years disposed of fully 500,000 cattle, which have been used to stock northern and western ranges, and which were not suitable to go direct to the beef markets. The drive of Texas cattle to the northern and western ranges began immediately after the close of the war, and were driven principally over what is known as the Chisholm trail to Kansas, a great many of them, however, going out in a western direction to New Mexico and Colorado. For the last twenty years Texas has probably furnished on an average 400,000 head of stock cattle, which have been distributed over the Indian Territory, Kansas, Colorado, New Mexico, Arizona, Wyoming, Montana, Dakota, and other northern Territories. As many of these were full-grown cattle it probably would not be an overestimate to put their value at an average of $15 per head, which would show an income to the State (not including the beef cattle shipped direct to market) of $6,000,000 per annum. The range-cattle business is now being carried on over almost the entire Territory of New Mexico and Arizona. These two Territories, but for their quarantine laws, would furnish an outlet for the present year for from 75,000 to 100,000 head of Texas cattle. A great deal of the territory of Old Mexico, especially the northern part of it, is well adapted to stock-raising, and is receiving more attention as a stock-growing country than ever before.

In reference to the number of cattle in Texas, will say that I know of no reason for changing the figures originally given you, except the heavy death loss during the past winter, which will probably decrease the number from one to one and one-half million. The rapid decline of cattle since my first report would probably justify a reduction in values of about $2 per head. I am of the opinion that your estimate of 5,000,000 of cattle for Texas is far too low, and that your estimate of one cowboy for each 500 will show a great many more cowboys than are actually engaged in that business; for instance, on many of our largest ranches owning 50,000 to 60,000 cattle, there are not more than 50 or 60 cowboys during the busy season, and probably not more than half that number during the winter.

In reference to the increase in the rainfall in Texas, will say that all the grazing part of the State is still subject to considerable droughts, often lasting for three or four months during the season, and taking it one month with another I am of the opinion that the rainfall is greatly increasing in this State during the last twenty years, and will, in my opinion, continue to increase as the country develops and is converted into an agricultural country. Instead, however, of the nutritious grasses giving way, I think the increased rainfall is having, and will have, just the opposite effect, and would greatly improve the range, were it not overstocked with too many cattle, besides being subjected in most parts of the grazing portion of the State to an increased supply of prairie dogs each year, which, in my opinion, are doing more damage to the grass of Western Texas than are all the cattle combined.

Replying to your telegram of the 10th, will say that there have been slaughtering-houses established at this place and Victoria, Tex., for the purpose of slaughtering and shipping in refrigerator cars beef in quarters to the Eastern markets. Neither of these houses are being operated at this time, principally on account of the scarcity of fat cattle, and partly on account of their inability to ever make it a success. My information is that both of the establishments have proved a losing business so far. The theory, I think, is a good one, but cannot be successfully run unless backed with an abundance of capital, and until the Texas people are willing to sell their cattle here at prices obtainable at Saint Louis and Chicago, less the freight.

For the want of time I cannot to-day carefully examine the different reports and documents sent me, but have simply answered briefly the matters referred to in your several letters. Would do so more fully but from the fact that I fear it will be too late to answer the purposes intended. If I can be of any further service to you, do not hesitate to command me.

Yours, very truly,

GEO. B. LOVING.

Hon. JOSEPH NIMMO, Jr.,
 Chief Bureau Statistics,
  Treasury Department, Washington, D. C.

APPENDIX No. 16.

AN ACT for the protection of cattle against Texas, splenic, or Spanish fever, and repealing chapter three of the special session laws of 1884.

Be it enacted by the legislature of the State of Kansas: No person or persons shall, between the 1st day of March and the 1st day of December of any year, drive or cause to be driven into or through any county or part thereof in this State, or turn upon or cause to be turned or kept upon any highway, range, common, or uninclosed pasture within this State any cattle capable of communicating or liable to impart what is known as Texas, splenic, or Spanish fever.   Any person violating any provision of this act shall, upon conviction thereof, be adjudged guilty of a misdemeanor, and shall for each offense be fined not less than $100 and not more than $2,000, or be imprisoned in the county jail not less than thirty days and not more than one year, or by both such fine and imprisonment.

SEC. 2.   It shall be the duty of any sheriff, under sheriff, deputy sheriff, or constable within this State, upon a complaint made to him by any citizen of the State, or otherwise having notice or knowledge that there are within the county where such officer resides, cattle believed to be capable of communicating or liable to impart the disease known as Texas, splenic, or Spanish fever, to forthwith take charge of and restrain such cattle under such temporary quarantine regulations as will prevent the communication of such disease, and make immediate report thereof to the live-stock sanitary commission, and such officer shall keep said cattle in custody as aforesaid until released by order of said live-stock sanitary commission, and no officer who shall take or detain any cattle under the provision of this act shall be liable to the owner or owners of such cattle for any damages by reason of such taking or detention, or by reason of the performances of any other duty enjoined in this act.

SEC. 3.   Whenever the live-stock sanitary commission shall determine that certain cattle within the State are capable of communicating or liable to impart Texas, splenic, or Spanish fever, they shall issue their order to the sheriff or any constable of the county in which said cattle are found, commanding him to take and keep such cattle in his custody, subject to such quarantine regulations as they may prescribe, until the 1st day of December next ensuing, on which date they shall direct such officer to deliver said cattle to their owner or owners or to his or their agents : *Provided, however,* That before any cattle so held shall be delivered as aforesaid, there shall be paid to said live-stock sanitary commission all the costs and expenses of taking, detaining, and holding said cattle ; and in case such costs and expenses are not so paid within ten days after the said 1st day of December, the said officer shall advertise in the same manner as is by law provided in cases of sales of personal property, that he will sell such cattle or such portion thereof as may be necessary to pay such costs and expenses, besides the expense of such sale ; and at the time and place so advertised he shall proceed to sell as many of said cattle as shall be necessary to pay such costs and expenses and the expense of sale, and shall forthwith pay over to the live-stock sanitary commission any amount so received in excess of the legal fees and expenses of such officer.   Any officer performing any of the duties enjoined in this section or in the next preceding section of this act shall receive the same compensation therefor as is prescribed by law for similar services, to be paid as other expenses of said live-stock sanitary commission are paid, as provided by law.

SEC. 4.   Any person or persons violating any of the provisions of this act shall be liable to any party injured, through such violation, for any damages that may thereby arise from the communication of Texas, splenic, or Spanish fever, to be recovered in a civil action ; and the party so injured shall have a lien for such damages on the cattle so communicating the disease.

SEC. 5.   In the trial of any person charged with the violation of any of the provisions of this act, and in the trial of any civil action brought to recover damages for the communication of Texas, splenic, or Spanish fever, proof that the cattle which such person is charged with driving or keeping in violation of law, or which are claimed to have communicated the said disease, were brought into this State between the 1st day of March and the 1st day of December of the year in which the offense was committed or such cause of action arose, from south of the thirty-seventh parallel of north latitude, shall be taken as *prima facie* evidence that such cattle were capable of communicating and liable to impart Texas, splenic, or Spanish fever, within the meaning of this act, and that the owner, or owners, or persons in charge of such cattle had full knowledge and notice thereof at the time of the commission of the alleged offense.

Provided, however, That if the owner or owners or person in charge of such cattle shall show by such certificate as shall hereinafter be designated by the live-stock sanitary commission of this State, that the said cattle had been kept since the 1st day of December of the previous year west of the east line of the Indian Territory and north of the thirty-sixth parallel of north latitude or west of the twenty-first meridian of longitude west from Washington and north of the thirty-fourth parallel of north latitude the provisions of this section shall not apply thereto : *Provided also,* That the provision of this section shall not apply to cattle which are owned or kept in this State and which may drift across the south line of the State when the said cattle are gathered in a general round-up and returned under the direction of any live-stock association of this State.

SEC. 6. Whenever two or more persons shall, in violation of this act, at the same time or at different times during the same year, drive or cause to be driven upon the same highway, range, common, or pasture within this State any cattle capable of communicating, or liable to impart, Texas, splenic, or Spanish fever, they shall be jointly and severally liable for all damages that may arise from the communication of such disease, at any time thereafter during the same year to any native, domestic, or acclimated cattle that shall have been upon the same highway, range, common, or pasture so previously traveled over by such first-mentioned cattle.

SEC. 7. Justices of the peace within their respective counties shall have criminal jurisdiction in all cases arising under the provisions of this act.

SEC. 8. It shall be the duty of the prosecuting attorney of the proper county to prosecute on behalf of the State all criminal cases arising under this act.

SEC. 9. Chapter 3 of the laws of 1884, and all other acts or parts of acts in conflict with any of the provisions of this act are hereby repealed.

SEC. 10. This act shall take effect from and after its publication in the official State paper.

Approved March 7, 1885.

I hereby certify that the foregoing is a true and correct copy of the original enrolled bill now on file in my office.

In testimony whereof I have hereunto subscribed my name and affixed my official seal. Done at Topeka, Kans., this 7th day of March, A. D. 1885.

[SEAL.]   E. B. ALLEN,
                                                   Secretary of State.

APPENDIX No. 17.

QUARANTINE LAW OF THE STATE OF COLORADO AGAINST TEXAS CAT-TLE APPROVED MARCH 21, 1885.

THE TEXAS FEVER LAW.

AN ACT to prevent the introduction of any infectious and contagious diseases among the cattle and horses of this State.

Whereas there is prevalent among cattle and horse stock in the States and Territories south of the thirty-sixth parallel of north latitude certain infectious and contagious diseases known as the Texas or splenic fever, Spanish itch, and other diseases of a dangerous and contagious nature; and

Whereas it is essential for the protection of the cattle and horses of Colorado to prevent the introduction and spread of all such diseases within this State; therefore

Be it enacted by the general assembly of the State of Colorado: It shall be unlawful for any person, association, or corporation to bring or drive, or cause to be brought or driven into this State, any cattle or horses having an infectious or contagious disease, or which have been herded or brought into contact with any other cattle or horses laboring under such disease, at any time within ninety days prior to their importation into this State.

SEC. 2. It shall be unlawful for any person, association, or corporation to bring or drive, or cause to be brought or driven, into this State between the 1st day of April and the 1st day of November any cattle or horses from a State, Territory, or country south of the thirty-sixth parallel of north latitude, unless said cattle or horses have been held at some place north of the said parallel of latitude for a period of at least ninety days prior to their importation into this State, or unless the person, association, or corporation owning or having charge of such cattle or horses shall procure from the State veterinary sanitary board a certificate or bill of health to the effect that said cattle or horses are free from all infectious or contagious diseases, and have not been exposed at any time within ninety days prior thereto to any of said diseases, the expense of inspection connected herewith to be paid by the owner or owners of such cattle or horses.

SEC. 3. Any person violating the provisions of this act shall be deemed guilty of a misdemeanor, and shall, on conviction, be punished by a fine of not less than five hundred dollars ($500), or more than five thousand dollars ($5,000), or by imprisonment in the county jail for a term of not less than six months and not exceeding three years, or by both such fine and imprisonment.

SEC. 4. If any person, association, or corporation shall bring or cause to be brought into this State any cattle or horses in violation of the provisions of section 1 or 2 of this act, or shall by false representation procure a certificate of health as provided for in section 2 of this act, he or they shall be liable, in all cases, for all damages sustained on account of disease communicated by or from said cattle or horses, judgment for damages in any such case, together with the costs of action, shall be a lien upon all such cattle and horses, and a writ of attachment may issue in the first instance without the giving of a bond, and the court rendering such judgment may order the sale of said cattle or horses, or so many thereof as may be necessary to satisfy said judgments and costs. Such sales shall be conducted as other sales under execution.

SEC. 5. Inasmuch as the public interest requires that this act should take effect at once, therefore an emergency exists, and this act shall take effect and be in force from and after its passage.

136

APPENDIX No. 18.

QUARANTINE LAW OF THE TERITORY OF WYOMING.

GOVERNOR TO APPOINT TERRITORIAL VETERINARIAN.

SEC. 31. The governor of the Territory is hereby authorized to nominate, which nomination shall be made upon the recommendation of the Stock Growers' Association of the Territory, and by and with the advice and consent of the council appoint, without unnecessary delay after the 8th day of March, 1882, a competent veterinary surgeon who shall be known as the territorial veterinarian, and on entering on his duties shall take an oath to well and truly perform his duties as provided by law.

AUTHORITY TO QUARANTINE.

SEC. 33. In all cases of contagious or infectious disease among domestic animals in this Territory the veterinarian shall have authority to order the quarantine of infected premises, and in case such disease shall become epidemic in any locality in this Territory the veterinarian shall immediately notify the governor of the Territory, who shall thereupon issue his proclamation forbidding any animal of the kind among which said epidemic exists to be transferred from said locality without a certificate from the veterinarian, showing such animal to be healthy.

GOVERNOR MAY PROHIBIT IMPORTATION.

SEC. 37. Whenever the governor of the Territory shall have good reason to believe that any disease covered by this chapter has become epidemic in certain localities in another State or Territory, or that the conditions exist which render domestic animals liable to convey disease, he shall thereupon, by proclamation, schedule such localities and prohibit the importation from them of any live stock of the kind diseased into this Territory, except under such restrictions as he may deem proper. Any corporation, or any person or persons, who after the publishing of such proclamation shall knowingly receive in charge any such animal or animals from any one of said prohibited districts, and transport or convey the same within the limits of this Territory, shall be deemed guilty of a misdemeanor, and upon conviction fined not less than one thousand dollars nor more than ten thousand dollars for each and every offense, and shall further become liable for any and all damages and loss that may be sustained by any person or persons by reason of the importation or transportation of such prohibited animals.

137

APPENDIX No. 19.

*OPINION OF DR. JAMES V HOPKINS, TERRITORIAL VETERINARIAN OF
WYOMING, IN REGARD TO THE RELATIVE LIABILITY TO DISEASE
RESULTING FROM THE MOVEMENT OF CATTLE FROM TEXAS BY RAIL
AND BY TRAIL.*

[From the annual report of the Wyoming Stock Growers' Association for the year 1884.]

SOUTHERN CATTLE.

It is reported that arrangements are being made to transport Texas and other southern cattle during the coming summer to Ogalalla for the purpose of stocking the ranges of Nebraska and Wyoming.

Gentlemen, this is a serious question, to which I hope you will give your earnest attention. When southern cattle are driven north, consuming three or four months on the trail, the change of feed and lapse of time have induced a change in the system of the animal—they no longer contain a virus spreading disease, and such cattle are perfectly safe to add to our home herds.

If there are any southern gentlemen here, I do not wish them to misunderstand me. Wyoming needs the Texan cattle, but experience has taught us that transporting Texas cattle north of a certain latitude by railroad, has been followed by the spread of Texas fever among northern cattle.

Texas fever is an enzootic disorder, probably due to the food on which southern cattle subsist, whereby the systems of these animals become charged with deleterious principles, that are afterwards propagated and dispersed by the excreta of apparently healthy animals.

In Texas, cattle of all ages, from the time they begin to graze, are afflicted with the malady in a latent or mild form.

138

APPENDIX No. 20.

EXTRACT FROM THE ANNUAL REPORT OF THE EXECUTIVE COMMITTEE AND SECRETARY OF THE WYOMING STOCK GROWERS' ASSOCIATION FOR THE YEAR 1885.

TEXAS FEVER.

In touching on the question of Texas fever the committee feel themselves on delicate ground. Some of our most valued members have always doubted the existence of such a disease, or that it could be dangerous in this climate and altitude; others are engaged in the business of bringing these cattle from the South. Nothing could be further from the intention of the committee than to antagonize the first class or injure the business of the other. The occurrences of last summer are now matters of history and as closely affecting this association are briefly recorded here.

It will be remembered that when we separated in April, 1884, the experiment of bringing cattle from Southern Texas by rail to Ogalalla, Nebr., and neighboring stations on the Union Pacific was about to be tried. The first shipment unloaded in May and others followed for two months. From these points they were driven north and northwest. The result was disastrous and realized fully the opinion expressed by our Territorial veterinarian, Dr. Hopkins. Within a few weeks the disease showed itself virulently among the Nebraska cattle which grazed near these unloading points, and large numbers died. Cattle which were brought east from of the Missouri River and grazed temporarily in the vicinity on their way westward, caught the infection, notably one lot of fifty bulls, all of which died within a month from the time of exposure to the contagion. The trail taken northward by the animals which had come by rail to Ogalalla became infected, especially the watering places and bed grounds, and the herds which followed later, both importations from Iowa and herds from Northern Texas, lost large numbers. Later on, the same route was followed unwittingly, and in the opposite direction by many bunches of beef cattle going southward to the railroad for shipment to Chicago. The time was very short for the development of disease in these cases, yet nearly every bunch lost from one to a dozen on the cars or in the Chicago yards. Still later, the cattle going to feeding lots in Iowa and Nebraska crossed this trail or drove upon it, and though the virus was undoubtedly mitigated by the time that had elapsed and increasing cold weather, some instances of death occurred in each herd after reaching their destination.

To ascertain beyond doubt the true cause of death your committee sent the veterinarian into the field at the earliest alarm and kept him there for some weeks. He pursued his investigations by autopsies upon the recent dead, and followed the various manifestations of this disease along the route of the Union Pacific and across country, for 200 miles northward from that railroad to the Cheyenne River. In his exhaustive examination he included many of the animals that went eastward for beef and feeding purposes. The evidence everywhere showed unquestionably splenic fever. This fever is disseminated in the dung and urine of the Southern Texans and the virus or poisonous germ is inhaled by the native cattle in grazing over these excretions.

Without enlarging further on this matter, which, however, it should be said, engrossed the entire attention of your secretary and a special force of inspectors for over a month, the conclusion of your committee is this, and they wish it clearly understood, they being actuated by no motive but that of protecting the cattle of this association: 1st. That Texan cattle brought from the southern part of Texas are dangerous to our cattle for about sixty days from the time the said Southern Texans leave their native ranges. Any method of bringing them which places them on our ranges in less than that time should be discouraged, and cattle so brought should be refused admittance. 2d. That the same cattle can be brought among our stock after said sixty days have elapsed with entire safety to us, and that recognizing the friendly and profitable relations which have for many years existed between us and our Texan friends, both those being among us and those residing in the South, we wish it to be distinctly understood, and believe we speak for the association in saying, that we do not favor or advocate the placing of a single unnecessary obstacle in the way of the Texas trade ; that we are not using, and will not allow to be used, any fictitious or exaggerated charge of danger as a lever against their interests, but, on the contrary, if they will bring their cattle here as harmless as they were from 1873 to 1883, the Wyoming association will raise no bar against them. In this connection the action of the Union Pacific deserves earnest commendation. The committee communicated at once with headquarters at Omaha, and, in the absence of other officials, Mr. P. P. Shelby immediately ordered a thorough cleansing of all infected yards and cars. Not only was this done at great expense in time to make them safe for the handling of beeves, but at a direct loss to the road he prohibited his agents and southern railroad connections from receiving any more animals of the dangerous class described. Such prompt care for our interests merits our cordial recognition.

APPENDIX No. 21.

CHAPTER XLIX.

AN ACT to prevent the introduction of diseased cattle into the Territory of New Mexico. Approved March 19, 1884.

CONTENTS.

Be it enacted by the legislative assembly of the Territory of New Mexico. It shall be unlawful for any person or corporation to drive or transport, or cause or procure to be driven or transported, into the Territory of New Mexico any cattle which are, or within twelve months prior to their introduction into this Territory have been, affected with or exposed to any contagious or infectious disease; or which within such period have been driven or transported from or through any district of country where such disease was known to exist at the time of such driving or transporting; or without the certificate of the inspector of cattle as hereinafter provided being first obtained.

SEC. 2. The governor shall appoint, at such convenient points as he may deem proper within the Territory, and as near as possible to the frontier, inspectors of cattle, whose duty it shall be to inspect all cattle destined for introduction into the Territory, and to ascertain whether any such cattle are or have been infected with or exposed to any contagious or infectious disease, or have been driven or transported from or through any district of country where such disease was known to exist as mentioned in section 1 of this act, and for this purpose he may require affidavits of the persons in charge of such cattle as to all the facts connected with their driving or transportation.

SEC. 3. If upon such inspection and investigation such inspector shall be satisfied that such cattle are free from contagious or infectious disease, and are otherwise proper to be admitted under the provision of section 1 of this act, he shall give to the person in charge of such cattle a certificate to this effect, and if not so satisfied he shall refuse to give such certificate.

SEC. 4. The said inspectors shall hold their offices during the pleasure of the governor, and shall be entitled to receive one dollar per head for all high-grade or thoroughbred cattle inspected, and twenty cents per head for all other cattle inspected, not exceeding 1,000 head at one time, and for any excess above 1,000 in the same herd or lot, ten cents per head, and ten cents per mile for the distance necessarily traveled in going from their usual place of abode to the place of inspection; such fees and mileage to be paid by the owner of the cattle before the delivery of the certificate of inspection, and in case a certificate is not given they may be recovered by the inspector from the owner in civil action.

SEC. 5. For the purpose of taking the affidavits mentioned in section 2 of this act the inspector shall have power to administer oaths, and any person who shall swear falsely in such affidavit shall be deemed guilty of perjury.

SEC. 6. The provision of this act shall apply to shippers and carriers as well as owners of cattle, and the certificate of the inspector shall not relieve them from liability, either criminal or civil, for the introduction of cattle contrary to the provisions of section 1 of this act.

141

SEC. 7. The inspector may appoint a deputy, who may act in his absence.

SEC. 8. Every person having in charge cattle destined for introduction into this Territory, whether as owner or carrier, or as agent of either, shall, at least ten days beforehand, notify the inspector nearest the proposed point of entrance to the Territory, of the time and place, when and where such cattle will be ready for inspection, which place shall be beyond the boundary line of the Territory, and he shall hold the cattle at the place so designated until inspected.

SEC. 9. Any inspector who shall knowingly give a false certificate, or shall without good cause under this act refuse to give a certificate of inspection, or shall willfully delay in making inspection when notified, shall be deemed guilty of a misdemeanor and shall be liable to the injured party for damages arising from such refusal or delay.

SEC. 10. Any person or corporation who shall violate the provisions of section 1 of this act shall be punished by a fine of $5,000 for each offense, to be imposed by the court on conviction upon indictment or information, or to be recovered as a penalty by the Territory in a civil action, and shall also be liable for all damages resulting therefrom. Each lot or herd of cattle unlawfully brought into the Territory shall constitute a separate offense.

SEC. 11. This act shall take effect from and after its passage.

CHAPTER LI.

AN ACT with reference to an act entitled "An act to prevent the introduction of diseased cattle in the Territory of New Mexico" [suspends operation of said act], approved March 19, 1884. Approved April 3, 1884.

Be it enacted by the legislative assembly of the Territory of New Mexico, That the governor of the Territory of New Mexico is hereby authorized, whenever in his judgment the circumstances and public interest warrant and require him to do so, from time to time, to suspend by proclamation the operation of an act entitled "An act to prevent the introduction of diseased cattle in the Territory of New Mexico," approved March 19, 1884, or by proclamation to put the same in force at any time when suspended that he may believe the circumstances or public interest require said act to be in force. Said act is hereby suspended in its operation and effect from this date until the same may by the governor be placed in operation and effect by his proclamation to that end.

This act shall be in full force and effect from and after its passage.

APPENDIX No. 22.

LETTER FROM THE PRESIDENT OF THE MEXICAN CENTRAL RAILWAY COMPANY IN REGARD TO THE RANGE-CATTLE BUSINESS IN MEXICO.

[Mexican Central Railway Company, limited Mason Building, No. 70 Kilby street.]

BOSTON, *April* 25, 1885.

DEAR SIR: I have your letter of the 23d instant, inquiring in regard to range and ranch cattle in Mexico.

Since the opening of our line the number of cattle in sight has evidently increased.

Between Paso del Norte and the city of Chihuahua there is a large extent of grazing country not excelled by any in the United States, with rich abundant grasses and a plentiful supply of water. It contains many fine lakes and ponds, and on it are pastured vast herds of neat cattle and horses.

In spite of the duties upon cattle there is some trade between Mexico and the United States, as you will see by our annual report for the year ending December 31, 1884 (a copy of which I send you), page 31, we carried two thousand two hundred and nineteen horses and two thousand eight hundred and fifty-five head of neat cattle. Nearly the whole of these were transported from different points in Mexico to the United States.

Our stock business is growing and the establishment of a stock-yard at El Paso would very materially increase the traffic. At present the buying of Mexican cattle is done wholly by individuals, who go to Mexico for the purpose of obtaining cattle and horses for their ranches in the United States.

Yours truly,

LEVI C. WADE, *President.*
Per G.

JONSPH NIMMO, Jr., Esq.,
Chief of Bureau of Statistics, Washington, D. C.

143

APPENDIX No.. 23.

[Office of Southern Texas Live Stock Association, 208 Main Plaza.]

SAN ANTONIO, TEX., *March* 21, 1885.

DEAR SIR: In answer to your telegram of the 13th ultimo, asking as to "success or lack of success in introducing high-bred bulls into Southern Texas," I answer: They have been and are being successfully introdued all over the State.

There are but few, very few, of the old long-horn Texans in the State. All show that good blood has been infused.

On the Gulf coast we have the Texas Land Cattle Company, near Corpus Christi, using as fine bulls as any in the United States. R. King, same county uses only well-bred bulls; in fact, every ranch in the South is now using one-quarter, one-half, and three-quarter full blood and registered bulls. South Texas has breeders of fine bulls, who do nothing else, and can show as fine pedigree stock as are bred in Kentucky.

A. W. Moore, Bastrop County; J. D. Snycro, Bastrop County; Hon. J. M. Miller, Gonzales County: Samuel A. Wolcott, Encinal County; A. E. Carothers, La Salle County; George B. Johnston, Bexar County, and hundreds of others are breeders of only fine cattle.

In former years the losses on fine stock deterred many ranchmen from importing them, but as the country was fenced up and ranch owners improved their homes, the importations increased, until to-day no ranch owner dare use any but good grade or high-bred bulls.

I have just returned from a trip south, Dimmit County; inspected two of the largest ranches in the south, on neither of them was there a common bull, and all of the young cattle show good breeding.

W. A. Pettus, Goliad County; H. T. Clare, Bee County; William Butler, Kames County; A. Milett, La Salle County, and hundreds of others of the largest ranchmen in the south use only fine bulls.

Hon. J. M. Miller, member of Congress, can answer as to his success with Holstein cattle; he has them as fine as are bred anywhere.

We have breeders who make specialities of the Durham, Hereford, Holstein, Devon, Brahma, Polled cattle, and (for dairy purposes) Jerseys. While in some instances losses have been heavy on imported stock, it is owing largely to the fact that the great change, not only in climate but in care, comes too suddenly, and in many instances to the swindle perpetrated by northern breeders in sending out animals that had been blanketed and stabled.

Hoping this may give you some idea of our business in this section,

I am yours, truly,

D. W. HINKLE.

JOSEPH NIMMO, Jr.,
Washington, D. C.

144

APPENDIX No. 24.

LETTER FROM E. V. SMALLEY, ESQ., OF SAINT PAUL, MINN., IN REGARD TO THE CATTLE INTERESTS OF MONTANA WITH RESPECT TO WATER-RIGHTS.

[Office of " The Northwest," Mannheimer Block, Third and Minnesota streets; E. V. Smalley, editor and publisher.]

SAINT PAUL, MINN., *April* 3, 1885.

DEAR SIR: In Montana it is membership of the round-up district association, and not ownership of water-rights, that determines a stockman's standing. Only within the last year or two has there been any marked movement towards taking up water-front lands under the desert act. Many of the largest stock-owners live in Helena, Bozeman, Deer Lodge, and Benton, and have neither pre-emption nor desert claims where their cattle range. Nor does the possession of water-rights necessarily secure admission to the associations. The water-right men are usually owners of small herds and do a little farming. Their feeling is one of hostility to the owners of large herds.

I am not as well posted on the conditions in Wyoming. The whole cattle industry on the ranges seems to me to be in a transition state, with many of the most important measures affecting it yet to be settled.

Yours, very truly,

E. V. SMALLEY.

145

APPENDIX No. 25.

THE RANGE-CATTLE BUSINESS OF MONTANA.

[From "The Rocky Mountain Husbandman" of April 2, 1885; published at White Sulphur Springs, Mont.]

The entire live-stock industry of Montana can at length be said to have fully recovered from the backset it received from losses precipitated by the severity of the winter of 1881-'82. During that memorable winter cattle herds were reduced from 25 to 35 per cent. and flocks from 50 to 60 per cent., and confidence in the industry was most fearfully shaken. Up to that date the operatives in the several branches of this pursuit had had plain sailing and felt perfectly secure. In looking back over the field now, it seems a little wonderful that a people should have placed such implicit faith in the elements or the country, or both, as they then did, for situated as we are--so far to the north—it is certainly remarkable that we should be blessed with a climate where stock can flourish the year round without being cared for, and nothing short of actual experience could have convinced any people that such was the case. The fact that our mountains abounded with elk, deer, and moose, and our valleys literally swarmed with buffalo and antelope, and that the few ponies which the first white men who ventured thither found in possession of the Indians who inhabited the country wintered without care was, to be sure, some evidence that Montana was naturally a stock country, but the fact did not fully assert itself until the gold stampede of 1-63, 1864, and 1865 began to see in what splendid condition their pack animals and old train cattle came out in the spring. And when it was noticed that old work-steers that had hauled trains all the way from Omaha and Nebraska City, and were so poor that they could have scarcely been wintered in the barn-yards of Missouri or Illinois, where hay and grain were plenty, recruited, nothwithstanding the winter blasts, and were ready for work again in the spring, the people began to think there was more than ordinary merit in Montana bunch-grass, and the experience of these twenty years proves the truth of this conclusion. It is true that there were sceptics even in those early days who pointed to the buffalo heads on our valleys as evidence against this, asserting that the animals had died from the severity of the weather, and that Montana caught a severe winter every few years that wiped animal life from the face of the country; but in spite of these adverse observations the business flourished exceedingly well for fifteen years, when the first and only disaster of great consequence in the history of the country occurred. But this is now a thing of the past. Herdowners and flock-masters are on their feet once more, and their reverses are forgotten. Not forgotten either, for all have learned a valuable lesson from the experience, and are now better able to cope with the winter blasts. Cattle-owners have learned that it will not do to crowd their ranges in summer, and that in winter they must have men with their herds to keep them out on high land, instead of allowing them to huddle in the willow groves along the creeks. Flock-owners have learned that a few tons of hay to every one thousand head of sheep is a great security, and that while it is possible to fetch them through nine winters out of ten without preparations, much better results are accomplished by a certain amount of feeding every winter. The truth is, civilization is death to range husbandry. In addition to the range being closely grazed, it is largely fenced. The presence of the fences catch so much snow upon our valleys that the animal that depends upon making its own living must resort to the hills, both winter and summer, a locality superior to our valleys, but somewhat limited in extent when compared to the whole country which was but a few years since one vast stock range. Yet even with the sure and gradual change that is being wrought from range husbandry to the tamer though surer modes, the interest was never more secure and cattle, horses, and sheep owners never felt so independent and their flocks and herds never increased more rapidly than now.

146

APPENDIX No. 26.

*STATEMENT IN REGARD TO THE SUBJECT OF GRAZING AND OF IRRI-
GATION IN THE STATE OF NEVADA, BY HON G. W. MERRILL.*

GRAZING.

The impression abroad is that Nevada is strictly a mining State, and that no other interests exist there. The error is very apparent when one notices the reports of constantly growing farming communities, and the large and constant shipment of beeves from the State. Nevada is fast assuming the position of a great cattle State. The bunch-grasses of the mountains afford excellent pasturage during the summer, while the seeming barren waste of deserts is the safeguard of winter. The snows of winter, falling deeply in the mountains, drive the cattle, horses, and sheep to the dry valleys and deserts where the snowfall is never deep, and they find good browsing on the white and black sage, and water in the pools of melted snow. The long stretches of wide prairie existing in the State, the fierce winds of winter do not gather that force that drives cattle for miles and miles against all resistance, but the high broken ranges of the mountains stand as bulwarks to break the winds and shelter is afforded in every valley.

Farming being confined to the lands in the valleys bordering immediately on a a stream, the vast territory outside is devoted to grazing, and instead of Nevada being a solitary mining camp among the barren mountains, thousands of cattle, horses, and sheep find fattening and nutritious food in the bunch-grasses that grow in the valleys and on the "barren mountains." The beef and mutton produced in the State are of exceptional quality, being juicy, firm, and tender, and are sought after by butchering firms of more noted States. On account of its superior climate Nevada is looked upon as the natural home of the horse, and for breeding purposes of both horses and cattle it is equal, if not superior, to Kentucky. Cattlemen of the south, who have examined different countries, claim Nevada as the best territory for that business. Cattle ranges are being sought for and a large acreage is being sold annually for that purpose.

Good grazing land is in demand, and large investments in stock ranges have been made in the last year by foreign firms. Several ranges have been disposed of to residents of California. English capital has also been used purchasing ranges in Elko County, and over a million dollars have changed hands in the last year. Although the assessors' reports do not show the fact yet it is ascertained from reliable authority, stockmen, associations, &c., that there are nearly 700,000 head of cattle in the State and 300,000 head of sheep.

"The hills and valleys," say the *Reno Journal,* "are fast being utilized by growing herds of improved stock. The superb climate, pure water, and nutritious grasses stand approved in the admitted superior health of the herds of horses, cattle, and sheep."

Blooded stock from the East and West has been imported during the past few years, and the farmers have taken a great deal of interest in the best breeds of cattle.

In the month of November, 1884, a gentleman in Churchill County imported a herd of the hornless Galloway cattle, costing him $40,000.

The Holstein as a fancy stock surpass all others. They cost about $3,000 to $4,000 a head and are credited with giving 50 quarts of milk a day, and have to be milked morning, noon, and night.

The Jersey, Guernsey, Alderney, Serk, and Herm have been, and are being, introduced into the State, but the general opinion coincides with the view that the Durham is the most profitable for two reasons : they produce large quantities of milk and beef, growing very large and taking on flesh in a short time. Up to within the past few years Nevada has received a large number of cattle from Texas, which were driven across the country, but of late years this source of supply has greatly diminished.

Concerning improved breeds of cattle, the *Silver State,* a paper published in Humboldt County, under date of October 28, 1884, has the following :

"The Nevada Land and Cattle Company whose headquarters are at Kelly Creek, in the eastern part of the county, sold last week to Chapman & Horn, of San Francisco, 1,000 head of beef cattle. Some 400 head of this purchase were shipped last week from Iron Point. Cattle dealers say the beeves will dress on an average nearly 700 pounds each. This shows the effect of introducing good breeds of cattle among Nevada herds. Some years ago T. D. Parkinson, who is managing the affairs of the company, bought some short-horn Durhams from Jesse D. Carr's herds in California, and took them to the Kelly Creek Ranch. From these and their progeny the company sell a number of thoroughbred bulls annually besides improving their own herds by crossing the ordinary stock with Durhams. The graded stock, some of which are as large as thoroughbreds, thrive as well as the native breeds on the plains and mount-ain ranges. Last year the Kelly Creek Ranch in this county, and the I. L. Ranch in Elko County, which adjoins it, and on which the cattle were also crossed with Dur-hams, were consolidated under the name of the Nevada Land and Cattle Company. On these ranches the beeves purchased by Horn & Chapman were raised, and stockmen say many of them are as fine-limbed and as large in size as pure-blooded Durhams. It is also said that these improved breeds are worth from $7 to $10 a head more than ordinary cattle, and as they stand the winters and do as well on the Nevada cattle ranges as the common breeds of cattle, that ought to be a sufficient inducement for all stock-owners to improve their herds. As the price of cattle keeps up, with no pros-pect of a material reduction, no doubt in a few years Nevada ranges will all be stocked with improved breeds of cattle."

The climate seems especially adapted to the growth of thoroughbreds, and when epidemics come the cattle can be driven to the mountains for safety.

It is quite impossible to obtain accurate figures showing amount of beef exported from the State for a given period, but, in order that some idea of this interest may be formed, I will say that on the 1st of December last it was estimated by cattlemen that there was about 35,000 head of beef cattle, which would average about 700 pounds each dressed, available for the winter season.

The price per pound is 7½ to 8 cents. During one week in the month of January, 1885, there were shipped from Winnemucca, a station on the Central Pacific road, to California, 100 cars of beeves, averaging 19 head per car, making a total of 2,014 beeves.

The principal markets for beef are San Francisco and Chicago, being transported over the Central Pacific Railroad and connecting lines, where it commands the highest market price.

HUMBOLDT EXPORTS.

Through the courtesy of J. A. McBride, the obliging agent of the Central Pacific Railroad at this place, we are enabled to give the following statement of the ship-ments of beeves, horses, wool, and fruit from Winnemucca during the year 1884, which is compiled from the railroad books: Of beef cattle there were shipped to San Francisco, 13,290 head; to Oakland stock-yards, 3,624; to San José, 1,270; to Merced, 1,053; to Suisun, 994; to Sacramento, 381; to Athlone, 375; to other points, 295; making the total shipments of beef cattle 21,282 head. There were shipped during the last year 341 horses, mostly to California. The wool shipments amounted to 309,375 pounds, of which 278,451 pounds were shipped direct to Boston and Philadel-phia, and 31,284 pounds to San Francisco. The shipment of green fruit is a new indus-try, and amounted during the summer and fall to 1,055 boxes, aggregating 62,495 pounds.

The cattle shipments in 1880 aggregated 21,302 head; in 1881, 29,382 head. This was exclusive of 1,600 dressed beeves shipped by the Refrigerator Company, and about 2,300 calves. In 1882 the cattle shipments aggregated 20,975 head, exclusive of 1,200 dressed beeves, shipped by the Refrigerator Company; in 1883 the cattle shipments aggregated 18,744.

In 1881 the wool shipments aggregated 227,127 pounds; in 1882, 349,585 pounds; in 1883, 400,575 pounds.

IRRIGATION.

Vast areas of land in the State need only water to be made productive and transform what is now apparently a barren waste into valuable farms. Several prominent cat-tle firms are at present irrigating large tracts of heretofore unproductive land with surprising results, having extensive reservoirs and canals. It is necessary for them to own large tracts for grazing purposes, and the best portions are being turned into created pastures. Whenever the test has been made and water has been brought from the mountains to the valleys by means of ditches and pipes or brought to the surface by artesian wells, the hitherto non-productive soil has literally blossomed with grain, fruits, grasses, and cereals of every description. Strikingly is this illustrated by rid-ing along through Humboldt County, on the Central Pacific Railroad, when, after traversing hundreds of miles of a barren, dreary country the traveler emerges from the car to find himself gazing upon beds of roses, fruit trees of every description, luxuriant fields of grass and farm products of all kinds adorning acres of land around, while a fountain of water, drawn from the mountains beyond, is a constant reminder of the secret cause of this beautiful oasis in the desert; notably, also, is this characteristic of the soil exhibited in Carson, Clover, Mason, Huntington, Ruby, Reese River, and, in fact, all the valleys of the State where the water has been systematically utilized.

No doubt that by means of a proper system of reservoirs a large area of Nevada could be made a garden of vegetation and the uninhabited regions dotted with towns and cities, and the waterless sage-brush plains transformed into green fields. Some general system of irrigation should be adopted, and doubtless will be, in the near future. Agitation has already commenced, and undoubtedly will continue to increase, directed to the idea of constructing large reservoirs for the purpose of holding in reserve large bodies of water for use in the dry season. Already much attention is being paid to this system of irrigation, and desirable sites for reservoirs for the storing of water are being sought after. It is evident a general system of irrigation is sadly needed, and to this end a bill was introduced during the last legislature to establish a State board of irrigation, whose business it was to be to investigate this matter and report desirable places for storing and saving water, and also to superintend the management of State canals for irrigating purposes. The object was to create a State investment whereby the waste water could be utilized on the sage-brush land at a profit to the State and to settlers, but by a local interest expressed in the bill it was defeated. A State board of irrigation doubtless will be formed, and laws enacted for the management of waterways of the State. The rivers and creeks furnish enough water to irrigate ten times the amount at present irrigated. More water is wasted by carelessness every year than is used, simply because there is no check.

A certain number of farmers unite and build a ditch from a river to irrigate their lands; an adjoining set build another for their lands, and so on until several ditches are in operation. The ditches being under separate management, conflicts ensue and damage suits follow, as one company fails to take care of its waste water, allowing it to run on to the farm of a stockholder of another company, thus wasting water that might be used to an advantage in another direction. The mill managers along the Carson River last year were complaining of the scarcity of the water, and upon examination by a committee appointed to investigate the matter it was found that while some ranchers were using the water economically others were allowing it to run to waste and receiving no benefits whatever by so doing, while still others were actually drowning out their grain to keep an unfriendly neighbor from getting his share of the water. The disposing of lands in elongated tracts along the course of a stream and forever debarring the using of that water for lands outside by another is encouraging a species of riparian rights that retards the country in its growth and settlement and puts a check on irrigation. There are now 800 irrigating ditches in the State, aggregating in round numbers 2,000, miles and successfully irrigating 150,000 acres of land. If the General Government could by persuaded to give the State all the unappropriated lands within its borders under due restrictions and proper precautions, a general system of irrigation could then be easily inaugurated, and a State now in the front rank as a producer of gold and silver bullion would soon take a similar position among the agricultural States of the Union, for it has been demonstrated beyond doubt that the lands of Nevada are sterile only because of aridity.

APPENDIX No. 27.

GRAZING.

The grazing interests of the Territory have largely increased during the last year ; quite extensive importations of improved breeds of cattle and horses have been made into Arizona, attracted by the unequaled advantages to be found here for the stock-owner in the mildness of the climate, the extensive ranges, the nutritious grasses, and the small amount of care required by the stock. There has been an entire absence of epidemic diseases among cattle and horses in this Territory, and the percentage of loss per year is stated to be about 3 per cent., being less than any other portion of the United States.

Much of the 60,000 square miles of grazing lands in Arizona, though bountifully covered with rich grasses, cannot be utilized at present for grazing purposes on account of the absence of water. It is believed, however, that this drawback can be largely, if not almost completely, remedied by the introduction of artesian water. In fact, where the experiment has been tried, in Sulphur Spring Valley, Cochise County, the result is most satisfactory, "sufficient water having been obtained in this way to water at least 30,000 cattle, besides affording sufficient irrigation to maintain the gardens that a population attending to this stock would require, and perhaps tree plantations for the relief of stock from sun and wind." (*Vide* report of commission appointed to examine and report upon artesian wells in Sulphur Spring Valley.)

The importance of this question of obtaining water by artesian-well process throughout the Territory where superficial streams are not sufficient to maintain stock, much less for agricultural purposes, is apparent.

Should all of the grazing land in the Territory be made available in this way it is estimated that there would be ample pasturage for five million cattle.

There are now in the Territory about three hundred thousand head of stock, with probably good pasturage, under present conditions, for one million more. During the prevalence of the Texas cattle fever last summer much apprehension was felt among stockmen that the disease might be communicated to the cattle of this Territory, and the question of establishing a quarantine against the admission of cattle from Texas was raised. The acting governor, at the earnest request of prominent cattlemen, issued a proclamation interdicting the admission of Texas cattle into the Territory for a limited period, thereby relieving the apprehension of contagion.

Upon examining this subject I find no provision of law covering such a question, and I would respectfully invite the attention of Congress to this matter, and suggest that authority of law be provided for establishing in the Territories quarantine restrictions should similar need arise.

AGRICULTURE.

The agricultural advantages of Arizona are, I think, generally underestimated abroad. There is no more productive soil in America than is to be found in the valleys of Arizona, and it is believed that a greater variety of productions can be raised here than elsewhere in the United States, providing water can be had for irrigation. Not only does the soil produce fine crops of cereals, but fruits of all kinds, and vegetables of the finest quality.

The yield per acre of wheat and barley is from 25 to 35 bushels, and after this is harvested corn can be planted on the same ground, and a fine crop raised the same season. Apples, peaches, pears, plums, figs, quinces, apricots, and nearly every other variety of fruit yield largely. Lemons, oranges, and olives can be raised with profit, and finer grapes cannot be produced anywhere. Sugar-cane and cotton have also been grown successfully.

In the valleys of Salt River and Gila River alone there are 400,000 acres, which can be brought under cultivation, although less than 50,000 acres are now being made productive. The principal lands now under cultivation in the Territory are confined to the two valleys above named and the valleys of the Verde, Santa Cruz, and San Pedro. Yet there are numerous fertile valleys throughout the Territory in every direction where considerable farming is done, among which may be named the Sulphur Spring and San Simon Valleys, in Cochise County; Williamson, Peeples, Chino, Aqua Fria, Skull, Kirkland, and Walnut Grove Valleys, in Yavapai County; the valley of the Little Colorado, in Apache County; and the fertile bottom lands of the Colorado and Lower Gila, in Yuma County.

Although most of the farming lands of Arizona are confined to the valleys and the bottom lands of the principal rivers, there are millions of acres among the hills and on the plains which could be made very productive if there was sufficient water for irrigation.

Irrigation is necessary to insure good crops in nearly every locality, although in a few of the northern valleys the subirrigation is sufficient from the rainfall during the wet season. Latterly special attention has been given to irrigation propositions.

In the Salt River Valley an immense canal is being constructed which will convey water enough, it is claimed, to reclaim at least 100,000 acres, besides furnishing motive power for an immense amount of machinery. With the 35,000 acres already under cultivation, when this canal is ready for use, which it is expected to be early in the spring of 1885, this valley will present as valuable and productive an acreage of farming land as any area of equal extent in America.

The possibilities for the immigrant in this and the adjacent valley of the Gila are wonderful. Land can be had reasonably cheap; "that which has not been improved can be had at from $5 to $10 per acre; improved land from $15 to $30 per acre, according to the character of soil and location. This price includes a water-right sufficient for crop-raising." (Hamilton's Resources of Arizona.)

In connection with agricultural pursuits, hog-fattening and pork-packing bids fair to become, ere long, an exceedingly profitable business. But little work is required in fattening; the hogs run on the alfalfa fields and keep in good order until the grain is harvested, and they are then turned upon the grain stubble-fields to complete the process of fattening. "The pork is solid, sweet, and finely flavored, and disease is unknown."

When the large canal in Salt River Valley is completed, ice can be cheaply manufactured by water-power, and pork-packing engaged in on a large scale.

In reference to the benefits of the canal to the Territory the following quotations from the prospectus of the canal company for 1884 are instructive:

WATER-POWER.

The water power is formed by a vertical fall of 15 feet of the entire body of the canal, made in solid rock, at a point about 8 miles northwest of Phœnix. The amount of power produced is 1,300 horse-power. This power will be of great value in this country, where fuel is scarce and expensive. It will be utilized to its full capacity. Flour for all of Arizona, Western New Mexico, Eastern California, and Sonora will be made here; ice for the use of the city and to refrigerate large rooms for dairy purposes. and pork and beef packing, and fruit and beef canning. It will also be used for quartz mills for the reduction of ores and for other purposes.

WATER SUPPLY.

The water in Salt River, from which this canal takes its supply, is found by measurement in the dry season of the year to be sufficient to fill the canal and supply such other canals as have been heretofore constructed.

It is the best supplied stream of water in the southwestern part of the United States. The canal is taken out the Salt River three-fourths of a mile below its junction with the Verde River. These two streams receive the total southern drainage of the high mountain ranges, extending for 200 miles through the northern and central part of Arizona. These mountains cover an area of 15,000 square miles, and some of them are 12,000 feet high. They receive heavy falls of snow in winter and of rain in summer, and are covered with a heavy growth of pine timber.

LAND RECLAIMED.

This canal reclaims fully 100,000 acres of land. This land is deep alluvial soil of surpassing fertility. The surface is remarkably even, being free from elevations and depressions, with an even grade of about 10 feet to the mile from the foot-hills to the river, rendering it perfectly adapted for irrigation. It is the one garden spot of Arizona.

AGRICULTURAL PRODUCTS OF THE VALLEY.

There are now in cultivation 35,000 acres under existing canals. The most profitable cereals are wheat, barley, and oats. The yield this year is estimated at 34,000,000 pounds. The wheat produced here is of extra fine quality, and makes a superior flour. The market for these productions comprises a radius of 400 miles of surrounding country.

The average yield of wheat per acre is fully 1,500, and 2,000 is not unusual. The cost of raising and marketing at Phœnix per cwt. is about 65 cents, and the average market price $1.60.

The means of watering crops being in the hands of the farmer, and with no frosts to interfere, the yield is very certain. There has not been a failure of crops in this valley since its settlement, thirteen years ago.

It is a notorious fact that in all countries lands that are supplied by water for irrigation rate at more than double the value of those lands that depend on rainfall, and this is owing to the larger crops produced and the greater certainty of crops on irrigated lands. In some countries—Spain, for instance—this disparity is even greater, the value of irrigated lands being more than three times that of other agricultural lands.

LIVE STOCK.

Alfalfa grows luxuriantly all the year and produces five crops per annum of from 1½ to 2 tons per acre each. It will sustain in pasture an average of three head of cattle per acre, and cattle raised on this alfalfa will weigh as much at two and one-half years old as those on the ordinary wild ranges at three and one-half.

Timothy, clover, and millet can be successfully raised, but alfalfa, being of a more rapid growth and excellent for hay and grazing, is considered by the old residents more profitable, and for dairy purposes it is unexcelled. With cheap power for manufacturing ice for creameries and cheese factories, dairying will become an extensive and profitable business. In Arizona alone 500,000 pounds of creamery butter can be sold annually at 50 cents per pound. It is now difficult to secure good butter in the Territory at any price, and fair ranch butter often sells at 75 cents.

The cost of raising hogs on alfalfa does not exceed 2 cents per pound. There was shipped into Arizona last year 2,000,000 pounds of bacon, at a cost of 18 cents per pound—$360,000—and the demand is rapidly increasing. Now, with our facilities for packing in the summer season, by means of the proposed ice-chilled rooms, this supply will, in a few years, all come from Salt River Valley. And, in addition to Arizona, we will supply Sonora, New Mexico, and Eastern California.

LAND GRANTS.

The present uncertainty existing regarding the final disposition of lands granted to the Atlantic and Pacific and Texas Pacific Railroads by Congress is preventing the settlement of Arizona to a great extent, and keeping from the Territory much capital that would be invested here could a title to these lands be obtained.

I most urgently present the fact that a determination by Congress of the question whether the railroads or the Government own the lands referred to, and the opportunity given citizens to acquire title from either one or the other of these sources, will be of incalculable benefit to Arizona.

ARTESIAN WATER.

I most earnestly suggest an appropriation by Congress to defray the expense of sinking artesian wells in several of the higher valleys of Arizona. Hundreds of thousands of acres of land which would be exceedingly valuable for grazing and in many instances agricultural purposes, if water could be obtained, are now comparatively without value to the Territory or the Government. Since my last report was rendered several artesian wells have been bored successfully by private enterprise in some of the valleys of the southern portion of the Territory where the altitude is not great, and an ample flow of water obtained at a very moderate depth.

The legislature of the Territory in 1875 offered a reward of $3,000 to the person first finding a flowing stream of water by means of a genuine artesian well. This reward was claimed in November, 1883, by Mr. W. J. Sanderson, of Sulphur Spring Valley, Cochise County, Arizona; and in order to determine the justice of his claim I appointed a commission of highly competent gentlemen, consisting of Hon. E. B. Gage, Prof. John A. Church, and Isaac E. James, esq., to examine and report upon the wells bored by Mr. Sanderson. The following is an extract from their report:

First. That flowing water has been obtained in Sulphur Spring Valley by boring.

Second. That the wells which furnish it are true artesian wells, in that they derive their supply from subterranean sources distinct from the surface by an impervious stratum, in this case clay 20 to 40 feet thick.

Third. That each of these wells inspected by them throws out water enough to supply 5,000 to 10,000 head of stock, and therefore is an important addition to the resources of the Territory.

Fourth. That the finding of the water is not accidental and doubtful, but is quite as regular and certain as can be expected of such enterprises.

Fifth. That no reasonable doubt exists of the possibility of carrying the same system of improvement into other valleys of Arizona and thus greatly extending her means of industry.

The deepest well bored was 83 feet. Mr. Sanderson's success stimulated others, and several other wells are reported in operation in the southern portion of the Territory; notably one near Florence, in Pinal County.

This is a subject of the utmost importance to the progress of Arizona, and the assistance of Congress is desired in demonstrating the feasibility of developing water on the uplands and higher valleys of the Territory, where great depth is required and the experiment is too expensive for poor settlers, and where under existing laws no inducement is offered to the rich to reclaim land by this means.

The Government still owns nearly all the table land of Arizona, and if water were procured on these uplands by artesian process the results would far more than repay the expense and the benefit to the Territory be very great.

APPENDIX No. 28.

STATEMENTS FURNISHED BY MR. ALBERT FINK, CHAIRMAN OF THE JOINT EXECUTIVE COMMITTEE OF EAST AND WEST TRUNK LINES, IN REGARD TO LIVE-STOCK SHIPMENTS FROM THE WEST TO THE EAST.

[Joint Executive Committee, office of the chairman, 346 Broadway.]

NEW YORK, *February* 26, 1885.

DEAR SIR: In compliance with your request of the 18th instant, I herewith inclose two statements of live-stock shipments:

First. Statement No. 233, E. B., showing the number of tons of cattle received at New York City, Philadelphia, Baltimore, and the New England States during 1880, 1881, 1882, 1883, and 1884, including all cattle shipped from the West which cross the Hudson River, and south of Saint Johns. Please understand that these are the arrivals at the seaboard of cattle from all parts of the country. The origin of shipments appears on the statement. Some of the cattle originated in New York State, some in Pennsylvania, some in New Jersey, some in Virginia, and some in Maryland. You can, from this statement, make out the cattle shipments from Western points, but we have no information showing where the shipments came from beyond Chicago or Saint Louis.

The same statement shows the dressed-beef shipments. You will notice that this traffic has been increasing, particularly to New England, since the year 1880; and this, of course, may account for the decrease in the shipments of live cattle, although there has been a general increase in the shipments to New England.

You will also bear in mind that these figures include all export shipments, which in some years are greater than in others. We have no statistics showing the export of cattle, but I suppose you can obtain that from other sources.

The weight of the live cattle will average about 1,200 pounds per head, and 100 pounds of live cattle, gross, will make about 57 pounds of dressed beef.

In the year 1884 the Delaware, Lackawanna and Western carried about 5 per cent. of the cattle to New York, which is not included in this table, and this will account for the decrease in the shipments as compared with the previous year.

Second. Statement No. 234, E. B., showing the cattle shipped in the years 1880 to 1884, from Chicago, Saint Louis, Indianapolis, and Cincinnati, of which we have accounts. The first total in the table shows the shipments to New York City, Philadelphia, Baltimore, and New England points. The shipments enumerated under "Other States" were made to interior points. For example, in 1880 the shipments from Saint Louis to Illinois were 16,823 tons, of which 13,000 tons went to Chicago, and the balance to interior points in Illinois. The 31,549 tons shipped from Chicago to Indiana in the year 1880, and the corresponding number of tons shipped in the subsequent years, go to a slaughtering establishment at Hammond, Ind., and are there made into dressed beef and shipped east. The dressed beef so shipped is included in Statement No. 233. The dressed beef arriving at the sea-coast is also included in the table of dressed-beef shipments contained in Statement No. 233.

You will notice that large shipments of cattle are made to interior points in the States of New York and Pennsylvania. This is partly for home consumption, but a large portion of this stock is fed in those States, and afterwards shipped to the seaboard; and that which goes to the seaboard would be included in Statement No. 233. The shipments to Buffalo, locally, are included in the New York State shipments, and all that is not consumed there, of course, comes east.

I hope this information is what you desire.

Respectfully, yours,

ALBERT FINK,
Commissioner.

JOSEPH NIMMO, Jr., Esq.,
Chief of Bureau of Statistics, Washington, D. C.

154

Special statement No. 233, E. B., showing cattle received at New York City, Philadelphia, Baltimore, and the New England States from points west thereof during 1880, 1881, 1882, 1883, and 1884.

Points of origin.	New York City.					Philadelphia.				
	1880.	1881.	1882.	1883.	1884.	1880.	1881.	1882.	1883.	1884.
	Tons.	*Tons.*	*Tons.*	*Tons.*	*Tons.*	*Tons.*	*Tons.*	*Tons.*	*Tons.*	*Tons.*
Chicago	243,569	259,906	260,634	247,686	173,553	20,585	27,539	32,406	24,034	19,558
Saint Louis	45,107	48,960	21,524	32,114	37,981	6,241	8,522	4,123	6,674	6,317
Peoria	1,703	2,418	507	2,698	1,033	169	608		159	
Indianapolis	1,991	2,060	1,832	5,205	6,085	170	60	199	99	21
Cincinnati	26,512	25,779	18,621	23,895	24,349	1,340	2,480	1,734	1,220	255
Buffalo	34,620	15,574	17,467	15,509	18,556		2,550	3,400	4,336	3,264
Pittsburgh	14,907	13,247	9,172	14,053	8,663	7,166	4,957	4,228	3,510	1,965
Illinois	10,096	3,173	537	105						
Iowa	680									
Indiana	4,884	2,156	2,091	2,277	2,094	101	267	12	10	
Michigan	110									
Ohio	15,360	11,417	9,199	16,093	13,839	6,476	5,351	4,623	2,648	3,105
Kentucky	6,608	2,635	6,606	3,635	3,403	3,573	1,901	2,303	2,406	2,947
New York State	5,171	3,619	3,758	6,051	6,939	363	100	40		50
Pennsylvania	2,231	4,323	5,070	9,251	14,727	16,268	16,546	12,248	18,181	17,910
New Jersey	100		40	193	347					
West Virginia	6,737	2,380	2,332	2,976	4,050	19,528	11,600	14,420	11,632	11,150
Virginia	470	290	5,849	9,014	9,912	1,693	1,460	8,642	8,337	6,393
Maryland and South			1,250	1,341	2,692	4,116	230	1,316	4,659	7,638
Grand total	420,856	397,937	366,489	392,096	328,223	87,789	84,171	89,694	87,905	80,573

DRESSED BEEF.

Points of origin.	1880.	1881.	1882.	1883.	1884.	1880.	1881.	1882.	1883.	1884.
Chicago			2,531	16,325	34,916			448	8,601	12,805
Saint Louis			10	33	20					10
Buffalo			92		10					
Ohio				7						
New York					9					
Total			2,633	16,365	34,955			448	8,601	12,815

Points of origin.	Baltimore.					New England States, including Boston.				
	1880.	1881.	1882.	1883.	1884.	1880.	1881.	1882.	1883.	1884.
	Tons.	*Tons.*	*Tons.*	*Tons.*	*Tons.*	*Tons.*	*Tons.*	*Tons.*	*Tons.*	*Tons.*
Chicago	4,193	4,456	4,243	8,136	5,843	28,239	106,386	53,077	78,373	55,343
Saint Louis	2,063	2,166	897	522	248	4,399	22,062	7,936	12,860	7,191
Peoria	190			447	77		31			
Indianapolis					31	277	353	510	280	
Cincinnati	440	873	1,273	221	201	260	226	80	151	205
Buffalo	540	550	490	106	2,150	6,760	4,769	6,024	2,004	8,753
Pittsburgh	20	63	504	37	44				36	309
Illinois						271	206	176	293	
Indiana					182	130	140	180		
Michigan						10	32	30		
Ohio	1,195	3,370	3,101	3,342	3,463	1,701	2,825	1,074	5,076	
Kentucky	11	90	22							
Tennessee	189	252								
Canada						10	255	4,980	490	90
New York State						1,253	3,230	2,201	1,366	2,257
Pennsylvania	1,059	1,158	503	906	1,269	23	91	109	87	64
New Jersey						10	3			
West Virginia	3,561	7,401	4,409	4,390	6,111					
Virginia	19,634	14,334	3,974	3,906	2,820					
Maryland and South	1,268	834	772	1,236	2,180					
Grand total	34,363	35,547	20,188	23,249	24,619	43,062	140,681	76,410	100,899	74,505

DRESSED BEEF.

Points of origin.	1880.	1881.	1882.	1883.	1884.	1880.	1881.	1882.	1883.	1884.
Chicago			879	4,149	4,181	15,680	75,259	87,970	116,737	120,922
Saint Louis					101			1,180	10	72
Buffalo										11
Illinois										10
West Virginia				9						
Total			879	4,158	4,282	15,680	75,259	89,150	116,747	121,015

Special statement No. 234, E. B. showing cattle from and via Chicago, Saint Louis, Indianapolis, and Cincinnati, fowarded east thereof during 1880, 1881, 1882, 1883, and 1884.

1880.

Destination.	Chicago.	Saint Louis.*	Indianapolis.*	Cincinnati.*	Total.
	Tons.	*Tons.*	*Tons.*	*Tons.*	*Tons.*
New York City	222,262	47,070	3,102	28,315	300,749
Philadelphia	19,280	4,220	190	376	24,066
Baltimore	4,053	1,120	....	400	5,573
New England.					
Boston	81,914	35,840	....	140	....
Portland	655	....	....	....	....
Vermont	10	....	....	....	....
Massachusetts	21,367	....	....	....	....
Connecticut	1,783	....	....	....	....
Rhode Island	21,331	....	....	....	....
Total New England	127,060	35,840	....	140	163,040
Other States.					
Illinois	....	16,823	....	....	....
Michigan	3,006	810	....	....	....
Canada	23	....	....	....	....
Indiana	31,549	1,290	30	....	....
Ohio	3,358	10,100	211	1,254	....
Kentucky	....	20	....	....	....
New York	43,272	9,850	17,172	14,100	....
Pennsylvania	10,599	170	6,800	560	....
New Jersey and Delaware	1,559	60	10	180	....
Maryland and South	368	600	....	80	....
West Virginia	970	....	....	....	....
Virginia	....	....	....	10	....
Total other States	94,704	39,723	24,223	16,184	174,834
Grand total	467,359	127,973	27,515	45,415	668,262

1881.

Destination	Chicago.	Saint Louis.*	Indianapolis.*	Cincinnati.*	Total.
New York City	265,367	40,830	6,079	26,532	338,808
Philadelphia	30,403	9,690	40	412	40,545
Baltimore	3,807	1,090	....	974	5,871
New England.					
Boston	96,222	25,160	380	170	....
Portland	2,392	....	....	....	....
Vermont	10	....	....	....	....
Massachusetts	1,934	....	....	....	....
Connecticut	1,068	....	....	....	....
Rhode Island	6,618	....	....	....	....
Total New England	108,244	25,160	380	170	133,954
Other States.					
Illinois	....	19,435	....	....	....
Michigan	2,856	760	....	....	....
Canada	55	....	....	....	....
Indiana	51,414	3,070	34	....	....
Ohio	6,247	16,530	140	3,677	....
Kentucky	....	60	....	....	....
New York	25,081	17,470	6,699	8,200	....
Pennsylvania	19,703	14,930	8,536	703	....
New Jersey and Delaware	1,017	10	....	218	....
Maryland and South	162	180	....	180	....
West Virginia	1,148	....	....	....	....
Virginia	....	....	....	2	....
Total other States	107,683	72,445	15,409	12,980	208,517
Grand total	515,504	149,215	21,908	41,068	727,695

* Excluding cattle from Saint Louis and Chicago.

Special statement No. 234, E. B., showing cattle from and via Chicago, &c.—Continued.

1882.

Destination.]	Chicago.	Saint Louis.	Indianapolis.	Cincinnati.	Total.
	Tons.	*Tons.*	*Tons.*	*Tons.*	*Tons.*
New York City	257,283	19,867	3,936	27,806	308,892
Philadelphia	36,137	3,350	12	420	39,919
Baltimore	5,085	891	10	946	6,932
New England.					
Boston	56,389	9,990	910		
Portland	115				
Massachusetts	10				
Connecticut	21				
Rhode Island		20			
Total New England	56,535	10,010	910		67,455
Other States.					
Illinois		23,357			
Michigan	3.785	2,363			
Indiana	56,218	7,771	80		
Ohio	10,744	18,604	380	3,776	
New York	30,826	20,930	13,158	2,024	
Pennsylvania	30,790	6,595	8,846	1,598	
New Jersey and Delaware	1,664		10	198	
Maryland and South	2,021			60	
West Virginia	1,162				
Total other States	137,210	79,620	22,474	7,656	246,960
Grand total	492,250	113,738	27,342	36,828	670,158

1883.

New York City	238,828	30,286	5,060	25,411	299,585
Philadelphia	20,225	8,712	76	198	29,211
Baltimore	8,167	593		130	8,890
New England.					
Boston	75,689	15,735	280	186	
Portland	983				
Massachusetts	10			10	
Connecticut	10				
Total New England	76,692	15,735	280	196	92,903
Other States.					
Illinois		19,150			
Michigan	5,364	3,891			
Canada	10				
Indiana	81,094	3,879	23		
Ohio	9,871	20,955	542	3,774	
Kentucky		20			
New York	36,562	18,945	11,565	751	
Pennsylvania	25,495	14,345	7,242	1,599	
New Jersey and Delaware	1,558			174	
Maryland and South	3,051	320		31	
West Virginia	5,909				
Total other States	168,914	81,505	19,372	6,329	276,120
Grand total	512,826	136,831	24,788	32,264	706,709

1884.

New York City	191,736	57,227	7,406	26,408	282,777
Philadelphia	15,759	7,398		132	23,289
Baltimore	6,211	255	20	257	6,743

Special statement No. 234, E. B., showing cattle from and via Chicago, &c.—Continued.

1884.

Destination.	Chicago.	Saint Louis.	Indian-apolis.	Cincin-nati.	Total.
New England.	*Tons.*	*Tons.*	*Tons.*	*To s.*	*Tons.*
Boston	54, 845	7, 532	20	190	....
Portland	163	....	....	....	....
Rhode Island	988	....	....	1	....
Total New England	55, 996	7, 532	20	191	63, 739
Other States.					
Illinois	....	36, 742	....	....	....
Michigan	2, 518	6, 310	....	....	....
Indiana	95, 057	2, 446	53	....	....
Ohio	7, 137	18, 604	525	1, 960	....
Kentucky	....	60	....	....	....
New York	16, 996	9, 650	9, 995	127	....
Pennsylvania	18, 589	8, 406	3, 948	958	....
New Jersey and Delaware	584	....	....	53	....
Maryland and South	1, 296	10	....	10	....
West Virginia	3, 243	....	....	....	....
Total other States	145, 420	82, 228	14, 521	3, 108	245, 277
Grand total	415, 122	154, 640	21, 967	30, 096	621, 825

APPENDIX No. 29.

LETTER ADDRESSED TO THE CHIEF OF THE BUREAU OF STATISTICS BY HON. JAS. F. MILLER, M. C., OF TEXAS, IN REGARD TO THE RELATIVE ADVANTAGES OF MOVING TEXAS CATTLE TO NORTHERN RANGES BY TRAIL AND BY RAIL.

HOUSE OF REPRESENTATIVES,
Washington, D. C., February 6, 1885.

MY DEAR SIR : Your favor of January 5, transmitting statement of the Missouri Pacific Railway system in relation to transportation of cattle is received, and as I think the statements made require some correction, I will therefore state briefly these points of difference:

1. I think the universal experience of cattlemen warrants me in saying that driving cattle (young or old) by trail, when grass and water can be had, is much cheaper than shipping by rail.

2. That cattle driven by trail arrive at their destination in much better condition than when shipped by rail. In fact, cattle driven by trail improve very much during the drive if properly handled.

3. That the losses in driving by the trail are much less than when shipped by rail.

4. That cattle driven over a regular trail, properly handled, become acclimated during the drive and are not liable, upon arrival at distributing centers, to communicate the cattle fever, while those shipped by rail must be quarantined during about the same period required to complete the drive to acquire this immunity, and at nearly as much expense as is required to complete the drive.

5. The railroad facilities and rolling-stock are not yet sufficient to enable them to handle the Texas cattle shipment in the time required within which the cattle must be gathered on the ranges (after spring opens) and delivered by June or July, so as to be able to get sufficient flesh to stand the winter.

These positions are, in my judgment, fully sustained by the experience of cattle drivers; and I may say further, that only those cattle are shipped by rail (except beef cattle for slaughter) which are so situated that it is not practicable to drive them by the trail.

Very respectfully,

JAS. F. MILLER,
|Member Congress Eighth District, Texas.

JOSEPH NIMMO, Jr.,
Chief of Bureau of Statistics.

159

APPENDIX No. 30.

A BILL TO ESTABLISH A QUARANTINED LIVE-STOCK TRAIL, AND TO REGULATE COMMERCE BETWEEN THE STATES AS TO LIVE STOCK—INTRODUCED IN THE HOUSE OF REPRESENTATIVES JANUARY 17, 1885, BY HON. JAMES F. MILLER, M. C., OF TEXAS.

A BILL to establish a quarantined live-stock trail, and to regulate commerce between the States as to live stock.

Be it enacted by the Senate and House of Representatives of the United States of America in Congress assembled, That the Secretary of the Interior be, and is hereby, directed to appoint, as soon as practicable, three commissioners whose duty it shall be to lay out and establish, by metes and bounds, a public highway to be known as a quarantined national live-stock trail, for the purpose of driving cattle, horses, sheep, hogs, or other live stock to market or from one location to another, and, further, to establish, by metes and bounds, at convenient points on said trail, suitable quarantined grazing-grounds where said live stock may be held and grazed for short periods during the drive.

SEC. 2. That said quarantined national live-stock trail shall begin on Red River, as near the one hundredth degree of longitude as may be deemed practicable for the purpose of this act; thence running in a northerly and westerly direction through the Indian Territory, following as far as may be practicable the present trail known as the Fort Griffin and Dodge City trail, to the southwest corner of the State of Kansas; thence over the unappropriated public lands belonging to the United States, in a northerly direction, on the most practicable route, to the north boundary line of the United States.

SEC. 3. That said quarantined national live-stock trail may be of any practicable width not exceeding six miles, and said quarantined grazing-grounds shall not exceed twelve miles square at any one place.

SEC. 4. That the unappropriated public lands upon which said quarantined national live-stock trail and grazing-grounds may be established shall be, and are hereby, withdrawn and withheld from sale, location, or settlement, and are set apart for the exclusive purposes of said trail and quarantine grounds for the term of ten years from the passage of this act.

SEC. 5. That as soon as said commissioners shall have laid out and designated said trail in accordance with the provisions of this act, they shall make a report thereof to the Secretary of the Interior, fully defining said trail; and if such report shall be approved by the Secretary of the Interior, he shall cause the same to be recorded in the General Land Office of the United States, and shall at once give public notice of the establishment of said trail by causing publication thereof in some newspaper published at the capitals of the States of Missouri, Kansas, Texas, Colorado, and Nebraska.

SEC. 6. That the sum of ten thousand dollars, or so much thereof as may be necessary, is hereby appropriated, out of any money in the Treasury not otherwise appropriated, for the purpose of paying the expenses of carrying out the provisions of this act, subject to the draft of the Secretary of the Interior.

APPENDIX No. 31.

STATEMENT BY MR. GEORGE OLDS, GENERAL TRAFFIC MANAGER OF THE MISSOURI PACIFIC RAILWAY SYSTEM, UNDER DATE OF DECEMBER 24, 1884, IN REGARD TO THE SHIPMENT OF CATTLE NORTH BY RAIL.

Two years ago it was not thought practicable to move young cattle from the breeding lands in Southern Texas, adjacent to the Gulf of Mexico, the drive over the old land trails being considered the cheaper means of removing the young stock to the grazing lands in Western and Northern Texas and the Indian Territory. This subject engaged the attention of Mr. Gould, our president, in April, 1883, and efforts were at once made to test the practicability of moving this class of live stock by rail from Laredo and other points on our southern lines to Northern Texas, especially to the Pan Handle, so called. Our efforts were rewarded with success, we having carried from Southern Texas points, since April, 1883, to Fort Worth and points west on the Rio Grande division and to Wichita Falls, the northern terminus of the Fort Worth and Denver City Railroad, from which point the stock took the land trail to Northwestern Texas, over 100,000 head of young cattle, and, as showing what the possibilities are, we carried several thousand head from Southern Texas to points as far north as Ogalalla, on the Union Pacific Railroad.

The old method of driving cattle overland is slow and tedious and always results in landing the stock in Nebraska and Dakota in a weak and exhausted condition; while that which we carried by rail was landed in five days' total time from date of loading, the distance hauled being, in round numbers, 1,400 miles, the drive over the same distance usually occupying six weeks' time. It has been stated by some of those who shipped by rail that the saving of interest on cost and the superior weight and condition of the stock when unloaded from trains went very far towards equalizing the excess cost of rail transportation over cost of driving overland. While this feature of railroad traffic is in its infancy in Texas, yet I am sanguine of the ability of the railroads to successfully compete with the old method of overland driving. In this respect it will appear the railroads of Texas, especially the Missouri Pacific system, is becoming a most valuable means of rapidly developing the enormous cattle resources of the State of Texas.

The question of overcoming the objections of the citizens of the Northwestern States, whose herds may be affected by the introduction of Texas cattle carried by rail direct from the extreme southern districts, is now engaging the attention of some of the railroad managers, and a plan of acquiring large tracts of land in Nebraska and Dakota, upon which the cattle carried by rail may be held in quarantine a sufficient length of time to acclimatize and get them into such condition as will remove all danger of spreading fever, is one which presents itself. The important features in connection with this plan are: Can land be had for this purpose, and are the profits to the railroad carrier likely to be such as to justify the cost of acquiring it?

161

APPENDIX No. 32.

STATEMENT FURNISHED BY MR. GEORGE OLDS, GENERAL TRAFFIC MANAGER OF THE MISSOURI PACIFIC RAILROAD SYSTEM, IN REGARD TO THE MOVEMENT OF CATTLE BY RAIL FROM TEXAS TO POINTS NORTH OF THE STATE OF KANSAS.

TREASURY DEPARTMENT,
BUREAU OF STATISTICS,
Washington, D. C., January 26, 1885.

DEAR SIR: Will you be so kind as to have a statement prepared for me showing the number of cattle which you have transported each year from Texas to the Northwest by rail?

I am, sir, very respectfully, yours,

JOSEPH NIMMO, JR.,
Chief of Bureau.

GEORGE OLDS, Esq.,
General Traffic Manager,
Misouri Pacific Railway Company,
St. Louis, Mo.

THE MISSOURI PACIFIC RAILWAY COMPANY,
OFFICE OF GENERAL TRAFFIC MANAGER,
Saint Louis, Mo., March 7, 1885.

DEAR SIR: Referring to your request of January 26, I beg to inclose herewith such information as I have been enabled to obtain from our general auditor relative to the movement northward of Texas cattle.

I regret that we cannot give the information in a more complete form. I also regret the delay in finally replying to your request, which has been entirely owing to pressure of business incidental to the preparation of the annual reports of this company.

You will observe that Mr. Warner's statement includes only such cattle as were moved by all rail to points north of the State of Kansas. The stock cattle (so called) moved by all lines from Southern Texas points to Wichita Falls amounted to 150,018. Besides this there were moved from Southern Texas points to points west of Fort Worth, on our Rio Grande division, about 200 head.

Yours, truly,

GEO. OLDS,
General Traffic Manager.

JOSEPH NIMMO, Esq.,
Chief Bureau of Statistics,
Washington, D. C.

THE MISSOURI PACIFIC RAILWAY COMPANY,
ACCOUNTING DEPARTMENT,
Saint Louis, Mo., March 6, 1885.

DEAR SIR: Referring to your favor of the 7th ultimo, in regard to statement, for Mr. Joseph Nimmo, of cattle transported via our line from Texas to the Northwest, I inclose to you herewith a memo. statement for the year 1884, that being the only year during which we had through billing arrangements, and to go any further back would necessitate going through the local billing.

Trusting that this will be satisfactory, and returning all correspondence to you, I remain,

Yours, truly,

C. G. WARNER,
General Auditor.

GEORGE OLDS, Esq.,
General Traffic Manager.

162

Stock from Texas to the Northwest, 1884.

[Through ways-bills via Burlington and Missouri River Railway.]

Month.	From—	To—	No. cars.
April	San Antonio	Culbertson, Nebr	11
May	Pearsall	Cambridge, Nebr	17
July	San Antonio	Culbertson, Nebr	19
September	......do	......do	6
			53

[Through way-bills via Union Pacific Railway.]

Month.	From—	To—	No. cars.
April	Fort Worth	North Platte, Nebr	4
Do	Taylor	Kearney, Nebr	8
May	Victoria	Brady Island, Nebr	50
Do	......do	Ogallala, Nebr	34
Do	San Antonio	......do	97
June	Denison	......do	32
Do	Forth Worth	......do	21
			246

[Billed locally via Papillion.]

Month.	From—	To—	No. cars.
June	San Antonio	Fremont, Nebr	5
July	......do	Kearney, Nebr	3
Do	......do	Madison, Nebr	2
Do	......do	Schuyler, Nebr	4
Do	Fort Worth	North Loup, Nebr	2
September	San Antonio	David City, Nebr	3
			19

[Billed locally via Falls City.]

Month.	From—	To—	No. cars.
May	Houston	Culbertson, Nebr,	16
Do	San Antonio	......do	10
July	Cisco	Brush, Colo	33
Do	San Antonio	McCook, Nebr	7
August	......do	Solem, Nebr	4
Do	......do	McCook, Nebr	7
			77
			396

396 cars, at an average of 22 head per car, 8,712.

APPENDIX No. 33.

STATEMENT FURNISHED BY MR. J. F. GODDARD, TRAFFIC MANAGER OF THE ATCISON, TOPEKA AND SANTA FÉ RAILROAD, IN REGARD TO THE TRANSPORTATION OF TEXAS CATTLE TO NORTHERN RANGES BY RAIL.

TOPEKA, KANS., *February* 21, 1885.

DEAR SIR : Your favor of the 13th to our general manager has been handed to me for reply.

Mr. Robinson wired you on the 13th as follows: "First shipment of Texas cattle from El Paso by rail over our road was made in 1884, in which year we moved about 30,000 head. With no unfavorable legislation we will probably move 75,000 head in 1885."

In answer to the latter clause of your letter, I have talked with several experts as to the danger of increasing or developing Texas fever by the movement of these cattle by rail as compared with the drive. It has been a much-discussed question as to what Texas fever is. Our best veterinarians differ on the subject. It is a well-established fact, however, that native cattle have taken the disease from passing over ground which had been previously passed over by Texas cattle, although several months may have elapsed between the time of passage of the two herds. From this it is supposed that the disease is propagated by a germ deposited either through the feet or mouth of the animals. Texas cattle themselves never have the disease; that is to say, if they contain the germs, the germs are never developed in themselves, they only having the power of communicating the disease to northern cattle. The cattle which take the disease, I am informed by the best authorities, have no power of communicating it to others. With these conditions, my judgment would be that it is altogether the safest plan of transportation for Texas cattle by rail. With proper sanitary precautions, by cleansing the cars and stock-yards where they are unloaded, before native cattle are allowed to be introduced (which was done by our company last year) will undoubtedly prevent any danger of a spread of the disease by means of shipment by rail. The only danger, then, remaining would be when the Texas cattle are turned out to graze, which danger always exists unless they are kept in separate pastures from the native stock. The advantage of shipment by rail is, I think, in the fact that in the movement from Texas to the point of unloading from the cars the country is kept entirely clear from the danger of contagion.

The Territories of New Mexico and Wyoming and the States of Colorado and Kansas have passed laws upon the subject; and it may be that such statutes will be passed as will make the shipment of Texas cattle by rail impracticable. I have not as yet investigated the subject as to whether such legislation would be constitutional as to inter-State traffic or not; but I can freely say that I believe that it would be ill advised, and work an injury to a very large industry which is an immense source of revenue to the country.

Very truly, yours,

J. F. GODDARD,
Traffic Manager.

Hon. JOSEPH NIMMO, Jr.,
    Chief of Bureau of Statistics,
        Washington, D. C.

TOPEKA, KANS., *February* 25, 1885.

DEAR SIR : Yours of February 20 to our general manager has been referred to me for reply.

I some days since wrote you stating that I did not believe in the theory that rail shipments of cattle increased the liability of a spread of the Texas fever; but, on the other hand, I believe the contrary is true. I stated in my previous letter the theories as to the spread of the so-called "Texas fever," that should the cattle be driven across the country, whatever ground they pass over is practically forbidden ground for native cattle, as the latter are liable to contagion from passing over the same ground. Whatever objection any of our people may have raised to a trail leading northwesterly, it doubtless emanates from the idea that shipments of native cattle, located at any point west of said trail, could not be driven to the shipping point unless such point was also west of the trail, as it would be dangerous for such native cattle to cross the trail so provided. I will here say that this objection is not on the part of the railroad company, but, as I look at it, in the interest, encouragement, and improvement of live stock. Cattle occupying the larger portion of the Indian Territory, the Pan Handle of Texas, and also of New Mexico, are graded cattle; that is to say, nearly all of the cattle raisers in that country have introduced into their herds, which were originally Texans, blooded stock to raise the grade far above the average Texan. My idea is that the best interest of the whole cattle industry would be served by the movement by rail rather than by trail. In other words, I consider the cattle interests of the country to be best served by a course which will induce, rather than the contrary, the improvement of the large herds of cattle raised in our section. I think this improvement will be very much more rapid if the parties so engaged feel sure that their herds will be protected from any ravages from Texas fever.

Yours, very truly,

J. F. GODDARD.

Joseph Nimmo, Jr., Esq.,
Chief of Bureau of Statistics,
Washington, D. C.

APPENDIX No. 34.

LETTER ADDRESSED TO THE CHIEF OF THE BUREAU OF STATISTICS BY MR. GEORGE B. LOVING, OF FORT WORTH, TEX., IN REGARD TO THE ESTABLISHMENT OF A CATTLE TRAIL IN TEXAS.

OFFICE OF DAILY AND WEEKLY GAZETTE,
Fort Worth, Tex., February 12, 1885.

DEAR SIR: I have your favor of the 7th, for which you will please accept my thanks. I answered your telegram of the 7th, stating that a bill was now before the State legislature proposing to open a cattle trail from the Colorado River to the crossing of Red River in Wilbarger County. I have very little hope of their being able to pass this bill, at least at this session of the legislature; in fact, there is no immediate necessity for the passage of such a bill in Texas, as there is no hindrance to the passage of cattle over any section of country in this State; but unless there is an outlet furnished for Texas cattle by the establishment of a national trail through the Indian Territory and Kansas (or the removal of all obstacles to their introduction to the ranges in the Northern States and Territories), I cannot but apprehend serious injury to the stock interests of this State, as the want of such an outlet for the surplus cattle of Texas must necessarily result in a very material decrease in values.

Very respectfully, yours,

GEO. B. LOVING.

Hon. JOSEPH NIMMO, Jr.,
Chief of Bureau of Statistics,
Washington, D. C.

A BILL to provide for the establishment of a State cattle trail and to make an appropriation for defraying the expenses of the same.

Be it enacted by the legislature of the State of Texas, That there shall be laid out and established a public thoroughfare in this State, to be known and designated as the "State Cattle Trail." It shall begin at some suitable point on the Colorado River, at or near the southwest corner of Brown County, and shall run from thence as nearly as practicable on a direct line to the initial monument on the one hundredth meridian, west longitude, where the same crosses the Prairie Dog Town Fork of Red River, and from thence with said one hundredth meridian to the northeast corner of Lipscomb County. Said State cattle trail shall be, as nearly as practicable, two miles in width from said beginning point to the said initial monument, and from thence to the said northeast corner of Lipscomb County it shall be, as nearly as practicable, one mile in width, and shall be laid out and marked as hereinafter provided.

SEC. 2. The governor shall appoint three disinterested and discreet citizens of this State, to be known and designated as the "Trail Commission;" they shall receive the compensation and perform the duties required of them by this act. Before entering upon the discharge of their duties each of said trail commission shall take and subscribe an oath to the effect that he will, to the best of his skill and ability, discharge and perform all the duties required of him by this act without favor or affection, malice, or hatred, to any person. Such oath shall be filed with the secretary of state.

SEC. 3. It shall be the duty of the trail commission to lay out and direct the surveying and marking of said cattle trail in accordance with the provisions of this act, and to report their proceedings in writing to the governor. Said report shall be accompanied by a plot or map showing the location of the trail, with field notes of the survey thereof.

SEC. 4. Said State cattle trail shall not be laid out across any farm, lot, or inclosure without first obtaining the written consent of the owner, or his agent or attorney, to the same, except as hereinafter provided. If such written consent should be refused, it shall then be the duty of said trail commission to carefully examine the country round about such farm, lot, or inclosure, and see whether the trail can be so diverged from its general course as to pass round such farm, lot, or inclosure without serious incon-

166

venience to the public; and if such can be done, it shall be their duty to so lay it out. In cases of the kind above mentioned said trail may be narrowed down to any width less than the maximum width of two miles, provided the same shall not be less than sixty feet in width at any place. But if, after such examination, the trail commission is of the opinion that such divergence cannot be made without great and serious inconvenience to the public, it shall be their duty to lay out said trail across such farm, lot, or inclosure, but in so doing they shall confine said trail to so much ground only as shall be necessary for the purpose. In laying out the said cattle trail, if the trail commission deem it expedient, they may adopt any or all lanes or other narrow passes along the route, and may confine said trail only to such lane or other narrow pass in order to pass the same through parts of the country where, by reason of inclosures or other obstacles, it would other otherwise incur unnecessary expense to lay it out the maximum width or less.

SEC. 5. If the owner, or his agent or attorney, of any land over which said trail may be laid out shall file with said trail commission a written protest against laying out such trail across his land, it shall then be the duty of the trail commission to assess the damages to such owner and make report thereof to the governor, and said written protest shall accompany such report; whereupon it shall be the duty of the governor to direct the comptroller to draw his warrant in favor of such owner for the amount so assessed by the trail commission, to be paid out of the fund appropriated by this act, after which such trail shall be opened across such party's land.

SEC. 6. In all cases of disagreement of said trail commission upon matters relating to their duty the decision of a majority thereof shall be sufficient to govern. Each member of the trail commission shall receive from the State, as compensation for his services, the sum of five dollars per day for every day he may be actually engaged in discharging the duties required of him by this act.

SEC. 7. Said State cattle trail shall be surveyed, and posts of cedar or other durable material set up every quarter of a mile on each side thereof. Said posts shall be at least six inches in diameter, securely set at least two feet in the ground, and shall extend at least five feet above the surface of the ground; they shall each be plainly marked on the side thereof next to the trail with the words, "State Cattle Trail." The surveying and setting the posts above mentioned shall be performed under contract, to be let by the governor after due notice thereof published in some newspaper of the State for at least four weeks. It shall be let to the lowest responsible bidder, who shall be required to enter into bond, payable to the governor and his successors in office, conditioned for the faithful performance of his contract. The trail commission shall superintend, direct, and control the surveying and marking of said State cattle trail, and it shall be their duty to personally lay out the trail, and the survey shall be made and the posts set along the trail as shall be directed by the trail commission. The commissioner of the general land office shall furnish said trail commission, free of charge, with such sketches, maps, field-notes, and other information necessary in laying out, surveying, and marking said cattle trail as he may possess.

SEC. 8. All lands belonging to the State situated within the bounds of said State cattle trail shall be, and are hereby, reserved from location, sale, or lease, os long as such trail shall be open as a public thoroughfare. And it shall be unlawful for any person to erect any fence or other obstruction on or across said State cattle trail. Any person violating the provisions of this section shall be fined in any sum not less than one hundred nor more than one thousand dollars, and such obstruction shall be removed by order of the court.

SEC. 9. After the governor shall have received the report of the trail commission provided for in section three of this act, and all claims for damages reported shall be adjusted, it shall be his duty to immediately issue his proclamation, declaring such trail as surveyed and reported by the trail commission to be a public thoroughfare. Such proclamation shall be published in at least three newspapers in the State of Texas for sixty days.

SEC. 10. From and after the expiration of sixty days from the date of the governor's proclamation provided for in the preceding section, every person with cattle bred in any part of the State south of the Colorado River, who shall desire to drive the same through the northern part of this State, shall be required to drive the same upon the State cattle trail, and shall be required to keep them thereon; and it shall be unlawful for any such drover to drive or permit his cattle to stray off from the said State cattle trail until after arriving at the shipping point or passed out of the State. Any person who shall violate the provisions of this section shall be fined in any sum not less than one thousand nor more than five thousand dollars.

SEC. 11. That the sum of one hundred thousand dollars, or so much thereof as may be necessary, be, and the same is hereby, appropriated out of any money in the State treasury not otherwise appropriated, for the purpose of carrying out the provisions of this act.

SEC. 12. That all laws and parts of laws in conflict with this act be, and the same are hereby, repealed.

APPENDIX No. 35.

LETTER ADDRESSED TO THE CHIEF OF THE BUREAU OF STATISTICS BY MR. W. H. MILLER, OF KANSAS CITY, IN REGARD TO THE TEXAS CATTLE TRAIL.

BOARD OF TRADE,
OFFICE OF SECRETARY AND TREASURER,
Kansas City, Mo., January 26, 1885.

DEAR SIR: Yours of January 23 has been received and noted. In reply to your first inquiry I would say that the sentiment of the cattle interest north of Texas, as I understand it, is against the national trail. That was my understanding when I received your letter, and I have since conferred with several live-stock men who confirm my opinion. The reason for this is, not that the people north of Texas are hostile to Texas interests, but because they have now occupied and stocked substantially all the ranch country in the West and Northwest, and do not need the supplies of young cattle from Texas which they have heretofore received. Besides this, the Texas fever, which is almost invariably engendered among native and northern herds of cattle by simply driving the Texas cattle across their ranges, is now much more to be dreaded because of the larger interests involved. Our cattle-men do not think the national trail would be an adequate protection against it, but hold that such of the Texas cattle as may be required north should in deference to northern interests be transported in railway cars.

Heretofore Texas cattle-men have devoted themselves largely to breeding and have sold their young stock for northern ranches; these ranches being now sufficiently stocked, and largely with northern cattle, the feeling has arisen that each State and Territory should do its own breeding and mature and market its own cattle. This will require a change in Texas methods, but it is not believed that it will injure Texas, as she can mature her cattle as well as other localities, and with present and prospective rail facilities market them as well as other sections.

The difference between the Oklahoma boomers and the cattle-men is that the boomers want the unassigned lands in the Indian Territory opened to white settlement like public lands in Kansas or Nebraska, so that it may be taken up and settled in the same manner and subject to the same laws, while the cattle-men have gone into the assigned districts and leased the lands for ranches from the Indians to whom it belongs. The cattle-men have a clear legal right to do what they have done, but the boomers have not. Their movement seems to be designed to coerce the Government into opening the unassigned lands. The Kansas and Missouri men who have leased lands in the Indian Territory are not hostile to the interests of the Texas cattle-men. On the contrary, they have left openings through their fences for the northward movement of Texas cattle, and the agitation of the Texas fever comes apparently less from them than from ranch owners and farmers farther north.

Any other information I can give you, in this or any other subject, I will furnish with pleasure.

Very respectfully,

W. H. MILLER,
Secretary.

Hon. JOSEPH NIMMO, Jr.,
Chief Bureau of Statistics, Washington, D. C.

APPENDIX No. 36.

VALUE OF EXPORTS OF INDIAN CORN, WHEAT AND WHEAT FLOUR, HOGS AND PORK PRODUCTS, AND CATTLE AND BEEF AND TALLOW FROM THE UNITED STATES DURING EACH YEAR FROM 1875 TO 1884, INCLUSIVE.

Year ended June 30—	Indian-corn.	Wheat and wheat-flour.	Hogs and pork products.	Cattle and beef products.
1875	$24, 456, 937	$83, 320, 303	$57, 923, 845	$11, 728, 358
1876	33, 265, 280	92, 816, 369	68, 508, 095	12, 029, 437
1877	41, 621, 245	68, 799, 509	82, 070, 671	20, 920, 148
1878	48, 030, 358	121, 967, 737	86, 955, 117	23, 677, 910
1879	40, 655, 120	160, 268, 792	79, 438, 936	29, 845, 036
1880	53, 298, 247	225, 879, 502	85, 259, 331	39, 233, 592
1881	50, 702, 669	212, 745, 742	105, 232, 203	39, 602, 333
1882	28, 845, 830	149, 304, 773	83, 362, 597	26, 696, 070
1883	27, 756, 082	174, 703, 800	71, 238, 784	28, 253, 495
1884	27, 648, 044	126, 166, 374	70, 380, 973	41, 080, 001

APPENDIX No. 37.

EXPORTS OF CATTLE AND THEIR PRODUCTS FROM THE UNITED STATES DURING EACH YEAR FROM 1875 TO 1884, INCLUSIVE.

Year ended June 30—	Cattle.		Beef.				Canned.*	Tallow.		Total.
			Fresh.		Salted or cured.					
	Number.	Value.	Pounds.	Value.	Pounds.	Value.	Value.	Pounds.	Value.	Value.
1875	57,211	$1,103,085	(†)	(†)	48,243,251	$4,197,956	$735,112	65,461,619	$5,692,205	$11,728,358
1876	51,593	1,110,703	(†)	(†)	36,596,150	3,186,304	998,052	72,432,775	6,734,378	12,029,437
1877	50,001	1,593,080	49,210,990	$4,552,523	39,155,153	2,950,952	3,939,977	91,472,803	7,883,616	20,920,148
1878	80,040	3,896,818	54,046,771	5,009,856	38,831,379	2,973,234	5,102,625	85,505,919	6,695,377	23,677,910
1879	136,720	8,379,200	54,025,832	4,883,080	36,950,563	2,336,378	7,311,408	99,963,752	6,934,970	29,845,036
1880	182,756	13,344,195	84,717,194	7,441,918	45,237,472	2,881,047	7,877,200	110,767,627	7,689,232	39,233,582
1881	185,707	14,304,103	106,004,812	9,860,284	40,698,649	2,665,761	5,971,557	96,403,372	6,800,628	39,602,333
1882	108,110	7,800,227	69,586,466	6,768,881	45,899,737	3,902,556	4,208,608	50,474,210	4,015,798	26,696,070
1883	104,444	8,341,431	81,064,373	8,342,131	41,680,623	3,742,282	4,578,902	38,810,098	3,248,749	28,253,495
1884	190,518	17,855,495	120,784,064	11,987,331	43,021,074	3,270,033	3,173,767	63,091,103	4,793,375	41,080,001

* During the years 1875 to 1883 inclusive, classified as "meats preserved."   † Included in "beef salted or cured."

APPENDIX No. 38.

VALUE OF THE EXPORTS OF CATTLE AND BEEF PRODUCTS FROM THE UNITED STATES DURING THE YEAR ENDED JUNE 30, 1884, STATED BY COUNTRIES, AND IN THE ORDER OF MAGNITUDE.

Order of magnitude	Countries to which exported.	Cattle.	Beef products.					Total value of cattle and beef products.
			Beef, canned.	Beef, fresh.	Beef, salted or pickled.	Beef, other cured.	Tallow.	
1	Great Britain and Ireland	$17,336,606	$2,542,122	$11,516,369	$2,059,433	$60,028	$2,941,008	$36,455,566
2	British North American Possessions	96,820	250,414	455,003	261,665	485	216,368	1,280,755
3	France		25,182		21,965	303	686,551	734,001
4	Germany	30,200	158,286		183,482	851	155,075	527,894
5	Netherlands		55,907		55,538	1,739	241,468	354,652
6	Belgium		26,688		19,124	1,564	270,838	318,214
7	British West Indies	98,968	8,703	15,423	177,194	952	3,850	305,090
8	Mexico	128,630	2,546		325	140	38,006	169,647
9	Cuba	145,024	1,436	529	5,143	68	7,049	159,249
10	British Guiana	150	237		72,343	110	8,600	81,440
11	French West Indies	1,320	110		65,284	324	147	67,185
12	Denmark		7,387		32,956	160	22,726	63,229
13	Italy		883		669		61,585	63,137
14	United States of Colombia	40	3,790		35,108		22,687	61,625
15	Central American States	150	8,077		13,224	438	37,749	59,638
16	Sweden and Norway		1,980		38,440			40,420
17	Hawaiian Islands	12,785	15,921		9,120			37,826
18	San Domingo		630		711	55	31,854	33,250
19	Hayti	65			19,004	27	9,696	28,792
20	British Possessions in Africa and adjacent islands		17,409		10,674			28,083
21	Brazil	1,625	13,748		8,961	42	679	25,055
22	Dutch West Indies		306		22,364	67	1,173	23,910
23	Dutch Guiana	75	767		21,882		100	22,824
24	Hong-Kong		11,497		8,494			19,991
25	Venezuela		1,771		3,286	90	9,807	14,954
26	Portugal						12,734	12,734
27	Peru		1,208		4,728		4,945	10,881
28	Chili	72	1,287		8,755	60	427	10,601
29	British Honduras	1,400	699		5,677		21	7,797
30	French Possessions, all other	1,030	3,467		2,194			6,691
31	Danish West Indies		161	7	5,948	226	211	6,553
32	Japan	375	3,230		2,608			6,213
33	Russia on the Baltic and White Seas						5,337	5,337
34	Azore, Madeira, and Cape Verde Islands		118		3,334		1,559	5,011
35	French Guiana		696		4,057			4,753
36	Porto Rico		141		3,252	29	944	4,366
37	Russia, Asiatic		150		3,984			4,134
38	Liberia				3,701			3,701
39	China		2,496		395			2,891
	All other countries	160	4,317		7,253		181	11,911
	Total	17,855,495	3,173,767	11,987,331	3,202,275	67,758	4,793,375	41,080,001

171

APPENDIX No. 39.

*LETTER FROM MR. T. C. EASTMAN, IN REGARD TO THE EARLY HIS-
TORY OF THE SHIPMENT OF FRESH BEEF AND OF CATTLE FROM THE
UNITED STATES TO EUROPE.*

NEW YORK, *April* 13, 1885.

DEAR SIR: In answer to your inquiry as to the shipments of dressed beef and live cattle to Europe: I commenced the shipments of beef in quantity the 1st of October, 1875. There were a few experimental shipments made of a few carcasses of beef in small refrigerators, on the deck of a vessel, which were failures, and were discontinued.

Nelson Morris, of Chicago, told me a year or two after I commenced shipping that he shipped a few carcasses of beef on the open deck of a vessel, which arrived in England in bad condition. This was previous to my shipments in refrigerators. The steamship companies running passenger boats carried all kinds of meats in their refrigerators for ship's use. The first meat shipped to Europe in quantity as a commercial article was shipped by myself, as before stated. The first live cattle shipped to England for beef for the English markets were shipped by Mr. Henry Bell, of the firm of John Bell & Sons, Glasgow, Scotland. They made several shipments by the Anchor Steamship Company in 1873 or 1874, but they discontinued in consequence of heavy losses on the voyages.

But in 1876, after I had got the beef shipments fairly opened, live cattle shipments commenced again from New York. I cannot now say who made the first shipment that year, but I am under the impression that Samuels Brothers, of New York, were the parties. I started in about the same time with live shipments, and have been shipping ever since.

Yours, respectfully,

T. C. EASTMAN.

JOSEPH NIMMO,
  Chief of Bureau.

172

APPENDIX No. 40.

LETTER FROM MR. T. C. EASTMAN, IN REGARD TO THE STATES FROM WHICH EXPORT CATTLE CHIEFLY COME, AND THE AVERAGE WEIGHT OF THE DRESSED BEEF OF SUCH CATTLE.

NEW YORK, *April* 18, 1885.

DEAR SIR: In answer to your inquiry about beef cattle and dressed beef exporting to Europe from this country, would say that most of it comes from the corn-producing States, Illinois, Missouri, Kansas, Nebraska, and Iowa, and they are generally purchased in the market at Chicago and Saint Louis. I should say that as much as nineteen-twentieths of all the export cattle come from those States. They are not all raised in those States, but they are finished up on corn for the markets, mostly in those five States. The grade of beef exported in quarters will average from 700 pounds to 750 pounds per steer. Those shipped alive will average from 800 pounds to 850 pounds per steer in the beef. The most desirable cattle for export are about the weights before named and of fine quality; the commoner grades being used at home, with a good share of the very best cattle, which are wanted in our eastern cities. There are a few cattle in the spring of the year exported from the State of Pennsylvania, where they are collected in the fall and stall-fed through the winter and sold in the spring. Kentucky also furnishes some cattle for export from the middle of June to the first of November. West Virginia, Ohio, Michigan, and the State of New York furnish considerable cattle from the first of August to the first of December. Very few of them are for export. About two-thirds of the export beef for the last two years has been slaughtered in New York, the other third in Chicago. All the cattle shipped from the west to eastern markets are slaughtered in the eastern markets, except those that are exported alive. The New England States are supplied mostly with beef slaughtered in Chicago. New York, Philadelphia, and Baltimore are also partly supplied with dressed beef from Chicago. I think about one-half of the consumption of beef in the Eastern States comes from Chicago in refrigerator cars.

Yours, respectfully,

T. C. EASTMAN.

CHIEF OF BUREAU OF STATISTICS.

173

APPENDIX No. 41.

STATEMENT IN REGARD TO CHICAGO BEEF PACKING AND THE CHICAGO BEEF TRADE—1884-'85.

(By Messrs. Howard, White & Co., publishers of the Daily Commercial Bulletin, Chicago, Ill.)

BEEF PACKING.

No distinction as to seasons is made in cattle-slaughtering operations, and a year's business under this head is based, by the trade, upon the calendar year, the same as in handling live cattle. Of the amount of beef packed last year other than that put into tin cans, there can be no reliable figures given. Indeed, the packing of beef in barrels is a comparatively insignificant branch of the business, and is carried on mainly by a few small firms who handle a few hundred head of cattle yearly, and ship their product abroad on special orders. The great bulk of the cattle-slaughtering business in Chicago is carried on by five firms, viz: Swift Bros. & Co., Armour & Co., Hammond & Co., Fairbank Canning Co., and Libby, McNeil & Libby. The latter do an exclusive but large canning business, while Swift Bros. & Co. and Hammond & Co. ship all of their cattle in the carcass. Armour & Co. do an immense business both in dressed and canned beef.

It is in the dressed-beef trade that the largest increase is shown during the year just closed. Early in 1884 butchers and other interested parties in the East made a great fight against western dressed beef, and an effort was even made to induce the New York legislature to enact a law hostile to it. Despite opposition, the business has flourished and grown beyond all expectations, and as a matter of fact is about the only local industry that can demonstrate by actual figures a marked increase over the previous year. Our operators now have cold storage rooms in all of the principal cities and towns of the Eastern and New England States, and as it has been demonstrated over and over again that meat can be kept in perfect condition for two months if need be, consumers have generally come to consider beef handled in this way with high favor.

The beef-canning business was rather on the drag during almost the entire season of 1884, by reason of a considerable accumulation of this product in the European markets, for it is there that a very large percentage of these goods finds an outlet. During November and December, however, the British Government purchased quite heavily for the Nile expedition, which relieved the markets of accumulations, and quite recently a heavy order was placed by them with a prominent firm here for canned beef to supply the troops in the Soudan country.

Following were the monthly and total receipts and shipments of live cattle at this point during 1884, with comparisons:

Months.	Received.	Shipped.
January	165, 124	80, 087
February	135, 417	64, 968
March	122, 633	59, 243
April	139, 082	68, 947
May	124, 150	53, 202
June	127, 187	54, 915
July	161, 008	62, 373
August	143, 015	57, 186
September	167, 801	65, 358
October	198, 717	86, 503
November	175, 143	68, 779
December	158, 420	70, 323
Total for year	1, 817, 697	791, 884
Total for 1883	1, 878, 944	966, 758

The receipts of cattle for the twelve months ending February 28, 1885, foot up 1,814,923 head, and shipments for the same time were 782,612, which is practically the same as for the calendar year. According to these figures there were left over for the use of dressed and canned beef buyers, and for local consumption, 1,025,813 head of cattle in the calendar year of 1884. For the past twelve months ending February 28, 1885, the number left over was 1,032,311 head. The January and February receipts of cattle this year amounted to 297,767, against 300,511 in 1884, and the shipments to 135,783, against 145,055 a year ago. While there was a falling off in the receipts in 1884, as compared with 1883, of 61,247 cattle, the number shipped out alive was 174,874 less, or a difference of 113,657 head, and this fairly represents the increase in the dressed and canned beef business of 1884, estimating the total local consumption of beef for the two years at the same number. Upon this latter point estimates made by those best posted in the matter differ very widely, but 6,000 cattle a week, or, in round numbers, 300,000 a year, is probably not far wide of the mark.

As nearly as can be ascertained, the number of cattle slaughtered here for shipment in the carcass, for canning, and for the city trade during the past year, were as follows:

	Head.
Swift Bros. & Co	401,617
Armour & Co	306,374
Fairbank Canning Company	163,423
Hammond & Co*	153,000
Libby, McNeil & Libby	112,215
Lees, Hendricks & Co	43,862
Schoeneman & Co	30,800
J. S. Smith & Co	18,995
Hess Bros	10,000
Total number	1,240,286
Total number 1883–'84	1,080,020

[Chicago beef trade—1884–'85.—Number of cattle slaughtered during the past twelve months 1,250,301, of which about 70 per cent. were required for the dressed-beef trade.]

While the hog-slaughtering interest of Chicago attracted considerable attention during the year ending March 1, the cattle-slaughtering interest was not neglected, and the returns show a further material enlargement of the business. Merchants engaged in this branch of trade have further increased their facilities for handling the product, and are now enabled, through branch agencies, to supply all the leading markets of the country with "Chicago dressed beef." Refrigerator cars are now forwarded direct over the various railroad lines diverging from the city, loaded with miscellaneous supplies of all kinds of fresh meats in the carcass—beef, mutton, and pork. The large territory west of our market is now largely devoted to raising live stock. More particularly has attention been given to this raising cattle in large numbers, and this has stimulated the dressed-beef trade to a great extent. The receipts of Indian Territory and Texan cattle during the year were about 360,000 head, and the arrivals of far western cattle were about 232,000 head, an increase in the aggregate of about 155,000 head over the returns of the previous year. These cattle were of better quality than usual, as the owners of the ranches are improving their stock, and endeavoring to place their cattle on sale in good condition, that they may compete with the native grades in the leading markets. The greater proportion of the cattle raised on the ranches fall into the hands of slaughterers and are devoted to the packing, canning, and local trade—the better qualities being accepted for the dressed-beef interest. The latter, however, absorbs the greater proportion of the good native cattle received, as the product comes in competition in the Eastern markets with home-raised cattle, and the meat must necessarily be of good quality. The receipts of cattle during the past twelve months ending March 1, 1885, were 1,824,923 head, and the shipments during the same period 782,612 head, including those forwarded to Hammond, Ind., leaving for the use of city slaughterers 1,042,311 head. Prices ruled somewhat irregular, depending greatly on the quality. Fair to extra native steers ranged at $4.10 to $8—the outside figures for extra droves during the holiday season. Far West and Texan cattle sold rather freely at $2.90 to $6, according to quality and condition—the inside figures for rough and mixed lots—though Texans were purchased freely within the range of $2.65 to $6.25, the bulk of the trading during the late summer

* The slaughtering establishment of Hammond & Co. is located at State Line. This house, however, is really a Chicago institution, and its slaughtering should be credited to this city. As the cattle handled by it—153,000 head—were all bought in the Chicago market and included in the shipments returned, they should, to make the numbers slaughtered approximate the *net* supply, be deducted from the shipments and added to the *net* supply. This would make the *net* supply left over for packers for the past twelve months 1,185,311 head.

and fall months, when the receipts were liberal, at $2.80 to $5.50. More cattle were packed during the year 1884–'85 for the domestic trade, and increased quantities of beef hams and all descriptions of barreled beef were produced. More attention was given to the canning trade, and it is understood that some large contracts have been made within the past two or three weeks with merchants in foreign markets.

CATTLE KILLED.

The following table exhibits the number of cattle slaughtered and disposed of by parties engaged in the different branches of the beef trade during the twelve months ending March 1, 1885, as compared with the corresponding time in 1883–'84 :

Firms.	1884–'85.	1883–'84.
Armour & Co	306, 374	287, 221
Eastland & Duddleston	17, 000	15, 400
Fairbank Canning Company	163, 423	131, 611
Hammond, Geo. H., & Co*	145, 010	130, 968
Lees, Hendricks & Co	43, 862	28, 786
Libby, McNeil & Libby	112, 215	116, 247
Shoeneman & Co	30, 800	25, 500
Swift Bros. & Co	401, 617	342, 890
Other houses	30, 000	86, 000
Total	1, 250, 301	1, 164, 623

*Slaughtered at Hammond, Ind., a short distance from Chicago, and reported in the shipments of live.

DRESSED-MEAT TRADE.

There is a very important branch of the dressed-meat trade which has been inaugurated within the past twelve months, and which is rapidly growing. It is the consignment of mixed car loads of beef, pork, and mutton, which are forwarded to the smaller distributing points all over the country, to supply the local trade. Merchants in the leading manufacturing districts of the Eastern and Middle States, and also in the lumbering districts of the Northwest, forward their orders to our markets for small quanties of fresh meats for immediate use, which are forwarded in refrigerator cars. Not only are the leading slaughterers engaged in this business, but smaller houses have commenced operations. It is estimated that outside of the number of hogs slaughtered for packing and city consumption during the winter, at least 50,000 were slaughtered for the dressed-meat trade, of the consignment of which there has been no special record kept. The number of sheep slaughtered for the dressed-meat trade is quite large—possibly one-third of the receipts—but no definite figures can be given.

MOVEMENT OF DRESSED BEEF.

In order to exhibit the enlargement of the trade in dressed beef, the following table is presented, showing the receipts and shipments during the past two years:

Years.	Received.	Shipped.
	Pounds.	*Pounds.*
1884	4, 407, 830	377, 955, 997
1883	1, 334, 769	314, 600, 149
Increase	3, 073, 061	63, 355, 848

The increase in the receipts is about 230 per cent., and the shipments were enlarged about 20 per cent.

CONCLUSION.

We extend our thanks to the manufacturers of hog products for their kindness in furnishing us with the complete details of their business. To the members of the provision trade, who have extended us many courtesies and favors during the past year, we also express our gratitude. Therefore, to all interested in the provision trade, we respectfully present our sixteenth annual report of the packing of this city.

HOWARD, WHITE & CO.,
Publishers of the Daily Commercial Bulletin.

APPENDIX No. 42.

States and Territories.	Original homesteads.		Final homesteads.	
	Number of entries.	Acres.	Number of entries.	Acres.
Arizona	534	74, 638. 07	158	22, 555. 69
California	29, 729	3, 946, 306. 91	12, 343	1, 565, 336. 39
Colorado	11, 154	1, 566, 184. 97	4, 406	618, 470. 68
Dakota	88, 880	13, 741, 654. 39	12, 100	1, 804, 924. 17
Idaho	4, 296	642, 542. 43	1, 113	158, 697. 28
Kansas	94, 032	12, 770, 450. 95	42, 358	5, 865, 088. 28
Montana	3, 592	533, 721. 21	970	139, 258. 56
Nebraska	77, 943	10, 211, 772. 38	33, 503	4, 183, 117. 94
Nevada	877	123, 314. 00	270	36, 009. 25
New Mexico	2, 939	459, 737. 22	1, 408	210, 553. 58
Oregon	14, 847	2, 014, 037. 02	5, 176	714, 129. 01
Utah	6, 536	869, 583. 11	2, 890	390, 203. 46
Washington	18, 018	2, 470, 263. 88	4, 740	630, 224. 28
Wyoming	927	131, 706. 32	197	24, 026. 93
Total	354, 304	50, 255, 912. 86	121, 632	16, 362, 595. 50

APPENDIX No. 43.

*STATEMENT OF THE NUMBER AND AREA OF ORIGINAL AND FINAL
DESERT-LAND ENTRIES MADE UNDER THE ACT OF MARCH 3, 1877,
FROM JULY 1, 1877, TO JUNE 30, 1884.*

States and Territories.	Original desert entries.		Final desert entries.	
	Number of entries.	Acres.	Number of entries.	Acres.
Arizona	347	154, 431. 26	45	17, 284. 30
California	1, 126	383, 548. 55	119	32, 547. 57
Dakota	22	18, 101. 00	1	300. 00
Idaho	563	169, 915. 79	65	17, 339. 97
Montana	1, 294	482, 281. 07	262	72, 598. 81
Nevada	563	160, 412. 37	102	25, 941. 20
New Mexico	429	121, 367. 60	16	5, 247. 03
Oregon	214	67, 292. 80	24	9, 749 14
Utah	943	188, 894. 17	228	31, 955. 30
Washington	117	106, 069. 64	18	2, 079. 10
Wyoming	1, 904	774, 096. 69	138	41, 030. 47
Total	7, 522	2, 626, 410. 94	1, 018	256, 092. 39

APPENDIX No. 44.

STATEMENT SHOWING THE NUMBER OF TIMBER-CULTURE ENTRIES AND THE TOTAL ACREAGE THEREOF IN THE FOLLOWING STATES AND TERRITORIES UNDER THE TIMBER-CULTURE ACTS OF MARCH 3, 1873, AND JUNE 14, 1878, TO JUNE 30, 1884, INCLUSIVE.

States and Territories.	Number of entries.	Acres.
Arizona	145	26, 376. 85
California	2, 046	276, 216. 42
Colorado	2, 414	347, 719. 74
Dakota	42, 667	8, 246, 3°4. 66
Idaho	1, 804	238, 001. 13
Kansas	24, 666	3, 938, 040. 45
Montana	1, 371	180, 509. 21
Nebraska	25, 031	3, 553, 479. 64
Nevada	33	4, 559. 79
New Mexico	377	51, 856. 78
Oregon	3, 315	497, 645. 16
Utah	285	34, 846. 67
Washington	5, 434	789, 720. 84
Wyoming	448	63, 830. 98
Total	110, 036	18, 249, 108. 32

APPENDIX No. 45.

NUMBER OF ACRES CERTIFIED OR PATENTED FOR RAILROADS UP TO JUNE 30, 1884.

States and Territories.	Acres.	States and Territories.	Acres.
Illinois	2, 595, 053. 00	Nebraska	4, 977, 585. 02
Mississippi	935, 158. 70	California	3, 453, 789. 12
Alabama	2, 884, 074. 03	Colorado	211, 279. 87
Florida	1, 760, 834. 98	Nevada	361. 981. 23
Louisiana	404, 664. 71	Oregon	322, 062. 40
Arkansas	2, 534, 608. 57	Utah	40, 196. 49
Missouri	2, 313, 996. 77	Wyoming	79, 042. 03
Iowa	4, 710, 961. 50	Washington	2, 896. 78
Michigan	3, 229, 010. 84	New Mexico	23, 037. 36
Wisconsin	2, 874, 088. 79		
Minnesota	8, 544, 842. 59	Total	47, 620, 046. 10
Kansas	5, 360, 881. 32		

180

APPENDIX No. 46.

STATEMENT SHOWING THE NUMBER OF ACRES OF LAND SURVEYED AND UNSURVEYED IN THE FOLLOWING STATES AND TERRITORIES TO JUNE 30, 1884.

States and Territories.	Area surveyed.	Area unsurveyed.	Total area.
	Acres.	*Acres.*	*Acres.*
Oregon	36,778,775	24,196,585	60,975,360
Nevada	31,767,405	39,970,195	71,737,600
Colorado	54,088,821	12,791,179	66,880,000
Nebraska	46,988,259	1,648,541	48,636,800
Kansas	51,770,240	....	51,770,240
Dakota	41,299,300	55,297,180	96,596,480
Montana	16,225,021	75,791,619	92,016,640
Idaho	8,887,362	46,340,798	55,228,160
Washington	19,950,395	24,845,765	44,796,160
Utah	12,269,828	41,794,812	54,064,640
Wyoming	43,054,987	19,590,133	62,645,120
Arizona	11,795,441	61,110,799	72,906,240
New Mexico	43,673,551	33,895,089	77,568,640
Total	418,549,385	437,272,695	855,822,080

APPENDIX No. 47.

STATEMENT BY MAJOR A. W. EDWARDS, OF THE DAILY ARGUS, FARGO, DAK., IN REGARD TO THE RANGE AND RANCH CATTLE BUSINESS OF DAKOTA.

Question. I suppose most of the old ranges in Dakota were originally stocked with Texas stock ?

Answer. Yes, originally. The range-cattle business in Dakota is quite young. The Marquis de Mores was the first party to introduce stock there. He has a large number of cattle and sheep. Theodore Roosevelt, of New York, is just establishing a range there. I think that the Marquis de Mores has 27,000 head of cattle and 10,000 sheep. Theodore Roosevelt has about 11,000 head of cattle. The Marquis de Mores has sub-let some of his herd to other herdsmen, upon the basis of a share of the profits, to some extent. The Marquis de Mores has established a large packing and slaughtering house at Medora, a point where the Northern Pacific crosses the Little Missouri. He has established cooling houses along the line of the Northern Pacific Railroad between Medora and Saint Paul—the principal one at Fargo—and supplies the large local trade both north and south of the Northern Pacific Railroad. He has at least three-quarters of a million dollars invested in the enterprise. Ranges are also being established at the south side of the Black Hills, in Custer County, and also on the Belle Fourche, on the north side of the Black Hills, in Lawrence County. These Lawrence County ranges are on the main roads entering Deadwood. The Marquis de Mores has constructed a wagon road from Medora to the Black Hills. About 240,000 young cattle were sent west last year over the Northern Pacific Railroad into Western Dakota and Eastern Montana.

There have been as many young cattle shipped west as there has been shipped east during the last two years. The Northern Pacific has stock-yards at Miles City, Glendive, Bismarck, Fargo, and Saint Paul.

There is a very active movement going on in Dakota toward improving the breed of cattle both for dairy purposes and for beef. President James J. Hill, of the Saint Paul, Minneapolis and Manitoba Railway, last year purchased some 200 fine bred young bulls, which he distributes over the lines of his road to responsible farmers free of charge, for the purpose of improving the breed. James B. Power, land and emigration commissioner of the Saint Paul, Minneapolis and Manitoba Railway, opened a stock farm in 1878 35 miles south of Fargo, where he has been breeding Durhams and Herefords. He is also breeding some fine trotting stock.

In Western Dakota the cattle are all on the range.

APPENDIX No. 48.

INTERVIEW WITH HON. JOHN HAILEY, DELEGATE IN CONGRESS FROM THE TERRITORY OF IDAHO, AND HON. JOSEPH K. TOOLE, DELEGATE IN CONGRESS FROM THE TERRITORY OF MONTANA, APRIL 2, 1885.

MEMORANDA, APRIL 2, 1885.

Hon. John Hailey, Delegate in Congress from Idaho, states that if they had artesian wells in that Territory a great number of cattle could be raised there. The sinking of artesian wells has not been experimented upon in Idaho.

Hon. Joseph K. Toole, Delegate in Congress from Montana, states that there are two artesian wells at Miles City, and the result has been reasonably satisfactory.

Mr. Hailey says that Texas cattle can do better at the north, for the reason that the air is more stimulating, and the grasses are more nutritious. There are at least 350,000 or 400,000 cattle in Idaho. The bulk of our stock comes from Oregon. We bring most of our stock for breeding purposes from the Eastern States. I do not think there are a hundred head of cattle in the Territory that have got any Texas blood in them.

Mr. Toole says that the range-cattle business commenced in Montana in 1868 or 1869 to a considerable extent. Some cattle were brought there as early as 1861.

In reply to the question as to what is the sentiment in Montana in regard to the Texas cattle trail, Mr. Toole replies that the sentiment is unanimously opposed to it, for the reason that it monopolizes the ranges of that country in the interest of people who are not actual residents of that country, and because it takes up the ranges by large companies foreign to Montana to the detriment of actual residents, and it tends also to deteriorate the breed of cattle.

Mr. Toole says that in Montana these large corporations from the South, which during the last five or six years have been driving up immense herds of cattle from Texas, have done so without pretending to acquire any water rights. Only to a very small extent have the great range owners of Montana acquired the ownership of land along the water. The same is true in regard to Idaho. Of the total number of cattle in Montana only a small proportion is owned by foreign individual proprietors. The sentiment of the people of Montana is opposed to allowing people to come in there with their large herds and eat out the ranges right up to the doors of the actual settlers. It is the general opinion that would follow the establishment of the cattle range. The Texas cattle destroy more grass by running over it and tearing the grass out of the roots than they do by grazing upon it.

Question. Is it not true that the Texas cattle are much better rustlers, and therefore better able to endure the rigors of the climate during the winter time, than the native cattle?

Mr. Hailey's reply is that as a general thing they do not stand it so well. In the first place, when they come from Texas, by the time they get to the northern ranges they are thin in flesh and are not prepared to go into the winter. Again, we find that cattle brought from the east during the first winter west will not take care of themselves and endure the northern climate as well as the Texas cattle. The pure blooded Texas cattle do not take on as much flesh as the native cattle, and, consequently, are not prepared to stand the northern climate as well as the cattle of the northern ranges.

Mr. Hailey says that the great cattle owners of Montana and Idaho who are regarded as citizens, including the foreigners, do not depend for the privileges of water upon the actual ownership of lands along the water.

Messrs. Hailey and Toole denounced the proposition to lease the public domain as an outrage upon the settlers.

APPENDIX No. 49.

INFORMATION FURNISHED BY HON. MORTON E. POST, LATE DELEGATE IN CONGRESS FROM THE TERRITORY OF WYOMING, IN REGARD TO THE CATTLE BUSINESS OF THAT TERRITORY.

THE IMPROVEMENT OF THE BREED OF RANGE AND RANCH CATTLE.

The most important points bearing upon this subject relate, first, to the class of bulls used; second, to the female stock; and, third, to the character of the increase. The Herefords and the Durhams, or Short-horns, are the favorite breeds. Our stockmen during the last few years have been doing their very best to get the best breeds, the highest class of bulls which they can procure. The cattle breeders of Wyoming have imported bulls quite largely from Europe. The very best specimens of the fine breeds have been procured. The importations from England have been principally Herefords. Durham bulls have been imported mostly from the States of Kentucky, Illinois, and other States of this country. The number of cows and heifers brought into Wyoming has been much less than that of bulls. The range-cattle business of Wyoming began along from 1868 to 1870. From that time to about 1876 or 1878 the great bulk of the cattle *were* brought from Texas. About three-fourths of the entire stock were steers, and the rest cows and heifers. After that the rangemen imported largely from Nevada and Oregon and the Territories of Montana, Idaho, and Utah, and also some from Colorado—mixed herds of cattle. The cattle imported from Utah, Nevada, Oregon, Idaho, and Montana were a good class of cattle, being composed mainly of improved natives, and largely also of improved Texas stock. The cattlemen of Wyoming realized at an early day the importance of improving the breed of their animals, and accordingly began as early as 1874 or 1875 to import graded and thoroughbred bulls. The result is that the general average of the range cattle of Wyoming to-day is improved stock, having large frames and small bones. They are well-developed animals, furnishing a superior quality of beef. We have done more in Wyoming toward improving the breed of cattle than has been done in any other section of the range-cattle area. Our cattle to-day are of a very high standard, and we have increased the value of our herds materially by systematic breeding. The success already attained in stimulating the cattlemen of Wyoming to still further efforts in the direction of improving the breed of their stock. The example of Wyoming is being followed very extensively throughout the range cattle area. The general quality of the cattle of Montana is about equal to that of Wyoming, but with that exception Wyoming is much ahead of all the rest.

THE WYOMING STOCK ASSOCIATION.

The Wyoming Stock Association is one of the best organized and most effective in its workings of any stock association in the United States.

It is controlled by stockmen for their mutual benefit. They have detectives and inspectors stationed at such points as may be necessary to look after stray cattle, and cattle being shipped or driven out of the country with brands belonging to any member of the association. They arrange for the spring "round ups," so as to work in harmony and have each man's interest looked after, and to see that each owner furnishes his proportion both of cowboys and supplies. These "round ups" are under the control of captains or officers appointed under the association, and have entire charge. In case of a dispute as to the different brands, instead of having recourse to law, such matters are referred to a disinterested party as arbitrator, and his decision is usually accepted as final.

In regard to the inspection system, it has proven very beneficial, as cattle sometimes stray some distance from the ranges. The inspectors are stationed at Omaha, Kansas City, and other points where cattle are shipped through by rail. When a train of cattle arrives at any one of these points the inspector looks through the cattle, and if he finds cattle whose brand indicates that they belong to a member of the Wyoming Stock Association, other than the shipper, such cattle are consigned to some commission merchant in Chicago for sale and the proceeds are remitted to the association, and by it handed over to the proper owners.

The stock growers' association of the State of Colorado and of Nebraska and Dakota work in harmony with the Wyoming association. The detectives of the associations look after cattle thieves and men guilty of altering brands, &c.

The cattle business up to the present time has been the great business of Wyoming. The laws of the Territory have been framed specially with the view of protecting this interest.

THE SOIL OF WYOMING.

The cultivation of the land of Wyoming is simply a question of water. The soil throughout the Territory produces the natural grasses in abundance, but there is not a sufficient rainfall for farming. Irrigation is necessary to produce crops successfully. All the agriculture carried on in Wyoming is by means of artificial irrigation. It is estimated that we have 10,000 square miles in the Territory which can thus be watered successfully. This constitutes about 10 per cent. of the 98,000 square miles in the Territory.

INCREASED RAINFALL.

The climatic changes in Wyoming have been very perceptible during the last two years. The increased precipitation of moisture has been very great; perhaps not so great as in the western part of Kansas and Nebraska. But if the increase continues for a term of years we shall undoubtedly be able to raise crops in almost any part of the Territory without irrigation. The season of 1884 was very favorable, and large quantities of hay were cut on the high lands.

THE NATURAL GRASSES OF WYOMING.

Of natural nutritious grass we have some 56 different varieties. The prevailing varieties are principally gramma or gamma, the bunch grass, wild oats, buffalo grass, and a peculiar kind of blue grass. This is different from the blue grass of Kentucky. I have had no personal experience in the cultivation of lucern, but know in a general way of the experience of others. Where it has been tried it has proved very successful. Usually three crops are grown during each year. Until it is well rooted it requires to be irrigated, but as the roots go down very deep it finally becomes self-sustaining. It is found to be a very nutritious and sustaining article of food for cattle, horses, hogs, and sheep. It is largely cut and used as hay, three crops a year being the average.

IMPROVING THE BREED OF RANGE CATTLE.

Doubts have been expressed as to the practicability of maintaining the high grade of cattle if unprotected the year round on the range. It may be true to some extent as to thoroughbred cattle, but we find by experience that our native-born stock maintain their finer characteristics—even those which are obliged to shift for themselves throughout their life-time. We find that their instinct leads even our higher bred animals to "rustle" and seek food for themselves without deteriorating. Our experience is that there is no class of cattle so well qualified to resist the rigors of our winters as cattle raised on the ranges, without regard to the standard of their breeding. We find that the Texas steers driven up into our country show a larger proportion of loss, especially during their first winter north, than among our own native-born cattle.

The losses of calves have been greatly reduced by taking the bulls away in the fall and holding them in a pasture until the proper breeding season.

THE BREEDING OF CATTLE ON THE NORTHERN RANGES.

Considering the inferior quality of stock and the prices which we have had to pay for young cattle from Texas, it is much more desirable to raise our stock in Wyoming than to import from Texas.

During the last eight or ten years our people have, to a considerable extent, bought Texas cattle, but it has been for the reason that we were not able to breed cattle fast enough to supply the demands of new capital seeking investment. I think we will have to be satisfied with what we produce, from the fact that it is impracticable under the present condition of affairs to import successfully, on account of the opposition to Texas cattle being driven across the States and Territories which they have to pass through in order to reach our Territory.

The increased price of young Texas stock within the last four or five years has been due to the increased demand for the purpose of stocking the northern ranges and to the high prices which have ruled for beef, and the depreciation in number of the stock cattle in the Western States, especially in Illinois, Iowa, Missouri, and Wisconsin. The tendency now is for the beef-cattle business to leave the old States and move out on the Territories. The farmers of those States are devoting their attention more and more to the dairy business.

Question. To what extent can the capacity of Wyoming for cattle raising be increased?

Answer. That depends entirely upon the increase of the water supply.

Question. How far can cattle range from water at the present time?

Answer. Five or six miles is as long a distance as cattle will successfully graze from water.

Question. So that the range lands now between the belts of lands following the streams are to-day practically unavailable for grazing purposes?

Answer. Yes; practically so.

Question. Has the experiment of artesian wells been tried to any extent in the high lands of Wyoming?

Answer. No; not at all.

Question. And for the reason, I suppose, that you still have an abundance of land within reach of a natural water supply?

Answer. Yes; that is so.

Question. What is the character of the soil of Wyoming as compared with that of the adjacent States and Territories?

Answer. In the greater portion of the Territory of Wyoming the soil is of a gravelly loam, carrying quite a sod, and for that reason it holds more moisture than the soil of the adjacent Territories and the State of Colorado. We are less liable to drought, and we find that with an increasing water supply we have an increased crop of grass. The grass of Wyoming does not "kill out" as the result of long drought and over-stocking of the ranges, for the reason that the soil is firm, and the roots of the grass well set, and the surface well covered, whereas in a large portion of the Southern country, also in Nevada, Utah, and Idaho, the soil is loose and sandy, so that when the seasons are dry and the wind blows the soil away from the roots it is apt to parch out, except in the mountainous country, where the soil is very firm. The soil of Montana and Dakota is quite similar to that of Wyoming.

Question. What is the percentage of loss on account of the severity of the winter?

Answer. The percentage of loss from all causes would be a general average of from 3 to 5 per cent. This loss occurs mainly from young heifers dropping calves too early in the season. Wyoming is not so much exposed to the cold, damp "blizzards" as Texas and the South generally, nor to the extreme cold of the North as is Dakota and Montana, therefore we are most favorably situated. This, in connection with our abundant supply of grass, enables our cattle to approach the winter in better condition, and to withstand the severe storms with less loss. The snowfall is about the same in Wyoming as in Montana, but the range of the thermometer is not so great in Wyoming. Our principal rainfall is during spring and summer months, and before the frosts occur, so that the grass cures in its natural condition, and retains its full nutritious qualities during winter.

Question. What per cent. of your cows drop calves each year?

Answer. I suppose about 50 to 60 per cent. The increase from two-year-old heifers is about 40 per cent.

Question. How does the increase in Wyoming compare with the increase in Texas and the South?

Answer. I should say that the increase was much greater in that country than in Wyoming; but every two animals raised in Wyoming are worth three raised in the Southern country.

Question. About what relation does the amount of capital invested in horses and in sheep in Wyoming bear to the amount of capital invested in cattle; also, how does the amount of capital in horses and in sheep compare with that in cattle in the adjoining States and Territories, in so far as you can judge?

Answer. The breeding of horses in Wyoming is, practically, a new industry. The immense cattle business has excluded almost every other branch of the stock business, but within the last four or five years some of our people have been turning their attention to horses to some extent, and there are now quite a large number of horse ranches or breeding establishments in the Territory, and the owners are showing the same foresight as our cattlemen have shown in the improvement of cattle. The business promises to grow and be profitable. It is impossible to state the relative magnitude of the two industries. The horse business, at the present time, is insignificant as compared with the cattle business. It is estimated that there is now invested in Wyoming over $100,000,000 actual valuation, including the cattle business alone, and not including lands, and probably not over $5,000,000 altogether invested in horses. Last year we shipped out of Wyoming somewhat over 160,000 head of cattle, and the previous year over 200,000 head. In 1884 the prices had fallen, and therefore stock was held back. Estimated at $50 a head, the shipments of last year of 160,000 head would be somewhat about $8,000,000, but that does not represent the increased value of the herds on the range, for the reason that at least five-sixths of the shipments consisted of steers, leaving the heifers and young cows on the range. Regarding the sheep business: We have, perhaps, altogether in the Territory in the neighborhood of half a million head of sheep, that would be worth from $1,500,000 to $2,000,000.

Question. Is the climate, soil, and natural food supply of Wyoming favorable to the raising of sheep?

Answer. Yes; the business has been reasonably successful.

Question. Do you brand your young horses?

Answer. Yes; by using a small brand, which does not disfigure the animal, or injure his market value.

Question. Do you allow your horses to mingle with those of other owners of horses, as the cattle of different proprietors intermingle on the ranges?

Answer. Horses that run on the public domain mix with other horses, but horses do not stray as badly as cattle, and become more attached to a range than cattle, and for that reason do not mix up so much as cattle. The horses are not "rounded up" by the association. In some instances horses are kept entirely within inclosures.

Question. Of late years have owners of herds of cattle who own no water rights, i. e., no land along the streams, come into Wyoming and allowed their cattle to intermingle with those of the ranchmen who own lands on the streams, and what position does the Wyoming Stockgrowers' Association take in regard to such cattle-owners without water rights?

Answer. The association has taken no action one way or the other as an association. But very few instances have occurred where cattlemen have turned their cattle loose on ranges already occupied. It would be unadvisable for any new-comer to undertake to graze a large herd upon ranges already sufficiently stocked. There is a common law or understanding among ranchmen, generally, with regard to the range which is supposed to be tributary to their watering privileges, and they would naturally feel aggrieved, and be likely to resent any attempt on the part of a new-comer to place cattle upon the ranges, and in case he had secured no water rights of his own, he would be regarded as an intruder. The intruder would, to some extent, jeopardize the interest of the occupants of the ranges, as well as his own, by turning loose more cattle than the range would support.

Question. Has there ever been any rule proposed, or even tacitly adopted, among ranchmen of any particular section as to proportioning the number of cattle which they shall keep according to the extent of the water privileges which they have?

Answer. None that I have ever heard of.

Question. The increase in the number of cattle on the different ranges will, of course, differ very much. Would it not be true in time, if it is not true to-day, that there will be a very great disproportion existing between the amount of water privileges which the different ranchmen will own and the number of cattle which they should own?

Answer. There is no present indication of any trouble of that sort. We have practically exhausted the supply of Nevada, Oregon, and Washington Territory, and the supply from Texas being shut off by the closing up of the trail will compel the cattle-owners of Wyoming to rely upon their own increase.

Question. What do you think of the proposition to slaughter beef in Wyoming and ship the carcasses east instead of the living animals.

Answer. I think it would be a desirable improvement and a great advantage to the stock interest, besides furnishing to consumers a clean and wholesome class of beef, free from the bruises and feverishness incident to shipping cattle alive, especially our range animals, which are highly nervous and excitable.

Question. Do you think it would be a paying investment to establish slaughtering places in Wyoming?

Answer. I am not posted as to the business of slaughtering, but it occurs to me that if it is a good business to be carried on in Chicago, it would certainly be more profitable to slaughter the cattle near the ranges.

Question. In view of the fact that the carcasses weigh only about 57 per cent. of the weight of the live animals, would not this difficulty arise—that the remaining 43 per cent., representing the hides, hoofs, horns, and other parts, including offal, which is now utilized in the varied industries of the city of Chicago, could not be so profitably disposed of in Wyoming?

Answer. In my opinion, it would cost less to ship the hides, blood, hoofs, horns, &c., of the animal, after being slaughtered, than to ship it in the shape of live animals. The railroad companies would lose very little in the matter of total weight haul, from the fact that the hides, hoofs, horns, and blood would also be shipped, but in more compact forms, making more desirable freights for the railroads. It seems that the railroad companies have lost sight of this. They think they would lose all but the carcasses. Besides, if we count the ice which is used in cooling them, they would probably, in the long run, haul more tons weight of dressed animals than they would of animals shipped alive.

Question. Has any attempt been made in Wyoming to slaughter cattle there and ship carcasses east ?

Answer. There has been no effort of any magnitude with the proper facilities.

Question. What is the average length of time in transporting cattle from Cheyenne to Chicago ?

Answer. About eight days.

Question. How many rests do the cattle take ?

Answer. They are usually unloaded about three times, for periods of twenty-four hours each time.

Question. What is the average shrinkage of stock in being transported from Cheyenne to Chicago ?

Answer. I think about 100 pounds to each 1,200 pound animal. Cheyenne is the great center for the cattle trade of the northern ranges.

Question. What is the cost per head of transporting cattle from Wyoming to Chicago, including all incidental expenses ?

Answer. The average cost of marketing cattle, including transportation from points in Wyoming, and feed, handling, and commissions in Chicago, is, say, $8 per head. Cattle weigh on the average 1,200 pounds apiece at Chicago, and lose about 100 pounds in shrinkage. This applies to Wyoming-bred cattle. I desire to add at this point that in speaking about Wyoming cattle, and particularly the shipments of them, I have had reference entirely to our native Wyoming cattle, and not to Texas-wintered cattle.

APPENDIX No. 50.

STATEMENT BY MR. W. H. MILLER, SECRETARY OF THE KANSAS CITY BOARD OF TRADE, IN REGARD TO CATTLE MOVEMENTS AT THAT CITY, AND NORTH BY TRAIL.

BOARD OF TRADE, OFFICE OF SECRETARY AND TREASURER,
Kansas City, Mo., April 17, 1885.

DEAR SIR: Your favors of April 4 and 8 came to my office during my absence at New Orleans, hence the delay in answering.

In reply to your inquiries concerning the Texas cattle drive, I would say that the statement published in my annual report includes all cattle driven northward from Texas. In the earlier years covered by this statement the cattle driven north consisted largely of beef cattle, and were shipped eastward from stations on the Atchison, Topeka and Santa Fé Railroad, the Kansas Pacific and Union Pacific Railroads, and from the southern terminus of the Kansas City, Lawrence and Southern Kansas Railroad, which was at that time Coffeyville, Kansas. Many of those cattle were marketed in Kansas City, and subsequently shipped eastward into the feeding districts of the Western and Northwestern States. Many, also, were slaughtered here. During the past six or seven years nearly all of the drive has been made up of stock cattle for ranges north of Texas. A greater or less number have been intended for the Indian trade, but most have been stock cattle. The Texas beef cattle during this time have been shipped out of the State by rail, and have been mainly carried by the Iron Mountain, the Southern, and the Missouri Pacific Railroads.

My information is that the drive of 1880 included but 300,000 head of cattle, 150,000 less than the statement made to you by Mr. Loving, of Fort Worth, Tex. I include, however, only cattle that crossed the State lines into Kansas, Colorado, and New Mexico, while his, most likely, includes all that passed Fort Worth, many of which stopped in the pan handle of Texas and in the Indian Territory. This probably accounts for the difference in his estimate and mine, and, if I am correct in this surmise, about that difference ought to exist.

No record is kept here, either by merchants or the stock yards, which distinguishes as to whether receipts are of native, range, or Texas origin. Hence it is impossible for me to make that distinction for you. I have applied to several of our merchants who handle range cattle largely for an approximate, but they say that they cannot make one. I can say, however, that no cattle now come to this market direct from Texas. Our receipts are all of native and range cattle; but the range cattle are mostly all of Texas origin, having been driven from that State in previous years as stock cattle. A few extra fine native cattle are shipped eastward from this city without entering the Saint Louis or Chicago markets, but the general fact is that cattle marketed here are afterwards marketed in one or other of those cities.

In reply to yours of the 8th, I would say first that no data has ever been preserved here which would enable me to give you the average weight of cattle shipped from here. The number shipped eastward during 1884 was 411,706. The total number shipped was 463,001, besides which there were 90,991 driven out of the yard for local consumption and packing purposes.

As before remarked, substantially all of those shipped went either to Saint Louis or Chicago on their way east.

My records show a shipment of 12,746,870 pounds of fresh beef from this point, of which 7,934,770 pounds went by eastward lines. Some of this beef has been shipped to the Atlantic seaboard cities, but how much I have no means of telling.

I regret that I have not been able to give you more information concerning the cattle product of Texas, and the ranges north of that State, but I know of no means of obtaining it.

Any further information I can furnish you at any time will be furnished with great pleasure.

Very respectfully,

W. H. MILLER,
Secretary.

Hon. JOSEPH NIMMO, Jr.,
Chief Bureau of Statistics, Washington, D. C.

APPENDIX No. 51.

Value of the exports of cattle and products of cattle from the United States, by countries, for the year ending June 30, 1884.

Order.	Countries.	Value.	Order.	Countries.	Value.
1	Great Britain and Ireland........	$36,455,566	22	Brazil...........................	$25,055
2	Dominion of Canada..............	1,210,035	23	Dutch West Indies	23,910
3	France...........................	734,001	24	Dutch Guiana	22,824
4	Germany.........................	527,894	25	Hong-Kong	19,991
5	Netherlands.....................	354,652	26	Venezuela.......................	14,954
6	Belgium	318,214	27	Portugal	12,734
7	British West Indies..............	305,090	28	Peru	10,881
8	Mexico..........................	169,647	29	Chili	10,601
9	Cuba............................	159,249	30	British Honduras	7,797
10	British Guiana	81,440	31	French Possessions, all other....	6,691
11	New Foundland and Labrador ..	70,720	32	Danish West Indies.............	6,553
12	French West Indies..............	67,185	33	Japan	6,213
13	Denmark........................	63,229	34	Russia on the Baltic and White	
14	Italy	63,137		Seas	5,337
15	United States of Colombia	61,625	35	Azore, Madeira, and Cape Verde	
16	Central American States........	59,638		Islands	5,011
17	Sweden and Norway.............	40,420	36	French Guiana	4,753
18	Hawaiian Islands	37,826	37	Porto Rico	4,366
19	San Domingo....................	33,250	38	Russia, Asiatic.................	4,134
20	Hayti	28,792	39	All other countries.............	18,503
21	British Possessions in Africa and adjacent islands...........	28,083		Total......................	41,080,001

Per cent. for Great Britain 88.7.

190

APPENDIX No. 52.

Value of the imports of cattle and beef products into Great Britain and Ireland for the year
1883.

Order.	Countries.	Values.	Order.	Countries.	Values.
1	United States of America	$33,504,401	15	Belgium	$230,911
2	Denmark	10,941,843	16	British East Indies	75,990
3	British North America	6,288,565	17	Falkland Islands	62,379
4	Australasia	4,361,898	18	Peru	8,760
5	Germany	3,247,398	19	British Africa	7,436
6	Sweden and Norway	2,399,242	20	Gibraltar	4,662
7	Portugal	2,278,914	21	Chili	3,407
8	Spain	2,132,004	22	Bermudas	2,759
9	Netherlands	1,399,328	23	Italy	973
10	France	801,391	24	British West Indies	584
11	Argentine Republic	779,443	25	Victoria	97
12	Uruguay	538,026		All other countries	8,146
13	Russia	338,703			
14	Channel Islands	311,198		Total	69,728,458

APPENDIX No. 53.

Statement showing the exports from the United States of cattle and cattle products, including dairy products, during the fiscal years 1790–1884, inclusive.

| Year ended— | Cattle and cattle products. | | | | | | | | | Cattle and cattle products, including dairy products. Dairy products. | | | | | Total values. |
| | Live cattle. | | Beef. | | Tallow. | | Hides. | | Total values. | Butter. | | Cheese. | | Total values. | |
	No.	Values.	Pounds.a	Values.	Pounds.	Values.	No.	Values.		Pounds.	Values.	Pounds.	Values.		
Sept. 30—															
1790	5,406	$99,960	8,932,400	$279,551	200,020	$20,722	230	$485	$400,718	469,224	$48,587	144,734	$8,830	$57,417	$458,135
1791	4,627	84,413	12,566,469	377,917	317,195	28,548	704	1,408	492,316	933,520	91,685	120,901	8,463	100,148	592,464
1792	4,551		14,942,692		152,622		1,602		b	658,616		125,925		b	
1793	3,728		15,021,200		309,366		9,278		b	514,640		146,269		b	
1794	3,495		20,173,200		187,212		35,531		b	2,171,232		601,954		b	
1795	2,510		19,229,800		49,515		27,865		b	1,589,784		2,343,093		b	
1796	4,625		18,504,200		187,403		40,363		b	2,554,885		1,794,536		b	
1797	3,827		10,362,400		26,012		106,862		b	1,255,435		1,256,109		b	
1798	4,283		17,884,200		16,610		11,838		b	1,313,563		1,183,234		b	
1799	5,304		18,264,200		19,926		72,650		b	1,314,502		1,164,590		b	
1800	9,824		15,009,000		15,079		33,003		b	1,822,341		913,843		b	
1801	8,486		15,066,200		37,142		3,691		b	2,830,016		1,674,834		b	
1802	9,039		12,304,000		32,863		953		b	2,361,576		1,332,224		b	
1803	7,563		15,586,800		59,217		4,814	c	1,145,000	2,489,954	o	1,190,867	o	585,000	1,730,000
1804	6,290	c	26,979,200	c	35,440	c	4,635	c	1,520,000	2,476,550	o	1,299,872	o	490,000	2,010,000
1805	5,822	c	23,106,400	c	13,681	c	5,692	c	1,545,000	1,656,724	o	843,005	o	415,000	1,960,000
1806	7,107	c	23,483,800	c	53,757	c	1,819	c	1,360,000	1,898,690	o	683,163	o	481,000	1,841,000
1807	8,148	c	16,841,800	c	53,115	c	4,801	c	1,108,000	1,963,480	o	879,697	o	490,000	1,598,000
1808	2,050	c	4,020,200	c	4,985	c		c	265,000	894,152	o	316,876	o	196,000	461,000
1809	3,981	c	5,711,000	c	4,562	c		c	425,000	1,366,374	o	588,907	o	264,000	689,000
1810	5,212	c	9,539,800	c	11,205	c	2,500	c	747,000	1,620,538	o	741,878	o	318,000	1,065,000
1811	8,522	c	15,348,600	c	44,775	c	800	c	1,195,000	1,878,789	o	944,116	o	395,000	1,590,000
1812	4,713	c	8,551,400	c	16,140	c		c	524,000	1,614,112	o	707,787	o	329,000	853,000
1813	460	c	8,748,200	c	300	c	277	c	539,000	419,395	o	276,552	o	95,000	634,000

Year															
1814	300,000	59,000		184,827		185,100	241,000		68		2,360		4,059,400		227
1815	649,000	242,000		468,609		844,029	407,000		51		37,541		2,626,000		4,604
1816	961,000	223,000		678,064		676,195	738,000	9,594	9,072	2,117	21,641	454,668	6,647,800	378,813	4,958
1817	1,058,616	213,424	59,235	394,903	154,189	670,387	845,192	6,794	6,396	1,810	17,641	479,375	7,577,800	160,310	7,975
1818	843,730	195,441	64,332	536,097	131,109	655,501	648,289	3,884	3,397	4,308	15,080	454,558	7,375,000	135,369	4,715
1819	895,281	297,162	114,838	1,148,360	182,324	911,621	598,119	2,393	1,942	11,146	35,897	638,292	6,993,200	205,800	3,471
1820	1,159,965	302,334	82,843	828,431	219,491	1,463,275	887,631		1,595		85,741		10,638,200		5,018
1821	888,610	190,287		766,431		1,069,024	698,323		13,558		81,691		13,377,400		4,116
1822	1,065,575	221,041		722,548		1,149,783	844,534		15,079		63,856		19,522,000		3,557
1823	932,239	192,778		591,689		1,171,701	739,461		42,499		735,333		12,283,400		2,865
1824	911,504	204,205		933,158		1,386,232	707,299		46,166		96,261		13,214,800		2,759
1825	1,178,252	247,787		1,230,104		1,442,197	930,465		56,043		533,451		17,605,000		3,427
1826	941,195	207,765		735,399		1,176,579	733,430		29,841		423,610		14,577,200		3,095
1827	956,685	184,049		641,385		1,148,480	772,636		22,883		301,983		18,137,000		3,768
1828	896,315	176,354		688,548		1,184,329	719,961		39,642		422,130		13,328,200		1,193
1829	851,160	176,205		916,695		969,137	674,955		44,282		491,106		10,220,000		2,044
1830	860,053	142,370		688,241		899,396	533,683		50,146		533,436		9,368,400		4,125
1831	1,094,778	264,796		1,131,817		1,728,212	829,982		299,473		679,623		12,154,000		5,881
1832	1,064,907	290,820		1,391,853		1,501,686	774,087		52,110		622,522		11,101,400		8,123
1833	1,216,528	258,452		1,213,092		1,346,364	958,076		58,179		676,841		12,864,400		6,837
1834	945,318	190,099		819,567		1,084,960	755,219		60,015		771,239		9,236,200		6,441
1835	803,570	164,809		887,000		684,624	638,761		41,495		491,412		7,605,600		7,348
1836	813,149	114,033		486,234		361,395	699,116		39,379		443,765		10,045,200		4,683
1837	681,322	96,176		411,338		281,989	585,146		112,096		168,795		5,615,200		3,237
1838	676,422	148,191		664,660		495,108	528,231		33,852		363,036		4,698,200		2,826
1839	499,196	127,550		519,017		424,609	623,373		56,762		118,037		3,237,800		4,775
1840	834,122	210,749		723,217		1,177,639	904,918		112,500		273,946		3,936,200		4,259
1841	1,409,733	504,815		1,746,471		3,785,993	1,212,638		45,898		980,027		11,307,400		7,861
1842	1,600,823	388,185		2,456,607		2,055,133			58,187		7,038,092		9,716,200		9,887
June 30—															
1843d	1,601,917	508,968	514,034	3,440,144	418,723	3,408,247	1,092,949	361,982	50,340	1,352,406	7,489,582	2,600,547	7,562,400	84,680	5,181
1844	2,569,380	758,829	887,705	7,343,145	580,286	3,251,952	1,810,551	101,174	62,558	829,086	9,915,366	1,983,151	21,294,800	133,743	10,822
1845	2,805,674	878,865	647,423	7,941,187	593,024	3,587,489	1,926,809	624,867	111,636	632,286	10,022,504	1,218,348	20,307,600	144,864	5,252
1846	3,537,295	1,063,087	731,910	8,675,730	541,863	3,436,660	2,474,208	875,753	143,323	824,910	10,435,696	2,081,856	29,844,600	1,238,769	3,101
1847	4,175,773	1,741,770	649,302	15,637,600	750,911	4,214,433	2,434,003	530,539	181,394	712,551	11,172,975	2,188,056	22,395,800	1,345,058	3,383
1848	3,267,009	1,361,668	1,565,630	12,913,305	1,144,321	2,751,086	2,058,958	1,036,100	36,145	1,598,176	8,004,135	2,674,324	20,657,200	1,052,426	1,919
1849	3,713,115	1,654,157	3,321,631	17,433,682	2,355,985	3,406,242	1,605,608	673,818	23,390	2,942,370	8,334,138	1,255,773	19,061,400	1,639,132	2,607
1850	2,821,071	1,215,463	2,216,804	13,020,817	4,164,344	3,876,175	689,459	518,687	71,940	4,026,113	5,858,459	2,017,077	18,129,600	197,019	1,848
1851	2,814,610	1,124,652	5,638,007	10,361,189	6,733,743	3,994,542	500,459	355,855	86,624	6,738,486	4,767,020	63,792,754	24,451,800	236,547	1,350
1852	2,279,820	779,391		6,650,420	6,140,031	2,222,264	2,214,554	305,111	55,421	6,215,260	4,198,278	2,185,021	25,208,200	117,573	1,078
1853	3,076,897	862,343		3,763,932		2,658,911	2,757,022		25,955		3,926,598	3,023,018	25,244,000		1,076
1854	4,015,425	932,757		7,003,974		3,774,634	3,047,154		23,622		3,325,471		29,898,795		1,501
1855	5,332,372	1,258,393		4,846,568		2,315,249	2,620,341		114,787		1,866,992		25,671,675		2,478
1856	4,515,145	1,467,991		8,737,029		2,936,491	2,021,348		40,184		7,458,415		25,747,650		4,325
1857	3,860,848	1,240,507		6,453,072		3,141,592			153,726		6,283,812		24,149,900		28,247
1858	6,295,121	1,273,773		8,098,527		3,082,117	4,766,204				7,103,045		31,059,290		32,513
1859	6,166,417	1,400,213		7,103,323		4,572,065	6,361,186				15,269,535		39,251,070		27,501
1860	9,071,137	2,709,951		15,515,799		7,640,914	5,515,297				29,711,108		35,849,310		3,885
1861	11,192,823	5,677,616		32,361,428		15,531,247	6,758,896				46,773,768		27,490,570		3,634
1862	13,639,132	3,321,631		34,052,678		26,691,247	6,516,809		56,071		63,792,754		23,792,754		3,509
1863	20,467,356	4,216,804		42,045,054		35,172,415	9,660,962				55,197,914		29,541,565		6,191
1864	21,439,000	10,950,547		47,751,329		20,895,435							35,666,400		

Statement showing the exports from the United States of cattle and cattle products, &c., during the fiscal years 1790–1884, inclusive—Continued.

Cattle and cattle products, including dairy products.

Year ended June 30	Cattle and cattle products									Dairy products					Total values.
	Live cattle		Beef		Tallow		Hides		Total values.	Butter		Cheese		Total values.	
	No.	Values.	Pounds.	Values.	Pounds.	Values.	No.	Values.		Pounds.	Values.	Pounds.	Values.		
1865	9,588	$159,179	27,333,960	$3,304,771	30,622,865	$4,979,135	205,950	$1,023,596	$9,466,681	21,559,892	$7,292,715	53,154,318	$11,697,746	$18,990,461	$28,457,142
1866	7,730	323,637	19,053,800	2,766,451	19,364,686	2,488,587	b	317,741	5,896,416	3,806,835	1,267,851	36,411,985	6,036,828	7,304,679	13,201,095
1867	10,221	268,236	14,182,562	1,727,350	23,296,931	2,747,618	b	286,381	5,029,585	4,912,335	1,184,367	52,382,127	7,893,535	9,077,902	14,107,487
1868	16,120	330,183	22,683,531	2,696,011	22,662,412	2,540,227	b	538,106	6,104,527	2,071,873	382,745	51,097,203	7,010,424	7,593,169	13,697,696
1869	c	c	27,299,197	2,430,357	20,534,628	2,362,630	b	292,491	5,085,478	1,324,332	484,094	39,960,367	6,437,866	6,921,960	12,007,438
1870		439,987	26,727,773	1,939,778	37,513,056	3,814,861	b	365,212	6,559,838	2,019,288	592,229	57,296,327	8,881,034	9,474,163	16,034,001
1871	27,530	403,491	43,880,217	3,825,666	33,859,317	3,025,035	b	700,604	7,954,796	3,965,043	853,096	63,698,867	8,752,990	9,606,086	17,560,882
1872	20,530	565,719	26,652,094	1,870,826	76,151,218	6,973,189	b	1,445,178	10,854,912	7,746,261	1,498,812	66,204,025	7,752,918	9,251,730	20,106,642
1873	28,033	695,957	31,605,196	2,447,481	79,170,558	7,068,471	b	3,605,023	13,816,932	4,518,844	952,919	80,366,540	10,498,010	11,450,929	25,267,861
1874	35,455	1,150,857	36,036,537	2,956,676	101,755,631	8,135,320	b	2,560,382	14,803,235	4,367,983	1,092,381	90,611,077	11,898,995	12,991,376	27,794,611
1875	56,067	1,103,085	48,243,251	4,197,956	65,461,619	5,692,205	b	4,729,725	15,722,971	6,360,827	1,506,496	101,010,853	13,639,603	15,166,599	30,889,570
1876	57,211	1,110,703	36,596,150	3,186,304	72,432,775	6,734,378	b	2,905,921	13,937,306	4,644,894	1,109,496	107,364,686			
1877	51,593	1,593,680	88,366,143	7,503,475	91,472,803	7,883,616	b	2,479,827	19,460,598		4,424,616	141,654,474	12,700,627	17,125,243	36,585,841
1878	80,040	3,895,818	97,878,150	7,983,090	85,505,919	6,695,377	b	1,287,840	19,862,125	21,827,242	4,103,529	147,995,614	13,931,822	18,035,351	37,897,476
1879	136,720	8,879,200	90,976,395	7,219,458	99,963,752	6,934,970	b	671,523	23,705,151	21,837,117	5,421,205	127,989,782	12,579,968	18,001,173	41,706,324
1880	182,756	13,344,195	129,954,666	10,322,965	110,767,627	7,689,232	b	649,074	32,005,466	39,236,658	6,690,687	141,654,474	12,171,729	18,862,407	50,867,873
1881	185,110	14,304,103	146,703,461	12,526,045	96,403,372	6,800,628	b	903,464	34,534,240	31,560,500	6,256,024	147,995,614	16,380,248	22,636,272	57,170,512
1882	108,110	7,800,227	115,486,203	10,671,437	50,474,210	4,015,798	b	1,449,737	23,937,199	14,794,305	2,864,570	99,220,467	14,058,975	16,923,545	40,860,744
1883	104,444	8,341,431	122,744,996	12,084,413	38,810,098	3,248,749	b	1,220,158	24,894,751	12,348,641	2,290,665	112,869,575	11,134,526	13,425,191	38,319,942
1884	190,518	17,855,495	163,805,138	15,257,364e	63,091,103	4,793,375	b	1,304,329	39,210,563	20,627,374	3,750,771		11,663,713	15,414,484	54,625,047

a The official returns from 1790 to 1865 state the quantity of beef exported in barrels and tierces, which have been reduced to pounds at the rate of 200 pounds and 305 pounds, respectively.

b Not specified.

c Not stated.

d Nine months ended June 30, 1843.

e Not including beef canned, $3,173,767.

APPENDIX No. 54.

WESTWARD SHIPMENTS OF CATTLE INTO NORTHERN RANGES BY RAIL

[Northern Pacific Railroad Company, General Freight Agent's Office; operating Northern Pacific Railroad, Saint Paul and Northern Pacific Railroad, Little Falls and Dakota Railroad, Northern Pacific, Fergus and Black Hills Railroad, Fargo and Southwestern Railroad, Sanborn, Cooperstown and Turtle Mountain Railroad, Jamestown and Northern Railroad, Rocky Mountain Railroad of Montana, Helena and Jefferson County Railroad. J. M. Hannaford, general freight agent; S. L. Moore, assistant general freight agent.]

SAINT PAUL, MINN., *April* 10, 1885.

DEAR SIR: Your telegram of the 9th instant, asking for the total number of cattle shipped west to the ranges over the line of our road during the year 1884 and the approximate average value is received. In round figures, we shipped west during the time mentioned 98,000 head of young cattle, averaging half yearlings and half two-year-olds. These cattle were worth about $23 per head at the point of delivery, or $2,254,000. I think there should be $225,000 added to these figures for the excess valuation of bulls, blooded stock, &c., which were mixed in with these shipments, and which we took under a release from the owner at the same rate and valuation, and cannot therefore tell how many there were.

Very truly, yours,

J. M. HANNAFORD,
General Freight Agent.

Mr. JOSEPH NIMMO, Jr.,
Chief of Bureau of Statistics, Washington, D. C.

[Union Pacific Railway Company. General Traffic Manager's Office.]

OMAHA, *May* 4, 1885.

DEAR SIR: In reply to your telegram of the 9th ult., we shipped over our line in Nebraska 1,025 car-loads of cattle in 1884 to the western ranges, and 284 car-loads over our Kansas lines. We average about 20 head per car-load, making 1,309 cars; 20 per car = 26,180 head of cattle; average, $30 per head.

Yours, truly,

THOS. L. KIMBALL,
General Traffic Manager.

Hon. JOSEPH NIMMO, Jr.,
Chief of Bureau of Statistics, Washington, D. C.

[Telegram.]

TOPEKA, KANS., *April* 17, 1885.

To JOSEPH NIMMO, Jr., *Washington, D. C.:*

Cattle shipped west to ranges during 1884 numbered 31,250; horses, about 7,000. Refer to C. J. Morse, Kansas City, as to valuation.

J. J. GODDARD.

11991 R C——14

APPENDIX No. 55.

*STATEMENT BY MR. LEVI C. WADE, PRESIDENT OF THE MEXICAN CEN-
TRAL RAILWAY COMPANY, IN REGARD TO THE RANGE AND RANCH
CATTLE BUSINESS OF MEXICO.*

[Mexican Central Railway Co., Limited; Mason Building, No. 70 Kilby street. P. O. Box 2813.
Levi C. Wade, president. S. W. Reynolds, treasurer.]

BOSTON, *April* 25, 1885.

DEAR SIR: I have your letter of the 23d instant, inquiring in regard to range and ranch cattle in Mexico.

Since the opening of our line, the number of cattle in sight has evidently increased. Between Paso del Norte and the city of Chihuahua there is a large extent of grazing country, not excelled by any in the United States, with rich abundant grasses and a plentiful supply of water. It contains many fine lakes and ponds, and on it are pastured vast herds of neat-cattle and horses.

In spite of the duties upon cattle, there is some trade between Mexico and the United States, as you will see by our annual report for the year ending December 31, 1884 (a copy of which I send you), page 31, we carried 2,219 horses and 2,855 head of neat-cattle. Nearly the whole of those were transported from different points in Mexico to the United States.

Our stock business is growing, and the establishment of a stock yard at El Paso would very materially increase the traffic. At present, the buying of Mexican cattle is done wholly by individuals who go to Mexico for the purpose of obtaining cattle and horses for their ranches in the United States.

Yours, truly,

LEVI C. WADE,
President.

JOSEPH NIMMO, Jr., Esq.,
  Chief of Bureau of Statistics, Washington, D. C.

196

APPENDIX No. 56.

STATEMENT IN REGARD TO THE EARLY SHIPMENTS OF CATTLE AND DRESSED BEEF TO EUROPE, BY MR. WILLIAM COLWELL, OF BOSTON, MASS.

BRIGHTON, MASS., *April* 13, 1885.

DEAR SIR : In reply to yours of the 11th instant, the first cargo of beef cattle that I shipped to Europe was in October, 1876. I believe those were the first shipped from any port in the United States, with the single exception of one small lot in the spring of same year. I have been across twenty-six times since, myself, with cattle. I am not certain as to the exact time when dressed beef was sent, but, as near as I can recollect, I think it was in the fall of 1874 or spring of 1875, from New York.

Respectfully, &c.,

WILLIAM COLWELL.

JOSEPH NIMMO, Esq.

197

APPENDIX No. 57

STATEMENT IN REGARD TO THE EARLY SHIPMENTS OF CATTLE AND DRESSED BEEF TO EUROPE, BY MR. NELSON MORRIS, OF CHICAGO, ILL.

UNION STOCK YARDS, EXCHANGE BUILDING,
Chicago, April 20, 1885.

DEAR SIR: In reply to yours of 11th inst., I beg to say that I was the first exporter of live cattle from the United States to Europe. I exported a few cattle to London and Glasgow in 1868. I also exported some dressed beef prior to 1870.

The difficulties attending the exportation of live cattle when this trade was in its infancy were many, but experience has removed most of them, and the mortality, under ordinary circumstances, has been greatly reduced, and now averages less than 1 per cent. The most serious drawback now attending the exportation of live cattle from the United States to English ports, is the law requiring all United States cattle to be killed at port of entry within five days after landing, and debarring them from being taken into the interior. No such restrictions apply to Canadian cattle. Many of the difficulties first encountered in exporting dressed beef have also been overcome.

Respectfully, yours,

NELSON MORRIS.

JOSEPH NIMMO, Jr.,
Chief of Bureau of Statistics, Washington.

198

APPENDIX No. 58.

STATEMENT BY MR. SILAS BENT, OF SAINT LOUIS, MO., IN REGARD TO THE METEOROLOGY AND CLIMATOLOGY OF NORTH AMERICA, WITH SPECIAL REFERENCE TO THE RANGE AND RANCH CATTLE AREA.

SAINT LOUIS, MO., *May* 4, 1885.

DEAR SIR: Thanks for your meteorological statement, which I herewith return with some verbal corrections and criticisms of one or two paragraphs of your quotations from Professor Elias Loomis, of Yale College, and Capt. Samuel H. Mills, Acting Chief Signal Officer, U. S. Army, and which I shall here repeat with additional comments, as you desired. Professor Loomis says that "near the Atlantic coast the amount of rainfall is evidently increased by vapor which comes from the Atlantic ocean. For the remaining portion of the United States east of the Rocky Mountains the vapor which furnishes the rainfall may come to some extent from these two sources (Gulf of Mexico and Atlantic Ocean), but it is chiefly derived from the chain of the great lakes, from the rivers, small lakes, and collections of water from the moist earth." The only criticism that I shall offer to this assumption is to ask the professor whence came the vapor which gave rise to this "chain of great lakes, rivers, small lakes, and collections of water from the moist earth" and whence comes the vapor that now keeps them in such unvarying supply of water from year to year if not from the prevailing west winds which come to this region from the Pacific Ocean? Captain Mills says, "It seems probable that evaporation from the Kuro-Siwo is no more important than that from the remainder of the Pacific Ocean.

The southwest wind that [prevails (?)] north of California passes over the Rocky Mountains and deposits rain on our Pacific coast undoubtedly draws most of its moisture from the Pacific Ocean." To this I reply that the only "remainder of the Pacific Ocean" not covered by the tepid waters of the Kuro-Siwo is a narrow strip of water lying directly along the eastern coast of Asia and to the west of a line drawn from the northeastern part of Japan to Behring Straits, and which, being of the same general temperature as the west winds that come from Siberia and Central Asia, it can, of course, impart but little or no moisture to those winds, and it is not until those winds reach the tepid waters of the Kuro-Siwo, which cover the whole Pacific Ocean from Japan northeastwardly and eastwardly to the shores of our continent and extending from Behring Straits to the Tropic of Cancer, that they begin to laden themselves with moisture by evaporation from the Pacific Ocean; for the power of the atmosphere to produce such evaporation is in exact proportion to the dryness and low temperature of the wind as compared with that of the water at the time and place of its contact with these tepid waters from the equator.

The climatic power in temperature alone of these tepid waters is forcibly shown by such distinguished writers as Mr. James Croll, of England, and Commander M. F. Maury. In his work entitled "Climate and Time," Mr. Croll says, "The quantity of heat conveyed by the Gulf Stream" (from the Gulf of Mexico through the Straits of Florida into the North Atlantic) "is equal to all the heat which falls upon the globe within thirty-two miles on each side of the equator;" that "the stoppage of the Gulf Stream would deprive the Atlantic of 77,479,650,000,000,000,000 foot-pounds of energy in the form of heat per day;" or, as the same fact is more popularly stated by Commander Maury in his "Physical Geography of the Sea," when speaking of the effect on the climate of Central America and Mexico arising from the excess of heat carried off from them by the Gulf Stream, says, "A simple calculation will show that the quantity of heat daily carried off by the Gulf Stream from those regions and discharged over the Atlantic Ocean is sufficient to raise mountains of iron from zero to the melting point, and to keep in flow from them a molten stream of metal greater in volume than the waters daily discharged from the Mississippi River." Mr. Croll further says that "were all ocean and aerial currents stopped, so that there could be no transference of heat from one point of the earth's surface to another, the difference between the temperature of the equator and the poles would amount to 218 degrees," and that "without ocean currents the globe would not be habitable." Now, *the sea, the atmosphere, and the sun are to the earth what the blood, the lungs, and the heart are to the animal economy,* and it is not only the transference and equalization of temperature over the face of the earth that is accomplished by the circulation of the currents of the ocean and of the atmosphere, but also, in the Divine economy, the parallel beneficence of such a distribution of moisture as is necessary for the sustenance of animal and vegetable life

199

throughout the world, and it is in this aspect of the question that it may be safely averred that were the Kuro Siwo shut out from the North Pacific, so that none of its moisture could be distributed over our continent, the whole of that part of North America lying north of the thirty-fifth parallel of latitude and west of the Alleghany Mountains would be an uninhabitable desert, and that if the ocean currents alone were stopped, so as to cut off the supply of moisture now obtained from them by the winds, and distributed over the continents and islands of the world, such stoppage would be death to the world as effectually and completely as the stoppage of the circulation of the venous system is death to the life of man. Any attempt, therefore, to solve the great and apparently intricate problems of meteorology, climatology, or even forestry, without starting the investigations from the ocean currents (which comprise a grand system of circulation, embracing all the oceans of the world, and which is as sublime in its simplicity as it is beneficent in its life-giving influences upon whom the animal and vegetable kingdom of the earth), will and must ever prove unreliable and unconvincing, because these currents—next to the sun—are the bases of meteorology and climatology, by reason of the heat and moisture which they throw off to the atmosphere for distribution in all parts of the world. For as Commander Maury says, "An examination into the economy of the universe will be sufficient to satisfy the well-balanced minds of observant men that the laws which govern the atmosphere and the laws which govern the ocean are laws which were put in force by the Creator when the foundations of the earth were laid, and that therefore they are laws of order. Else why should the Gulf Stream, for instance, be always where it is, and running *from* the Gulf of Mexico and not somewhere else, and sometimes running *into* it? Why should there be a perpetual drought in one part of the world and continual showers in another; or why should the winds and waves of the sea ever "clap their hands with joy, or obey the voice of rebuke?"

With apologies for my delay in answering your letter, which was occasioned by unavoidable engagements, and regrets that I am compelled to touch so briefly upon the abundance of evidence that I find on every hand to sustain the hypothesis advanced in my address to the Cattle-Growers' Convention upon the Mountains and Plains of North America, I beg you will accept my grateful acknowledgment for your earnest interest in this matter.

Believe me, very respectfully and truly, yours,

                                        SILAS BENT.

Hon. JOSEPH NIMMO,
    Chief of Bureau of Statistics, Treasury Department,
                Washington, D. C.

Use and Abuse

of

America's Natural Resources

An Arno Press Collection

Ayres, Quincy Claude. **Soil Erosion and Its Control.** 1936

Barger, Harold and Sam H. Schurr. **The Mining Industries, 1899–1939.** 1944

Carman, Harry J., editor. **Jesse Buel:** Agricultural Reformer. 1947

Circular from the General Land Office Showing the Manner of Proceeding to Obtain Title to Public Lands. 1899

Fernow, Bernhard E. **Economics of Forestry.** 1902

Gannett, Henry, editor. **Report of the National Conservation Commission, February 1909.** Three volumes. 1909

Giddens, Paul H. **The Birth of the Oil Industry.** 1938

Greeley, William B. **Forests and Men.** 1951

Hornaday, William T. **Wild Life Conservation in Theory and Practice.** 1914

Ise, John. **The United States Forest Policy.** 1920

Ise, John. **The United States Oil Policy.** 1928

James, Harlean. **Romance of the National Parks.** 1939

Kemper, J. P. **Rebellious River.** 1949

Kinney, J. P **The Development of Forest Law in America.** *Including,* Forest Legislation in America Prior to March 4, 1789. 1917

Larson, Agnes M. **History of the White Pine Industry in Minnesota.** 1949

Liebig, Justus, von. **The Natural Lawss of Husbandry.** 1863

Lindley, Curtis H. **A Treatise on the American Law Relating to Mines and Mineral Lands.** Two volumes. 2nd edition. 1903

Lokken, Roscoe L. **Iowa**—Public Land Disposal. 1942

McGee, W. J., editor. **Proceedings of a Conference of Governors in the White House, May 13–15, 1908.** 1909

Mead, Elwood. **Irrigation Institutions.** 1903

Moreell, Ben. **Our Nation's Water Resources**—Policies and Politics. 1956

Murphy, Blakely M., editor. **Conservation of Oil & Gas:** A Legal History, 1948. 1949

Newell, Frederick Haynes. **Water Resources:** Present and Future Uses. 1920.

Nimmo, Joseph, Jr. **Report in Regard to the Range and Ranch Cattle Business of the United States.** 1885

Nixon, Edgar B., editor. **Franklin D. Roosevelt & Conservation, 1911–1945.** Two volumes. 1957

Peffer, E. Louise. **The Closing of the Public Domain.** 1951

Preliminary Report of the Inland Waterways Commission. 60th Congress, 1st Session, Senate Document No. 325. 1908

Puter, S. A. D. & Horace Stevens. **Looters of the Public Domain.** 1908

Record, Samuel J. & Robert W. Hess. **Timbers of the New World.** 1943

Report of the Public Lands Commission, with Appendix. 58th Congress, 3d Session, Senate Document No. 189. 1905

Report of the Public Lands Commission, Created by the Act of March 3, 1879. 46th Congress, 2d Session, House of Representatives Ex. Doc. No. 46. 1880

Resources for Freedom: A Report to the President by The President's Materials Policy Commission, Volumes I and IV. 1952. Two volumes in one.

Schoolcraft, Henry R. **A View of the Lead Mines of Missouri.** 1819

Supplementary Report of the Land Planning Committee to the National Resources Board, 1935–1942

Thompson, John Giffin. **The Rise and Decline of the Wheat Growing Industry in Wisconsin** (Reprinted from *Bulletin of the University of Wisconsin,* No. 292). 1909

Timmons, John F. & William G. Murray, editors. **Land Problems and Policies.** 1950

U.S. Department of Agriculture—Forest Service. **Timber Resources for America's Future:** Forest Resource Report No. 14. 1958

U.S. Department of Agriculture—Soil Conservation Service and Forest Service. **Headwaters Control and Use.** 1937

U.S. Department of Commerce and Labor—Bureau of Corporations. **The Lumber Industry,** Parts I, II, & III. 1913/1914

U.S. Department of the Interior. **Hearings before the Secretary of the Interior on Leasing of Oil Lands.** 1906

Whitaker, J. Russell & Edward A. Ackerman. **American Resources:** Their Management and Conservation. 1951